AGAINST THE GRAIN

THE LOUIS I. KAHN VISITING ASSISTANT PROFESSORSHIP
YALE SCHOOL OF ARCHITECTURE

MARCELO SPINA AND GEORGINA HULJICH
DAN WOOD
LISA GRAY AND ALAN ORGANSCHI

EDITED BY NINA RAPPAPORT AND JACQUELINE KOW

Yale School of Architecture
180 York Street
New Haven, Connecticut 06520
www.architecture.yale.edu

Distributed by Actar-D
355 Lexington Avenue, eighth floor
New York, N.Y. 10017
www.actar-d.com

This book was made possible through an endowment for the Louis I. Kahn Visiting Assistant Professorship at the Yale School of Architecture. It is the seventh in a series of publications of the Louis I. Kahn Assistant Professorship published through the dean's office.

Editors: Nina Rappaport and Jacqueline Kow
Design: MGMT. design

Library of Congress Control Number: 2016942285
ISBN: 978-1-945150-08-1

LOUIS I. KAHN *VISITING ASSISTANT* PROFESSORSHIP

The Louis I. Kahn Visiting Assistant Professorship is Yale's second endowed chair to honor Kahn. Established in 2004, the professorship brings to the school younger architects who practice and teach, offering them the opportunity to lead advanced design studios and seminars. The Kahn Visiting Assistant Professorship carries with it the expectation that the work of the visiting professors and their students will be published so that others may benefit from the ideas developed and exchanged in the studios and seminars.

Louis I. Kahn (1901–1974), perhaps the greatest American architect of the post-World War II era, was closely associated with Yale as a teacher and practicing architect. Yale is home to his first important building, the extension to the Art Gallery (1951–1953), and his last, the Center for British Art (1969–1977). Kahn was fresh to teaching when he came to Yale, in 1947, to begin what would be ten years as chief critic in the architecture school. As a teacher, he worked closely with students and encouraged them to go beyond their initial ideas about architecture, as he himself was trying to go beyond his own ideas. Kahn inspired a generation of architects, leading them to new insights that became the basis of their independent work.

Twenty-four studios have been offered by Louis I. Kahn Visiting Assistant Professors, beginning with Gregg Pasquarelli, whose studio—along with that of successor appointees, Galia Solomonoff and Mario Gooden—was published in the book *Layered Urbanisms*, in 2007. The studios of the next three appointees to the chair, Jeanne Gang, Sunil Bald, and Mark Tsurumaki, were documented in *Negotiated Terrains*, in 2009. The studio led by FAT Architects—Sean Griffiths, Sam Jacob, and Charles Holland, collaborating with Edward P. Bass Visiting Fellow and developer Nick Johnson of Urban Splash—was published in *Urban Integration/Bishopsgate Goods Yard*, in 2010. The studios of Christopher Sharples, William Sharples, and Ali Rahim were represented in the volume *Turbulence*, in 2011. *Architecture Inserted*, published in 2012, presented the work and studios of Eric Bungé and Mimi Hoang, Chris Perry, and Liza Fior with Katherine Clarke. *Renewing Architectural Typologies*, published in 2013, documented the work and studios of Makram El Kadi and Ziad Jamaleddine of L.E.FT, Tom Coward, Daisy Froud, Vincent Lacovara, Geoff Shearcroft of AOC, and Hernán Díaz Alonso of Xefirotarch. The previous volume in the series, *Cultural Cues*, presented the studios of Joe Day of Deegan Day Design, Tom Wiscombe of Tom Wiscombe Architecture, and Adib Cúre and Carie Penabad of Cúre & Penabad.

This volume, *Against the Grain*, reflects, as do its predecessors, Yale's studio pedagogy, providing students numerous approaches toward architecture as a building art and encouraging independent thinking for the future of design.

INTRODUCTION

Against the Grain is the seventh book to feature the work of the Louis I. Kahn Visiting Assistant Professorship and the work of the advanced studios at the Yale School of Architecture.

This book begins with the research and designs that emerged from the studio "Brutal Beauty: Piles, Monoliths, and the Incongruous Whole" offered by Marcelo Spina and Georgina Huljich of the Los Angeles–based architectural practice P-A-T-T-E-R-N-S. The firm, founded in 1999, was named an Emerging Voice in 2011 by the Architectural League of New York and noted in *Architectural Record's* Design Vanguard in 2012. Dedicated teacher-practitioners, Spina and Huljich have taught at SCI-Arc and University of California, Los Angeles. Their built projects include art institutions in Los Angeles and apartment buildings in Rosario, Argentina, as well as exhibition installations and large-scale projects for international competitions. In their Yale studio, Spina and Huljich introduce the problem of the monolith as a way of countering current trends in computation-driven architectural design. While most parametric form is smooth and articulated, the formal experiments examined in this studio are mute and segmented. These qualities were achieved by developing contrasting relationships between volume and texture on the interior and exterior of the various student proposals.

The second studio, "Boulevard Triumphant: Ecological Infrastructure, Architecture, Modernization, and the Image of the City," was taught by Dan Wood, who started the New York City-based practice WORKac with his partner, Amale Andraos, in 2003. Wood has taught at numerous architecture schools, including at Princeton and Columbia. The firm's work ranges from master plans to commercial and cultural institutional projects, including Wieden + Kennedy's new headquarters in New York City and the Blaffer Art Museum, in Houston, Texas. In his studio, Wood asked students to study the culture, infrastructure, and history of Gabon, Africa, to create a new architectural language that goes beyond merely modernizing the vernacular or implementing a Western style. With a focus on the governmental boulevard in Libreville, Gabon's capital city, the studio attempted to develop projects that critiqued the clichés and nostalgic themes of the adjacent architecture, which relies heavily on the aesthetics of Tropical Modernism, to create new forms that merge infrastructure with a vision for the city and country.

Lisa Gray and Alan Organschi of the New Haven, Connecticut-based practice Gray Organschi Architecture taught the third studio, "Timber City Innovation District." The firm has strong ties with Yale: Organschi has led the Vlock Building Project for the past ten years. The firm primarily works on residences and small infrastructure projects, finding innovative uses for traditional materials and construction techniques. Gray and Organschi's Yale studio examined ways to expand the use of wood beyond the single-family house and focused on the environmental benefits of wood as a construction material. The studio projects were sited to create a district showcasing the potential of various timber technologies for multi-family housing, infrastructure, commercial and industrial buildings.

Against the Grain divides the three studios into three separate sections, each of which begins with an interview with the architects about the work of their firms. The essays and project briefs framing the studio explorations highlight the variety of these practitioner-educators' pedagogical approaches and the current diversity within the discourse of architecture. The studios led by these young practitioners challenge conventional academic inquiry, producing work that explores alternate implementations of form, style, and material.

The editors would like to thank the professors and the students for helping to make this document possible. From Marcelo Spina and Georgina Huljich's studio, we would like to thank Constance Vale, Justin Nguyen, Hochung Kim, Craig Rosman, Kate Warren, Robert Cannavino, Cristian Oncescu, Chessin Gertler, and Jonathan Meier. From Dan Wood's studio, we would like to thank Bryan Maddock, Robert Cannavino, Rushyan Yen, Ann Morrow Johnson, Evan Wiskup, William Sheridan, Adam Wagoner, Henry Chan, Hochung Kim, Jacqueline Kow, and Yoojin Han. From Lisa Gray and Alan Organschi's studio, we would like to thank Haelee Jung, Perry Wexelberg, Ben Smith, Amy Su, Boyuan Zhang, Mengran Li, Maya Alexander, Karolina Czeczek, and Peter Mcinish. Special recognition is due to Constance Vale and Ben Smith for their editorial work on their respective studio sections.

We extend our utmost appreciation to Sarah Gephart of MGMT. design, copy editor David Delp, and Dean Robert A. M. Stern. We hope this volume presents new possibilities for exploration and elicits debate on the future of architecture.

—Nina Rappaport and Jacqueline Kow
Editors

MARCELO *SPINA* AND *GEORGINA* HULJICH

BRUTAL BEAUTY

INTERVIEW

MARCELO SPINA *AND* GEORGINA *HULJICH*

Marcelo Spina and Georgina Huljich discuss their approach to design with Nina Rappaport.

Nina Rappaport Can you talk about how you established your firm, P-A-T-T-E-R-N-S, and what the initial objectives were in terms of work and approach?

Marcelo Spina P-A-T-T-E-R-N-S began in Los Angeles, in 2002, as an attempt to establish a platform to produce architecture at a global scale and in close relation with new technologies. We were pursuing an extended version of formalism, very much in sync with Sanford Kwinter's writings and a Deleuzean philosophy of materialism. We were operating under the assumption that form could not be reduced to a notion of "object" but, rather, attained the "field" around it—that is, the pattern of habits and behaviors enabled by it in both space and time. While some of those ambitions still remain, our work can't be fully explained according to only this notion.

NR When you refer to patterns as physical organizational systems, one aspect you mention is the idea of surface ornamentation as a sign of formal weakness. What do you mean exactly, and how do you avoid it in your own work?

MS Right, we think that surface ornamentation, as a default, is not only a sign of formal weakness but also a complete cliché. The level of refinement is such that even corporate offices, with the aid of similar software packages available in the most advanced schools, are already patterning their buildings façades left and right. As a result, architecture becomes a cartoon of itself. Victor Shklovsky suggested that the role of art and architecture is to defamiliarize things around us so we can look at them as if for the first time and see how strange they are, "to make the stone feel stony again." This is why the notion of monolithicity is so important now, the idea that, in order to preserve the effects of mass, a certain muteness in architecture is not only desired, but essential.

Georgina Huljich We are interested in articulating form, not decorating surfaces. So, it is a question of not only what, but where and how much. For us, it is a functional means to generate scalar transitions, obfuscate the metrics of building, introduce depth and tactility, relate interior to exterior, and so on. I also think that the notion of patterns relates to the idea of convention as something that is recurring and the contrast between how different materials behave and how someone can engage them at the scale of a building. Behavior is a rhythm of doing things more than once. The idea of rigor is not a priori but acquired, so the notion of innovation emerges out of testing and experimenting with the behavior of many normative aspects of a project.

NR How does your Prism Los Angeles art gallery, which opened in 2009, attract people through the bending of the envelope and the experience of the space? How do you explore materiality through the translucence and opaqueness of the plastic façade?

MS This project is a great example because, with a façade, we had to address social and cultural aspects of an environment that is completely driven by images and advertisement. The project produces two opposing torsional moments, which cause a visual and physical instability. It is not just the spectacle of the building that is important but the theatricality of its surfaces—a sense of anticipation, like the lifting of curtains in a theater. The real spectacle is the art you are going to see inside—a sculpture or a painting.

GH We had to be responsive to two kinds of movement at the urban level. The first is the vehicular movement on Sunset Strip, with the upper-helix twist of the façade, and the second is the movement at the scale of the human body, engaging pedestrian activity at the gallery entrance. This duality informs the selection of materials, both translucent and opaque. It is about creating a dichotomy that operates continuously throughout the day.

NR In terms of maneuvers that respond to changes of scale in the folded plates, wrapping surfaces, and oblique angles, what happens when these geometries jump to a larger scale, so that the diagonals become surface to volume to structure? Is it a much more holistic form than one would imagine?

MS We are interested in the oblique, not only in the sense that Paul Virilio described it, but also, as a way to tie together formal, spatial, and social problems. We were interested in hyperbolic paraboloids and saddle-surface geometry as a means to destabilize assumed understandings of space. That is why we looked at architects such as Le Corbusier, Iannis Xenakis, and Felix Candela. In our Jujuy Redux residential tower, in Rosario, Argentina, the balconies are twisting out of the concrete, vertical surface. We don't like the idea of a one-liner, and we don't think that is the right scale for the plasticity of the building to express itself; we, rather, look for the layering of conditions—functional, formal, and aesthetic. The balcony projects out of the building mass, expressing its

01

02

03

plasticity in a transition from mass to volume to surface. We challenged the local building code to adjust notions of envelope and managed to be innovative with a very tight, developer-driven typology in South America.

GH We also try to connect things that wouldn't otherwise be connected. These challenges become opportunities for us to engage a problem that, while proposed before, can lead to a different answer. The idea of innovation interests us. That's why conventions and constraints are so important in our work. In terms of surface and volume, we are deeply interested in mass as a combination of both. The idea of exposing the thickness of the surface while embedding it within a much larger formal logic promotes the idea of articulated transitions, rather than pure continuity.

NR I am very interested in the way you talk about robustness as a structural attribute that becomes part of the massing, volume, and design of the building, especially in the Rosario project. What do you mean by "robustness"? Is it more than just the weight or physical structure of a building?

MS Yes. There are two aspects to the way we understand it. One is conceptual and has to do with the monolithic aspect of our work, including a proclivity for certain material finishes and construction methods. The other has to do with a particular sensibility toward articulation and the necessary lack of it at certain essential times. The two are intrinsically related in achieving this sense of robustness.

01–02 Jujuy Redux in Rosario, Argentina
03–04 Prism Gallery in Los Angeles

04

GH It is also a problem of building assembly and the effective disguising of it.

MS It is a question of suppressing tectonics in the traditional sense so as to produce "objects" of a scale that cannot be easily discerned in the context of a building. "Robustness" refers to qualities of the mass, its lack of articulation and sense of weight, its defiance of gravity, its relation with the ground, and so on. These are significant issues that, in our opinion, can be both read and experienced. In our projects for Keelung Crystal, in Taiwan, and the library in Helsinki, the mass is deliberately chunky; a layer of rustication enters at a different scale and, nearer to interior regions, more as a disruption than as refinement.

NR Both the Keelung Crystal and the library are similar to your approach to designing the Zhixin Hybrid Office Park, in Chengdu, China, where you are kind of cutting away the solid mass and creating a pattern from the structure beneath.

GH Like with most of our work, there are two intersecting systems at play. One is strictly formal and relates ordering, geometric, and functional principles to the idea of mass. The other is material and physical and is directly connected to the way the building expresses itself as mass. This duality relates to the idea of the monochromatic materiality and monolithic form, which we subvert by conceiving difference through refractive qualities of the material, instead of the color or contrasts between two materials. In Chengdu, the flat portions of the façade are clad in aluminum panels, and the torsion sections are GFRC [glass-fiber-reinforced concrete]. The building appears to be, materially, monolithic when, in fact, it is not. The articulated areas underneath the overhangs are, in fact, monolithic, and the flat and smooth are not. The way you perceive the material in close proximity and the way that you can perceive it from farther away creates a sense of mysteriousness. I think this connects back to the idea of the robust.

NR In terms of spatial organization, how do you foreground and resolve interstitial spaces?

MS Our interest in interstitial space reflects an attention to interiority, not just the idea of interiority but the interior itself. Only architecture can produce and deliver interior experiences. We have discussed this in our book, *Embedded* [2011], in which we relate the interstitial to the political, conceptual, and physical. Continuing our interest in mass, an interstitial understanding of space is a way to deliver its effects in the interior. In our Collective Void dormitory project for the Pontifical Catholic University of Puerto Rico, in Ponce, the interstitial space is a zigzagging void that articulates both interior and exterior. It brings the idea that architecture has a core that

---

05 Rendering of proposal for the New Keelung Harbor Service Building, Taiwan

06 Chendu Fluid Core-Yard

06

07

08

can't be reduced to only an external appearance. In our project in China, the building's mass appears pure and simple, but it completely restates itself once you examine it at close range. From the outside, it could be confused with just another corporate box. It is only when you get closer that you see it is something else. That aspect of producing a project that is both familiar and strange at the same time interests us a lot.

NR There is an element of surprise in the complexity of the massing, as though the interstitial spaces, rather than left over, are purposeful.

MS Exactly. Those interstitial moments are compressed by architectural volume and mass. Underneath these overhangs are the most intense areas of the building, and a sense of tactility is introduced by the coffered surfaces. Neil Denari refers to this notion as "optical tactility," the notion that the sense of sight operates as a parallel to the sense of touch.

NR Yale was your first time teaching together. How did that go?

GH Yes, this was the first time. We have taught in different institutions. We talk about each other's studios, look at each other's syllabi, and attend each other's reviews, but we never actually teach together. It was an interesting experience to do this, since we combined not only our interests but also our different approaches to pedagogy.

NR How does your focus on massing and volume relate your Yale studio?

MS At Yale, we explored mute forms of iconicity in architecture. Our studio reconsidered the formal economy and ruthless aesthetics of Brutalism, especially its reliance on robust massing, volumetric piling, and a sensibility that leaned toward monolithicity. All these issues were considered in the context of a renewed interest in the object in both architecture and philosophy and problems of posture, legibility, and near autonomy. We imagined our studio as an alternative to the recent excess in ornamentation. If ornament is small and beautiful, Brutalism is large and disgusting. We wanted to find the uncanny in it, its "brutal beauty."

NR In your own practice, what are you working on now and excited about going forward?

MS We have been working on various projects, ranging in scale, location, and scope. One of them is a large, two-million-square-foot mixed-use project in downtown Los Angeles. It's a challenging scale and program for our office. Because of its central location, accessibility to nearby infrastructure, and potential amalgamation

09

of old and new, the project has the potential to become a different architectural icon and a catalyst for new social and cultural development at the south end of the downtown district.

GH The politics of this project are extremely complicated and certainly new to us, so we are really excited about the possibility of connecting the polemics of our work with a larger audience and a wider discussion of a city such as L.A., which is in desperate need of densification and urbanity.

MS Another project, at the opposite end of this spectrum, is a resort on Rottnest Island, just off the city of Perth, in western Australia. This project confronts our current interest in muteness and monolithicity with notions of nature, the rural, and their associations with the vernacular.

NR And how does this idea of brutal beauty apply to your own projects?

MS Brutal beauty was just the title and maybe one of the effects the architecture we are after can produce. I guess the central theme of what we are really interested in is that of "mute icons," the working title of our next book, which is very influenced by the studio and seminar we taught at Yale and have been teaching at both UCLA and SCI-Arc ever since. There have been a series of projects since our Yale studio that have dealt with this subject. Probably most significant among them is our proposal for Budapest City Park, which consists of four independent and familiar buildings in a large Neo-Classical park. This project, its representations, some of the most recent images, and even a reincarnation of it for the Chicago Architectural Biennial—we are really excited about all of it and committed to continue. In a way, these four buildings are mute icons, captivating and off-putting, participating in their context and estranging it at the same time. Paradoxical in nature [as brutal beauty], we think of them and the work we are currently pursuing as possessing dichotomic qualities in projective and mysterious ways.

---

07 **Rendering of proposal for Helsinki Library**
08 **Rendering of student dormitory for the Pontificia Catholic University**
09 **Rendering of proposal for Budapest City Park**

BRUTAL *BEAUTY*:

PILES, *MONOLITHS*, AND THE *INCONGRUOUS* WHOLE

"Rcyner Banham insisted that a Brutalist building should produce an affecting image, 'something which is visually valuable'; and while classical aesthetics would presume this value to accrue in pleasure of something beautiful, for New Brutalism, 'image may be defined as *quod visum perturbat*—that which, seen, affects the emotions,' with pleasure, displeasure, or, pointedly, an admixture of the two."

Mark Cousins, "The Ugly," *AA Files 28* (1994): 61.

"With the exception of monuments, architecture requires space for inhabitation. If the term *monolith* is taken literally to suggest material solidity, monolithic architecture would be impossible by definition. However, we understand "monolithic" to signify monolith-like, confer a sense of solidity and homogeneity on objects that are not and could not be integrally solid and homogeneous."

Rodolfo Machado and Rodolphe el-Khoury, *Monolithic Architecture,* Munich: Prestel, 1995.

—Marcelo Spina and Georgina Huljich
with Nathan Hume

Introduction: Monolithic Architecture

Used by Rodolfo Machado and Rodolphe el-Khoury, in 1995, to describe a series of projects that deliberately avoided the articulation of part-to-whole relationships as dictated by classical doctrine, "monolithic architecture" became the predominant architectural formal modality of the "avant-garde" in the past two decades. In their preface to the exhibition catalog, they rightly acknowledge that the projects they designate as monolithic architecture "exist in their most radical aspect as paradoxical representations: radical in the sense that they self-consciously elaborate their monolithic character into an aesthetic strategy and carry it out to its extreme realization; paradoxical, in the sense that they undermine their own fixity and solidity when their lapidary countenance stands as something totally other with respect to internal and external realities, program, and context."[1]

Paradoxical in its representations, monolithic architecture engages complex material and tectonic assemblies that are in contrast to its formal aspirations. The studio aimed to engage the disciplinary riddle innate in the impossibility of a truly monolithic architecture and to explore its dichotomous ambitions, which connect issues ranging from abstract representation all the way to material and building assembly. Dwelling in the very incongruity of the term as a productive dichotomy, the class aimed to bring contemporary relevance to the critical lineage of monolithicity in architecture.

Mute Icons: A Pressing Dichotomy

In the wake of 9/11, the financial market crash, and a new age of cultural and economic austerity, there followed a reexamination of the architectural icon and its role in contemporary culture. The icon has become an object of public scrutiny, putting into question its social significance in the present milieu with its typical associations with both spectacle and civic allure. While the icon has traditionally produced a strong, emblematic urban image, monolithicity favors a suppressed formal legibility and an introverted approach to building in the city. The turn away from the icon, as such, and the contemporaneous interest in the monolithic indicate a strategy of formal muteness as an alternative mode of cultural production.

Specifically, in the context of the discipline, the perceived exhaustion with digital design processes, driven purely by aesthetics of excess, added to the almost formulaic

01

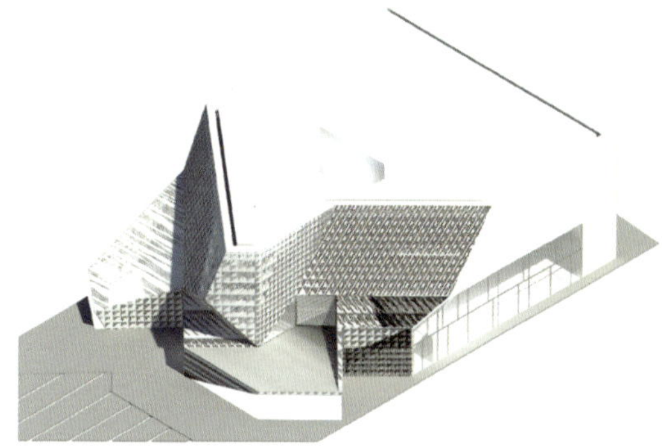

02

03

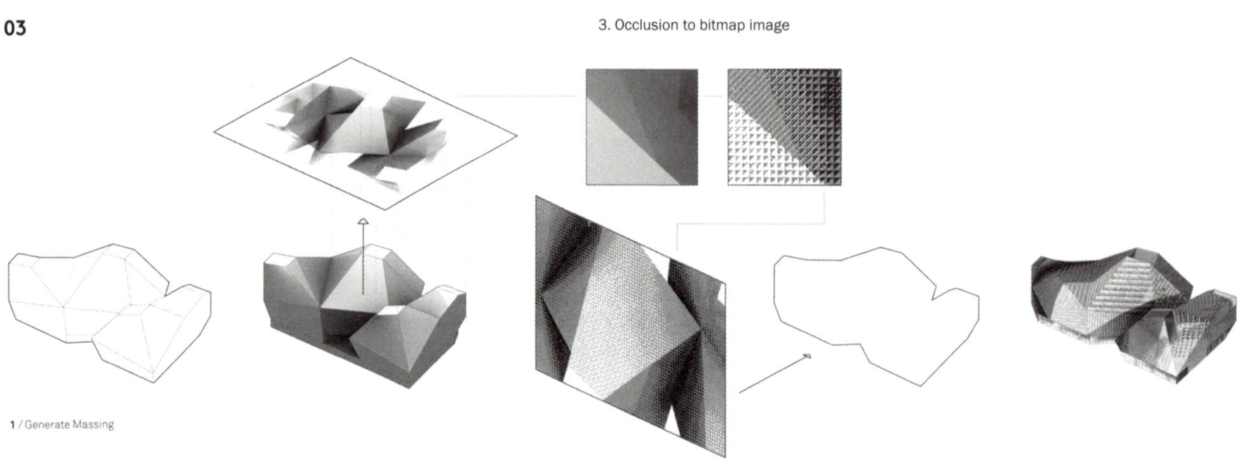
3. Occlusion to bitmap image
1 / Generate Massing
1. Generate massing
2. Extract top occlusion
4. Project to front elevation
5. Texture result

"parametric" approach to form, and the failure of the single surface to produce substantive qualities of volume and mass have engendered a renewed interest in solid objects. Part of this reaction against the icon has generated a demand for a new simplicity, an absolute, pure, and even autonomous architecture.

The studio aimed to find a critical and progressive approach to the problem of the image or icon in architecture and contemporary culture. Issues of form, mass, volume, interiority, and articulation were seen as key components from which to speculate on the status of the icon as the ultimate architectural object. In that regard, the studio intended to position a new regime in which the real thing—its functionality as a thing—and its image could coexist together in a dichotomous whole.

In its representational and iconographic nature, scalar ambiguity, and indifference to both program and context, the monolithic project finds itself in the territory of the mute icon. Dwelling in the paradox between silence and sign, mute icons debunk a false dichotomy between critical discourse surrounding form and the attainment of social ethics. The mute icon manages disciplinary autonomy in its capacity for both resistance and resilience— what Sarah Whiting refers to as "engaged autonomy."[2]

Mass: The Monolith and the Pile

With the objective of exploring mute forms of iconicity in architecture, the studio reconsidered the formal economy and ruthless aesthetics of Brutalism, especially its robust massing, volumetric piling, and monolithic sensibility. Moving beyond the past two decades of what would now be described as a process of cohesive formal homogenization, the studio aimed to explore the formal and aesthetic possibilities of incongruity in architecture. Formal ambiguity and ambivalence of reading were mobilizing mechanisms to subvert notions of typological and aesthetic fixity, challenging the role and current status of the icon. Consequently, the studio pursued dichotomies as a way to defy fixed notions of part-to-whole relationships. Rather than pursuing a naive return to collage and its collision of multiple opposites to produce disjunction and fragmentation, dichotomies combine opposites to generate a formally indeterminate and visually inconsistent whole. Here, contrasts would neither exist as oppositions nor dissolve altogether but, rather, become blurred, with the whole entering into a more complex state of dualism.

Understood as incongruous and ambivalent, mute icons are in direct opposition to fluidity and singularity, and, thus, the studio moved well past Brutalism's regularity, uniformity, and much-critiqued atmosphere of totalitarianism. In addition to the well-known Brutalist buildings and social experiments from the 1960s and 1970s, the studio also considered the embryonic nature of the monolithic fortifications documented in Paul Virilio's *Bunker Archeology.* The formal autonomy, "objectness," and lack of relation with the ground of these "defensive architectures" are in diametrical opposition to the ambition for physical movement and social connectivity of Brutalist doctrine. In fact, it is this opposition between a discrete static object (the bunker) and a continuous dynamic system (Brutalist building) that the studio was interested in studying as a duplicitous condition internal to each project. This dichotomy was all the more relevant when considering a similar antagonism between logics of "object" and "field," the former exemplified by the work on object-oriented ontology by Graham Harman and the latter by the philosophy of Gilles Deleuze and Felix Guattari.

For all the baggage of the term, "formal incongruity" was not an a priori quality set but, rather, a problem to be tracked and hypothesized by each student through rigorous processes and in the context of specific design experiments. In this first phase, the projects were designed completely independent from their site. Students focused on autonomous objects with the idea of generating prototypical masses, rather than specific buildings. Students relied on rigorous digital modeling techniques and scripted mathematical definitions to simultaneously deploy packing organizations of various platonic solids and articulate monolithic compositions. In this way, each project explored formal and organizational contrasts between two extremes: cohesive wholes and random piles.

Turning its attention to both platonic solids and figural outlines, the studio began with two parallel and interrelated lines of research. The class interrogated the potential of the random packing of platonic solids to generate unstable, lumpy masses. The intention was to continue contemporary investigations into the development of mass with the use of platonic solids as well as explore the qualities emerging from their accumulation

01 Budapest House of Music

02 Budapest Architecture & Photo Museum

03 Diagram, showing the progression from mass to texture

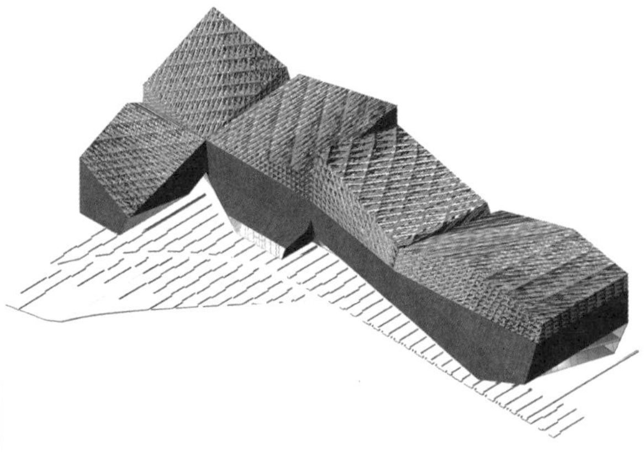

04

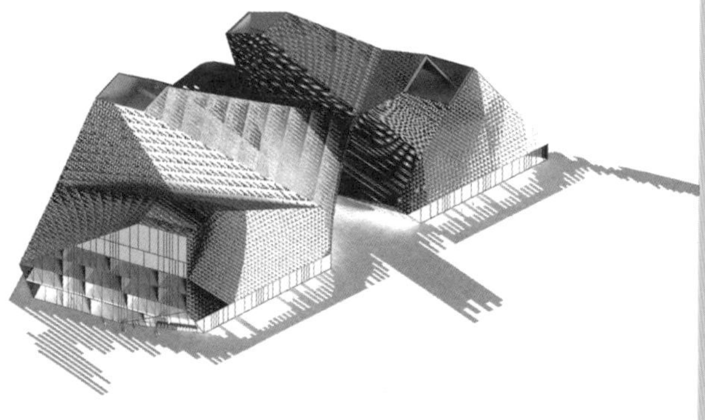

05

and interpenetration. In tandem with this work, students were asked to examine an overlay of saddle-surface geometry with defined, linear-edge conditions. These surfaces produced figural and prickly qualities when associated with the piles, making them appear to be more cohesive and monolithic. Rather than seeing these two languages as being in opposition, students looked for ways to combine and hybridize them into a language of volume and mass at the scale of building.

Surfaces: A Materiality of Shade and Shadow

Going back to "Beton Brut" and Le Corbusier's work on the Unite d'Habitation, in Marseille, and, later, Chapel of Notre Dame du Haut, in Ronchamp, and Sainte Marie de La Tourette, in Lyon, two ideas have been associated with Brutalist architecture. The first one is the roughness of the concrete, particularly evident in the texture of building surfaces produced by the uneven wooden planks. The second one is the reliance on simple volumes and a strong contrast among discrete elements, exemplified by shade and shadows within the building mass. The studio integrated the problem of materiality and contrast through the study of shade, shadow, and noise. Projects paid special attention to the means by which renderings are translated into a language of 2D drawing by using bitmap patterns as well as other means of visual and optical distortion. Aimed at delaying and concealing legibility, this visual grain came from the massing source, which was modified so as to acquire a dimensional quality and misapplied, again, into the mass. Much like a glitch, this subtle "noise" was meant to emulate a fake materiality.

Aiming to connect theoretical concerns with design ambitions, the studio interrogated what implications these representational problems could bring to bear upon physical reality through the media of drawing, rendering, and physical models.

1. Rodolfo Machado and Rodolphe el-Khoury, *Monolithic Architecture*, Munich: Prestel, 1995.
2. Sarah Whiting, "I am interested in a project of engaged autonomy," *Log 28*, Anyone Corporation, summer 2013.
3. Gilles Deleuze and Félix Guattari, *A Thousand Plateaus: Capitalism and Schizophrenia*, Continuum, 2004.

04 Budapest Museum of Ethnography
05 Budapest New National Gallery & Ludwig Museum
06 Model of proposed Prishtina Mosque
07 Aerial site plan of proposed series of mute icons

06

07

LOS ANGELES:

ACADEMY MUSEUM OF *MOTION* PICTURES @ *LACMA*

“I don’t want to live in a city where the only cultural advantage is that you can make a right turn on a red light.”

Annie Hall, 1977, directed by Woody Allen

“A typical criticism of Los Angeles: if you don’t like one thing, complain about its opposite as well: ‘The architecture is too eclectic, but it’s also too uniform.’ ”

Los Angeles Plays Itself, 2003, directed by Thom Anderson

—Marcelo Spina and Georgina Huljich
with Nathan Hume

The studio project required students to consider a new building for The Academy of Motion Picture Arts and Sciences Museum at the Los Angeles County Museum of Art (LACMA). Renzo Piano’s recently unveiled proposal, a 290,000-square-foot addition to the existing May Company Building on Fairfax and Wilshire, served as a basis for the studio’s programmatic requirements. The new project included a 1,000-seat theater, more than 10,000 square feet devoted to the history of the movies, a public piazza, the museum lobby, a café, a gift shop, and a 12,000-square-foot “making of. . .” demonstration room for 150 people to re-create the experience of a real cinematic production.

The LACMA campus brackets an eclectic collection of buildings by diverse architects, from different time periods, and of varied sizes, all coexisting horizontally on a connecting ground. In this way, the museum mimics the dispersed and unstructured quality of the city of Los Angeles itself. Consistent with the “tabula rasa” trend initiated by Rem Koolhaas’s proposal for LACMA, in 2001, and continued by Peter Zumthor’s latest plan, Piano’s current proposal repurposes the existing May Company Building and suggests an addition at the rear of the building. The studio contemplated alternatives to the current proposal and pursued bold new visions that reconsidered the museum’s urban presence within its immediate context and the so-called Wilshire Corridor, as well as the cultural implications of making a different kind of icon in a city of icons.

Project Conclusions

The studio addressed the problem of the contemporary icon by developing a discourse surrounding muteness and monolithicity. The projects focused on these two aspects by engaging formal and digital techniques that offer a high degree of representational abstraction and formal autonomy. In this context, muteness and monolithicity implied three main aspects.

Objectness, or the Denial of Ground

Projects emphasized a reading of mass and the qualities associated with it, including weight, instability, discreteness, and autonomy. These aspects implied a certain discomfort in the posture the building assumed relative to its context and ground. A majority of the studio projects altogether denied or ignored the ground, as both context and as a viable datum, by asserting a formal indifference and independence from it.

Noise: Ornament and Crime

In support of this reading of mass, projects exhibited a level of visual noise through texture, coarseness, and grain just a degree below what might otherwise be viewed as ornamentation or surface articulation. This noise was employed to irritate the surfaces of the mass in order to produce openings and fenestration consistent with its monolithic qualities. This tactic created a problem, in general, for the openings and fenestration, which became a rich source of discussion and controversy within the studio. To preserve the perceived weight of mass, students had the challenge of incorporating a realistic number of windows without altering the monolithic nature of the surfaces.

Incongruity: Discontinuity between Exterior and Interior

To convey solidity and impenetrability, projects exhibited a radical disassociation between interior and exterior, a quality that was invoked by solid-void diagrams. The idea here was as obvious as it was strange: if an architectural project was to be solid, the interior would have to be either full or void and compressed in such way that the effects of mass and volume would continue to exert pressure on the interior. In that way, some of the projects produced a building within a building—that is, an interior that was equivalent in its formal dominance to the exterior and only loosely dependent on the form of the exterior. The exterior-interior relationships were neither one-to-one nor totally detached.

The seeming opacity of an exterior and the impenetrability of its mass led to a constant misreading of building objects. To many jurors' surprise, most projects treated the auditoriums not as part of the larger internal volumes or as voids but as indistinct from the rest of the program. That caused the a priori volumes of the auditoriums to be completely indistinguishable from the larger mass of slabs.

Last, the studio approached representation so as to support the preceding aims and maintain a sense of distance between object and subject. Perspective views were avoided in favor of orthographic projection and axonometric drawings. With the intention of estranging the conventional relationships between subject and object, projects purposely appear to be both wild and indifferent. Elevations and sections were particularly important devices to evaluate, refine, and judge the projects. In fact, the problem of orthographic projection and drawing as two-dimensional endeavors was foregrounded by the studio to bring the medium of drawing and its projective abstraction into full flesh. This process allowed all the projects to disregard perspectival articulation and imprecise sculpting in favor of rigorously developed orthographic projections.

As a consequence of all these exercises, the studio results were as virtuous as they were controversial. The projects were unsettling, managing to be, at the same time, brutal and sophisticated, pervasive in their formalism, and withdrawn in their sensibility.

Studio Bibliography

Banham, Reyner, *The New Brutalism: Ethic or Aesthetic?* New York: Reinhold, 1966.

Boullée, Étienne-Louis. *Boullée's Treatise on Architecture,* edited by Helen Rosenau, London: A. Tiranti, 1953.

Breuer, Marcel, and Blake, Peter, *Marcel Breuer: Sun and Shadow: the Philosophy of an Architect*, New York: Longmans Green, 1956.

Breuer, Marcel, *Marcel Breuer: Design and Architecture,* first edition Weil Am Rhein: Vitra Design Stiftung, 2003.

Cousins, Mark, "The Ugly," in *AA Files,* Vol. No. 28 (Autumn), London: Architectural Association School of Architecture, 1994 (61–64).

Kaufmann, Emil, *Three Revolutionary Architects: Boullée, Ledoux, and Lequeu,* Philadelphia: American Philosophical Society, 1952.

Kipnis, Jeffrey, *A Question of Qualities: Essays in Architecture*, edited by Alexander Maymind, Cambridge, Mass.: MIT Press, 2013.

Le Corbusier, *Towards a New Architecture*, edited by Frederick Etchells, New York: Dover Publications, 1986.

Machado, Rodolfo and Rodolphe el-Khoury, editors, *Monolithic Architecture*, Munich: Prestel, 1995.

Nouvel, Jean, *Jean Nouvel, 1994–2002: The Symbolic Order of Matter = El Orden Simbólico De La Materia,* Madrid: *El Croquis*, 2002.

Shklovsky, Viktor, *Theory of Prose*, 1st ed. Elmwood Park, Ill.: Dalkey Archive Press, 1991.

Vidler, Anthony, *Claude-Nicolas Ledoux: Architecture and Social Reform at the End of the Ancien Régime*, Cambridge, Mass.: MIT Press, 1990.

Virilio, Paul, and Collins, George, *Bunker Archeology: Texts and Photos,* New York, N.Y.: Princeton Architectural Press, 1994.

Whiting, Sarah, and Somol, Bob, "Notes around the Doppler Effect and Other Moods of Modernism," in *Perspecta, Mining Autonomy*, Vol. 33, (72–77). Cambridge, Mass.: MIT Press .

STUDIO WORK

01 WITHDRAWN *FIGURE*

The incongruity between the interior and exterior of these projects resulted from retaining the piles of platonic geometry as interior volumes. Despite the divergent formal languages that occur on either side of the envelope, the interior is still loosely related to the exterior, as both share a number of surfaces. The piles divide two dissimilar interior realms, defining the edge between solid and void at their perimeter. On one side, there is a thick poché of dense programmatic volumes and, on the other, a void that contains large, open volumes. Many of these projects exhibit the qualities of a single object wrapping around or folding back on itself due to their interior voids encircling or excavating the dense programmatic mass. The exterior texture results from portraying artificial shadows, which provoke false readings of the geometry.

CONSTANCE VALE

INCONGRUOUS MONOLITH

In order to achieve monolithic qualities, this proposal employs three primary formal strategies. First, like the monolithic structures described by Paul Virilio in *Bunker Archaeology*, mass is made to appear "upturned" and "tilted," as if the weight were displacing volume over time, an effect that is reinforced by the shadows in the façade's texture. Next, the earth is seen as "no longer being good lodging," due to an apparent "dematerialization of the ground" through a formal insistence on verticality and in the shift of the predominant mass above the ground plane. Similarly, the internal primitive volumes, over which saddle surfaces are arranged, rotate from the horizontal to the vertical, reinforcing this reading of terrestrial dematerialization. Finally, the pile of platonic geometry is made to "interpenetrate," leading to a "confusion of the animate and inanimate." Their forms are coincident and rotate around a hinge point, creating an internal sense of motion.

The resultant monolith is, in effect, a slightly lifted pyramid, with its internal primitives acting as narrow tunnels. A solid-void relationship is created in which solid program acts as a thick poché, wrapping around the central void of the primitives. The convergence of these primitives produces an atrium that carries light to the interior, provides circulation space on the lower horizontal levels, and allows views from the adjacent floor plates through the pores of a micro-texture in the vertically oriented prisms above. These platonic solids can be read as a vestige of the monolith's creation, but they are intended to act as an unexpected inner world that is incongruous with its exterior. The monolith retains its status as such, not only for its formal qualities, but also

01–03 Elevations, showcasing the interplay of the textured façade with the monolith's lifted form

01

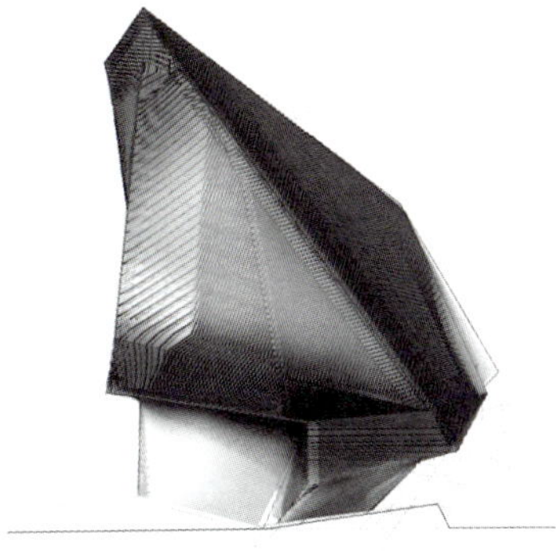

02

03

for its "inward-looking" attitude. It becomes, like Virilio's bunkers, "a single object folding back on itself."

In addition to creating an exaggerated top-heaviness, the texture employed conveys a false transparency of the figure in its multiple, overlaid offsets and rotations. The texture also produces a multitude of small "firing slits," loosely related to the original geometry. On the interior, this strategy was reproduced as a moiré pattern of columns that provides structure and suggests a thick, transparent volume, affording further visual density to the poché space. Because of this, occupants sense the "incredible pressure" and "singular heaviness" of the surrounding monolithic interior. Ultimately, it is read in the conceptual proximity of its presence to its absence, through the overlay of "two dissimilar realities."[1]

1. All quotations used in the project description indicate a theoretical framework shared with Paul Virilio

---

04 Generative diagrams, showcasing three different elements: monolithic form, interaction of the form's shadow and texture, and the stacked primitives
05 Final massing model in context
06 Unrolled section, showing circulation through the building
07 Section, illustrating the connection of interior voids and the nesting of theaters around them

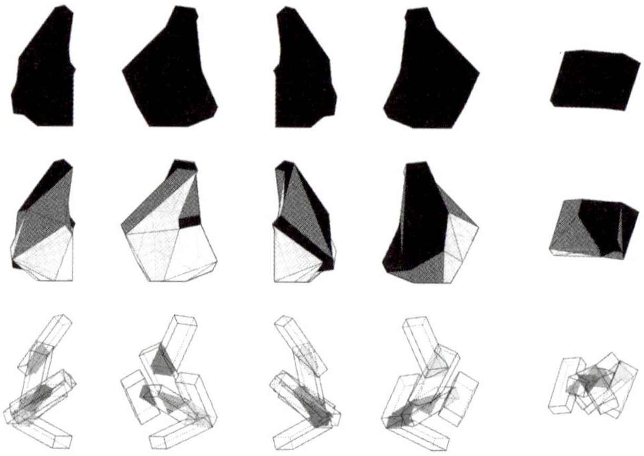

04

05

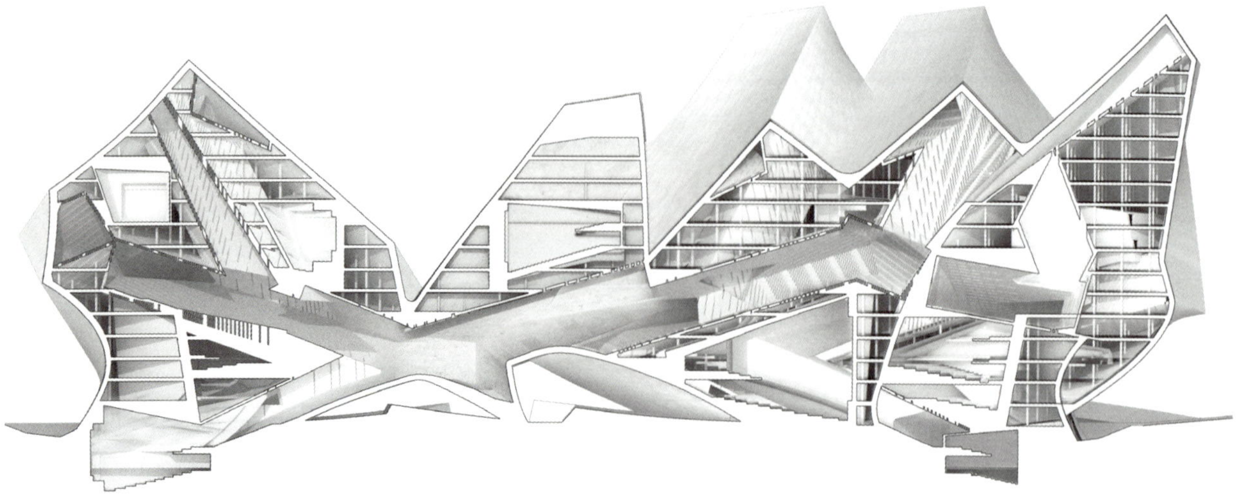

06

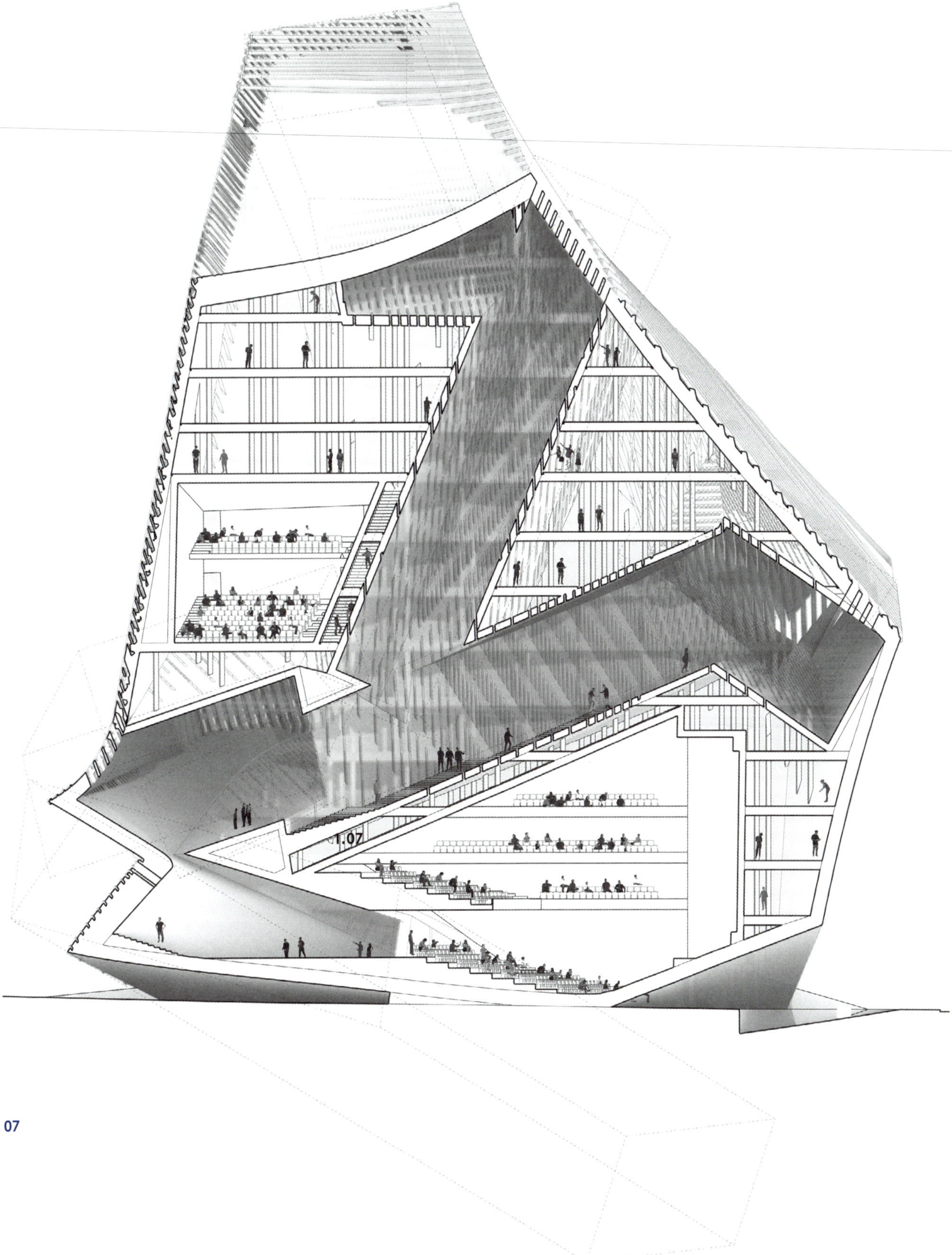

07

JUSTIN NGUYEN

MEDUSA

"But in Ovid's text it is not Medusa's 'head,' or even her gaze, that petrifies. Rather, it is primarily her silenced 'face' or 'mouth' (os, oris) that does its enigmatic work."
— Lynn Enterline, *The Rhetoric of the Body from Ovid to Shakespeare*

Considering the incongruous formal relationship between cohesive wholes and random piles, this project is interested in the possibility of multiple and paradoxical readings within the monolith. Rather than assuming the mute iconicity of the architectural monolith as a lack of articulation, blankness is defined here in terms of multiple and contradictory part-to-whole relationships as described by Kipnis' concept of "intensive coherence," further recalling his account of Frank Gehry's Vitra Design museum.

The monolithic arrangement is additive rather than subtractive, such that a heterogeneous yet cohesive whole suggests no single dominant form in either the organization of the initial massing or the internal volumes, the wrapping of the envelope, or the dematerialization of the texture. Multiplicity through layering produces an unstable and ambiguous dialogue between inside and outside, background and foreground, and vertical and horizontal. The Medusa-like form distorts and dislocates elements that "seek to engender shifting affiliations that, nevertheless, resist entering into stable alignments".[1] While these elements keep the reading of a theater at each elevation, they are otherwise contradictory; this strategy explores the idea of a consistent yet heterogeneous interior and exterior. The misalignment and miscoupling of the original organization of primitives within the pile attempt to create a reading that is both and neither part (pile) or whole (monolith).

1. Jeffrey Kipnis, "Towards a New Architecture," *Folding in Architecture*, Profile No. 102, London: John Wiley & Sons, 1993, pp 40–49.

---

01 Exploded axonometric diagram, showing relationship between an unraveled interior and its corresponding elevation

02–04 Elevations, showing how texture and shadows are used to blur the reading of the building's volume, edges, and openings

05 Detail of final model, showing exterior texture and aperture

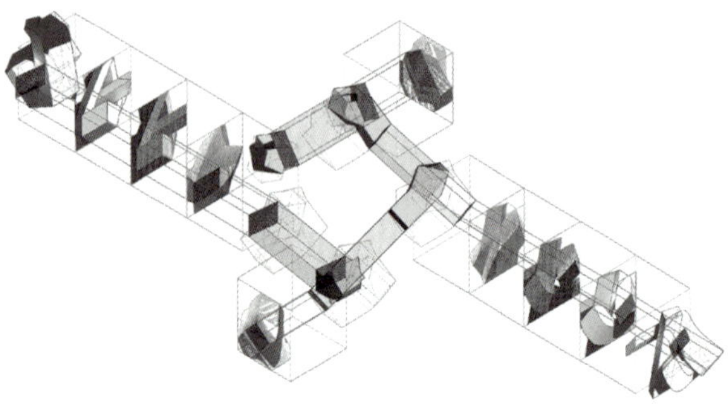

01

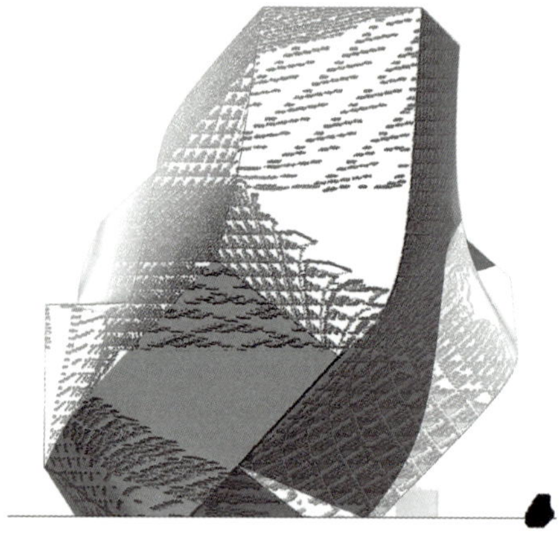

02

03

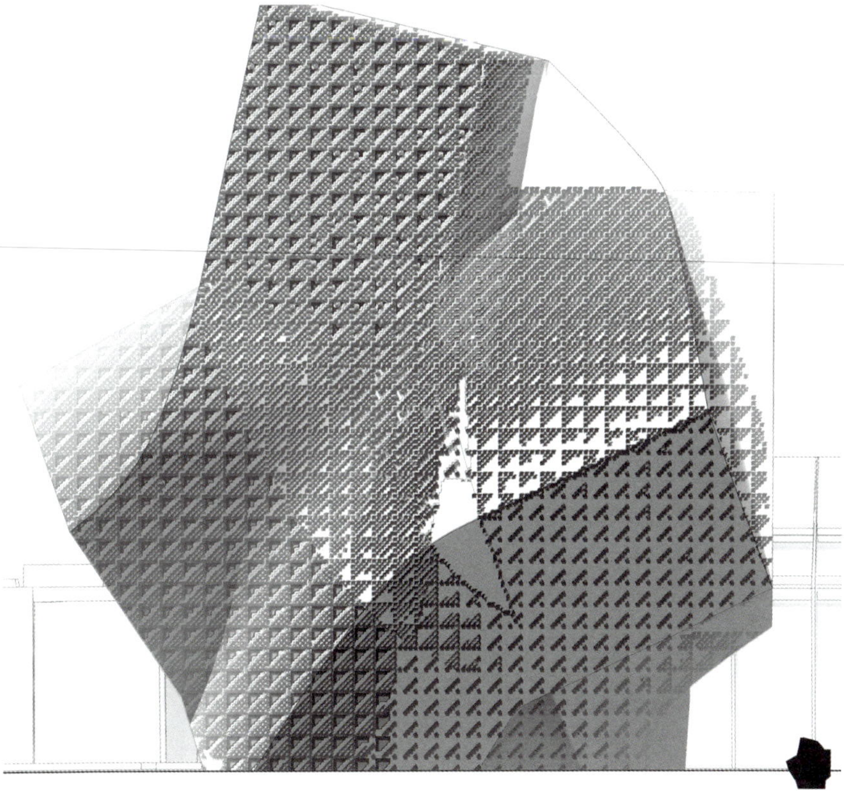

04

05

JUSTIN NGUYEN

06 Section, showing the interior primitives and theater halls suspended over the lobby

07 Final massing model in context, showing how the building holds the corner of South Fairfax Avenue and Wilshire Boulevard while opening up a large public plaza that aligns with the grand entrance and walkway

08 Site plan, showing monolith's adjacency to LACMA's campus

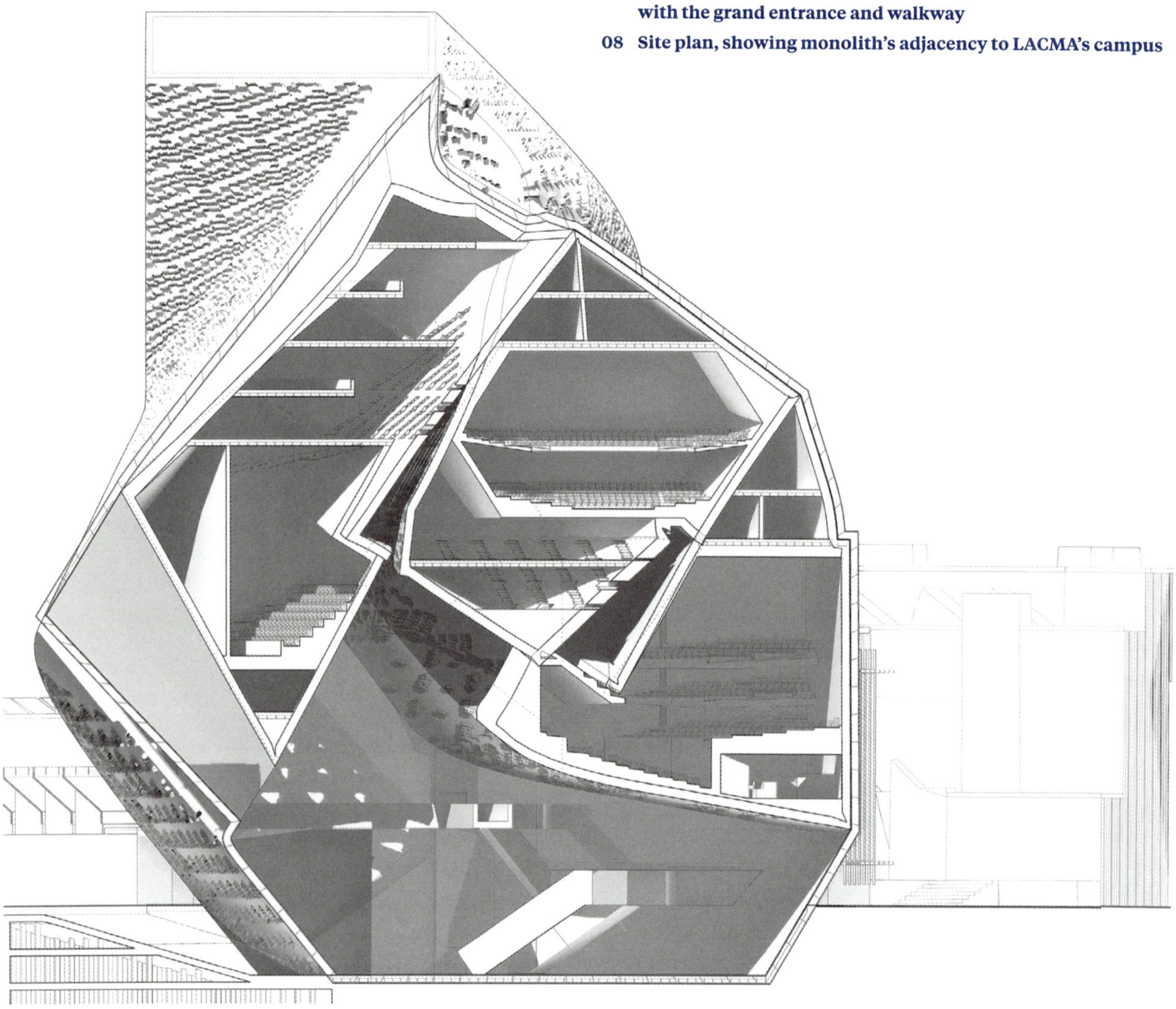

06

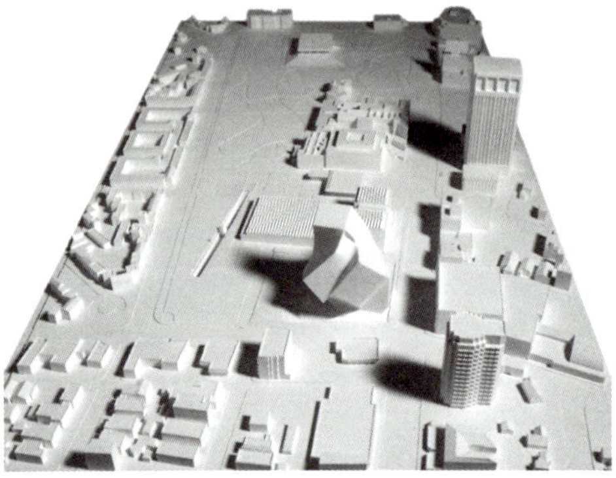

07

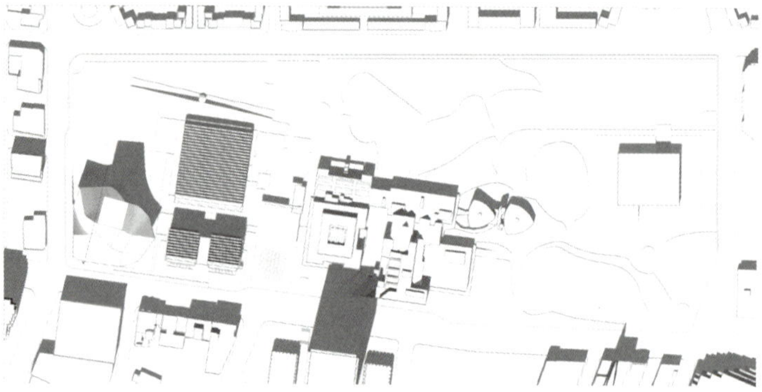

08

HOCHUNG KIM

ENIGMATIC THEATER

The theaters in this project are located within three corresponding primitive geometries, that are connected at a center point and rotated into different axes. The three geometries serve as a framework for different kinds of theater programs. The primitive geometries, consisting of cones, cubes, and saddle surfaces, are modified to create obscured, non-platonic solids which hold the theaters. By locating these solids in different corners of the project, it allows for a centralized public circulation to exist between them.

The surface of the monolith is treated as an autonomous system, like a shell or a skin, and the building is treated as an object that is autonomous from the ground. In his book *Monolithic Architecture*, Rodolfo Machado frames a similar thought concerning monolithic exteriors, stating, "The outer shell form betrays faintly the contours of the instrument while negotiating the regularity of its geometry with subtle curves, depressions, and protuberances." As Paul Virilio notes in *Bunker Archeology*, bunkers, which are truly monolithic architecture, remain autonomous from the ground; while "most buildings are embanked in the terrain by their foundations, the casemate is devoid of any, aside from its center of gravity, which explains its possibility for limited movement when the surrounding ground undergoes the impact of projectiles." Jean Nouvel's New National Theater, in Tokyo, served as a precedent for this project. The theater stands higher and is broader than the adjacent buildings and masks the three auditoriums within it.

Just like an instrument case that has a layer of soft material to mediate between the case's generic geometry and the particular contours of the instrument inside, the building has a cavity between the object and the building skin. The openings in the envelope are small, hybrid apertures that produce a moiré pattern and a high contrast similar to the style of film noir. The patterns are created by contouring the outlines of primitive geometries. There are no direct visual connections between the transparent openings and the interiors.

---

01 Axon rendering of the site

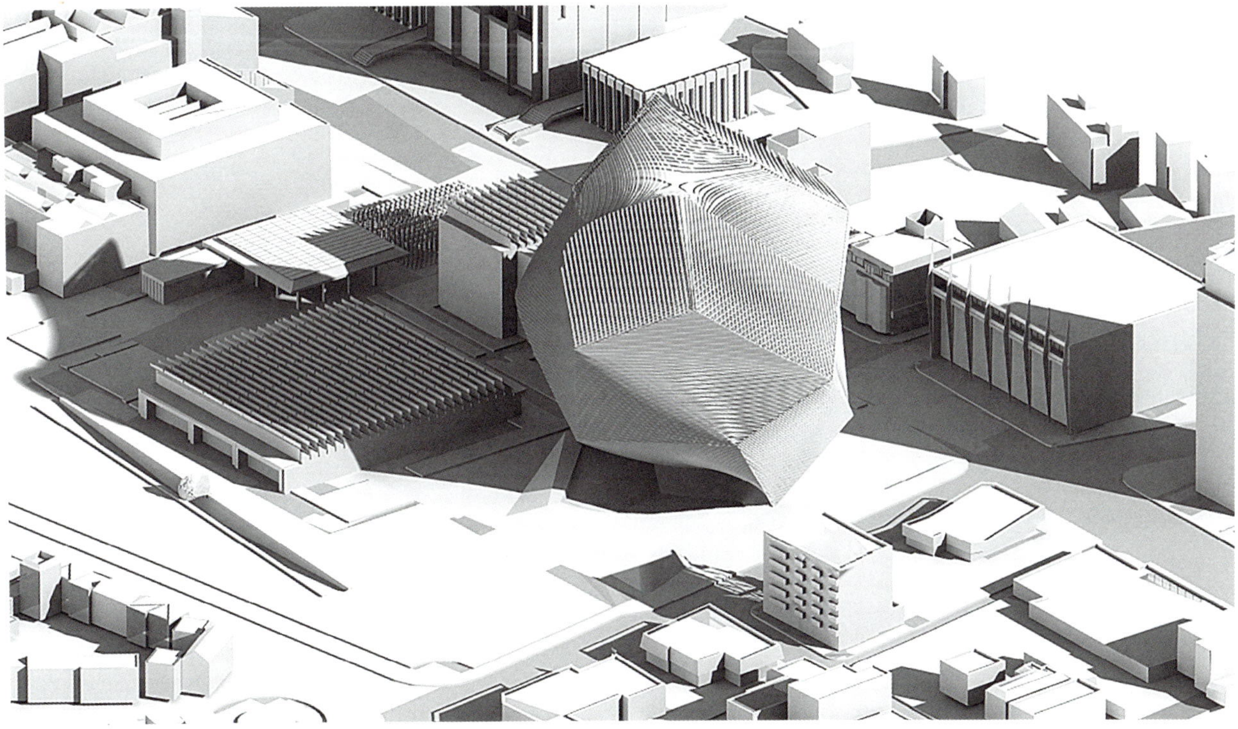

01

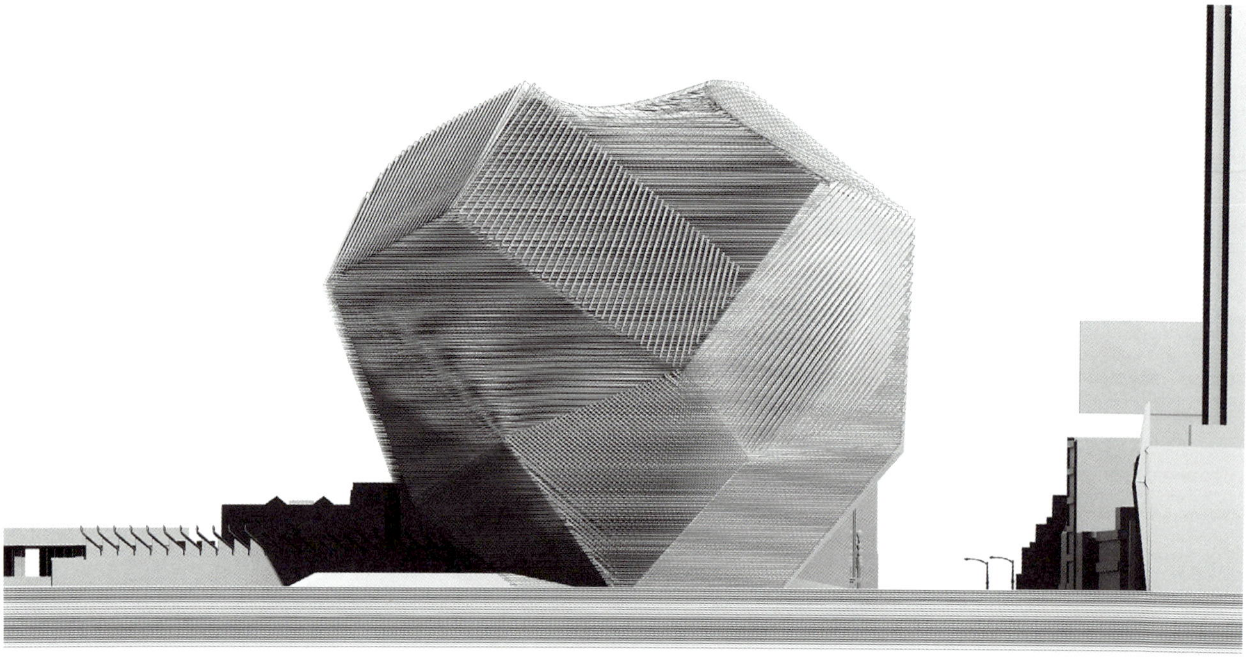

02

03

04

02 Elevation from Fairfax Avenue

03 Section revealing the three nested theaters within the monolith

04 Early study models, showing progression from piles to building form

02 FUZZY *MONOLITHS*

Volumetric density and diagrammatic complexity increase on the interior of these student projects. Rather than exploring programmatic bifurcation at a large scale, each project demonstrates a gradient of chambers, with fluctuating scales and intensities, on the interior. A porous, gridded poché is derived from controlled sets of data, either point clouds or vectors. These indeterminate ripples of data yield an object that evades singularity in favor of internal subdivision. The interior subdivisions are transmitted on the exterior as a façade texture that de-emphasizes any singular legibility of the monolithic form.

CRAIG ROSMAN

POROUS MONOLITH

Within a broader understanding of monolithicity, this project investigates the potential for indeterminate objects to exhibit muteness. Disregarding standard sources of architectural genesis (program, context, and so on), the object must generate its own internal set of data. The project focuses on techniques to produce internal information and, in turn, transform that data into several aesthetic outcomes, including the object's envelope, texture, and volume. The overlap of aesthetic regimes negates the possibility of a singular, sensual object but, instead, proposes a multi-layered, eidetic object.

Research that started in an object-oriented programming environment was employed to create a set of vectors, which define the discrete primitives and monolithic boundary in aggregate. The vectors also are defeatured, thus complicating a reading of figures. In order to test this process, the results were treated as found objects and considered for their eidetic properties, specifically, sphericity, top-heaviness, and chunkiness.

Rather than reinforce the perceived qualities of the exterior, the original vector data is further analyzed and translated to produce the interior volume and texture of the object. In the interior, a point cloud is produced from the density gradient of the primitives. This point cloud is then pixelated to create a series of overlapping boxes. Countering the smooth reading of the object's silhouette, the voxeled texture converts the curvature graph of the form into a gradation of resolutions. The alternating patches of smooth and textured skin further confuse the object's scale and relationship to the sun.

Rather than a central atrium or a pile in a skin, the object's interior spaces are distributed to define multiple experiences. In its envelope, volume, and texture, the monolithic object is never truly a singular object but, instead, a fluctuating nexus of intensities.

01 Elevations of monolith, showing variable orientations and solar conditions
02 Site plan, showing monolith's adjacency to LACMA's campus
03 Final model, showing the continuity of language on the interior and exterior of the building
04 Section, showing main theaters

01

02

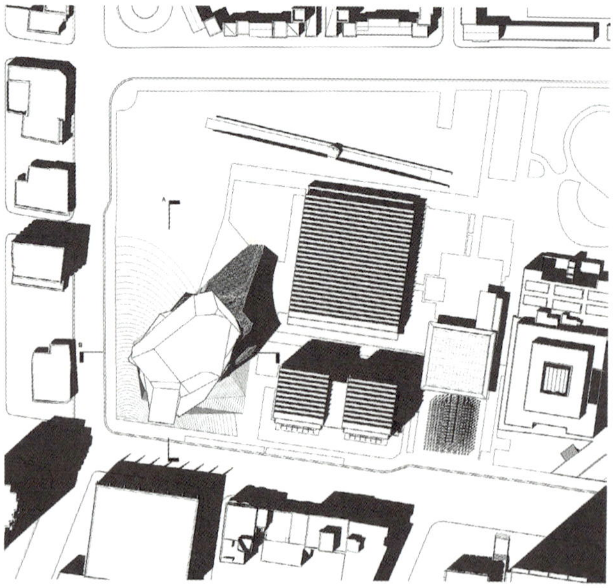

03

04

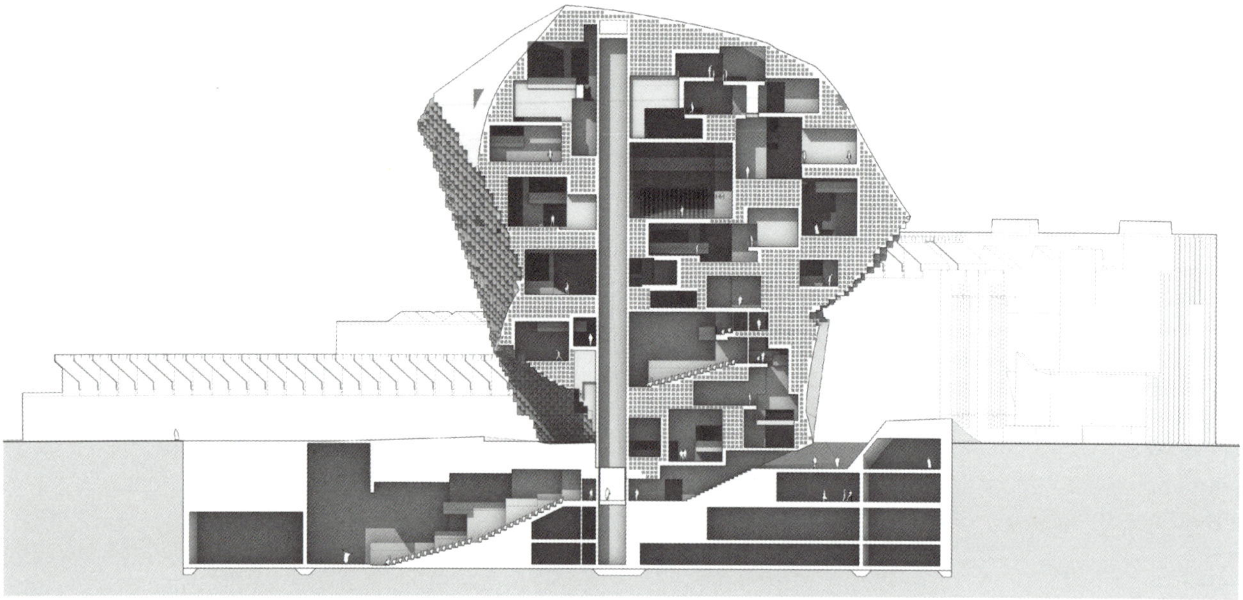

04

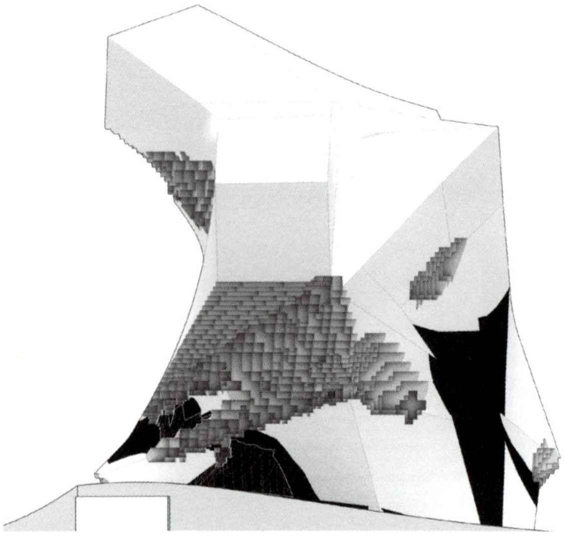

05

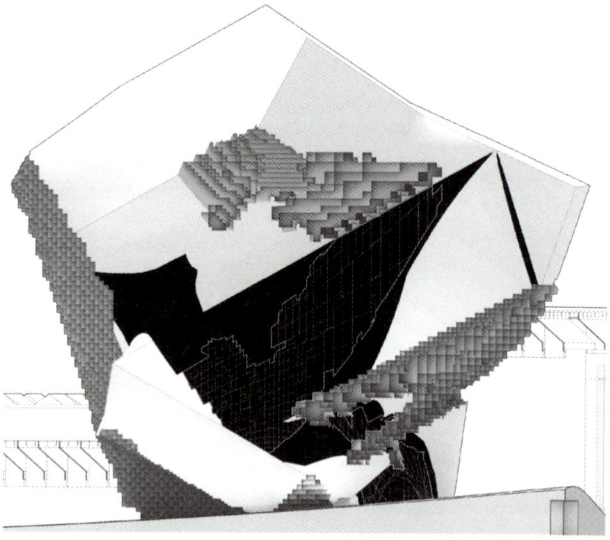

06

04 Section, showing main entrance and underground theater
05 Elevation from Wilshire Avenue, highlighting contrast between the smooth and voxeled textures
06 Elevation from Fairfax Avenue, highlighting the juxtaposition of light and shadow on the monolith

KATE WARREN

MONOLITHIC MOIRÉ

This proposal for the Academy Museum of Motion Pictures questions the studio's formal proposition of muteness and monolithicity as being equal to solidity through the use of two layers of louvered surfaces, applied to a form generated by the subtractive carving of a cube by spheroids. The horizontal outer layer of louvers emphasizes muteness and monolithicity and de-emphasizes the prismatic exterior. The curving inner layer responds to and reflects the generative platonic solids, produced by fragments of the spheroids that carve away from the initial cube. This tactic preserves a record of the inner layer's form within the building. This layer is visible in only brief glimpses, depending on one's physical relationship to the building, as the outer louvers obscure the internal complexity. In addition to generating the curved layer of louvers, the spheroids also create the interior spaces of the building. Four theaters are formed by the intersection of these spheroids, while the circulation areas result from the residual spaces between the theaters and the louvers.

The primary influences for this project were Herzog & de Meuron's Signal Box building, in Basel, and World War II bunkers, as discussed by Paul Virilio in *Bunker Archaeology*.

Using the Signal Box as a cue, this project incorporates the idea of a mute exterior appearance that, when the building is illuminated, reveals a more complex interior form. This effect is achieved in the Signal Box by wrapping the building in a thin layer of twisting metal strips. This project attempts to achieve the same result through the use of a very deep layer of poché, formed by the louvers. In Paul Virilio's analysis of bunkers, he notes that the interior space and exterior form of a bunker are often unrelated and created through the use of a massive layer of solid poché, necessitated by the bunkers' function. However, because the poché is created by louvers, the building is never solid; in fact, the only fully enclosed elements within the building are the theaters, an architectural gesture that questions whether solidity, as exhibited by Virilio's bunkers, is a requirement for monolithicity.

01 Detail of final model, showing moiré texture
02 Final model, showing exterior elevation of monolith
03 Final section model, showing the disjunction between the interior and double-layered exterior

01

02

03

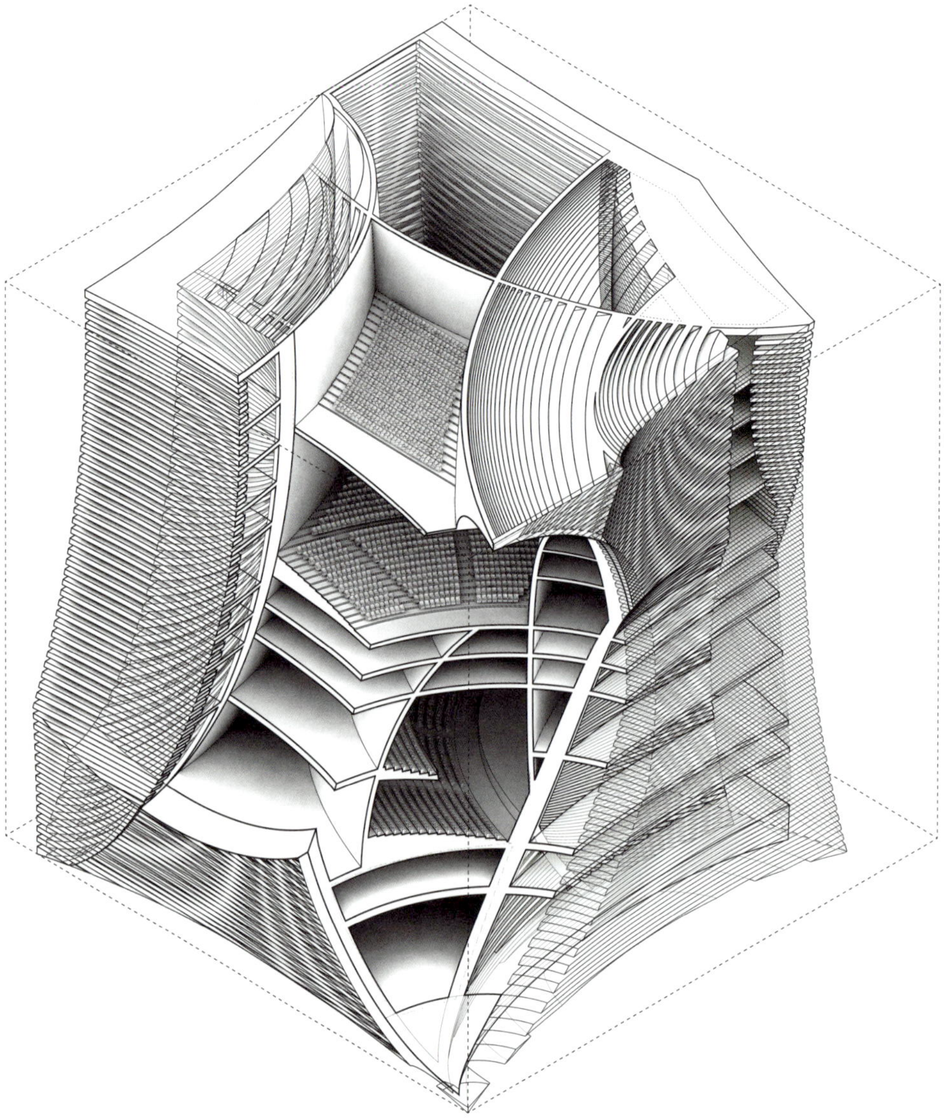

04

05

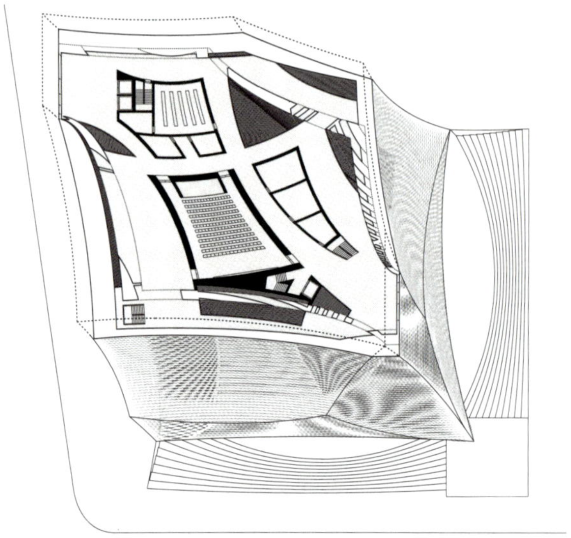

06

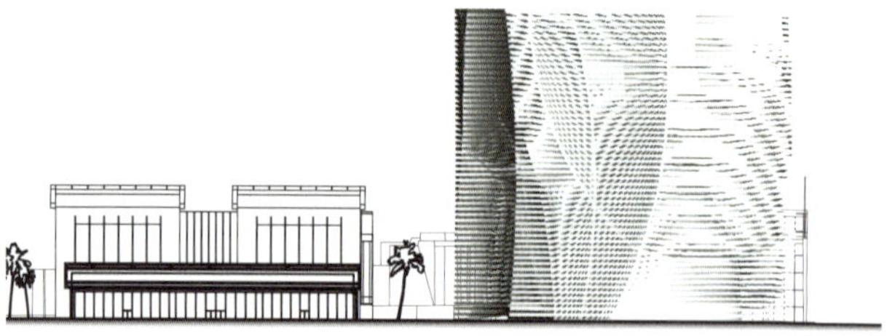

04 **Cutaway axonometric, revealing how theaters stack within the monolith**

05 **Oblique floor plan, showing theater geometry in relationship to exterior envelope**

06 **Elevations, showing moiré pattern wrapping around the building**

03 DICHOTOMOUS *GEOMETRIES*

In these projects, a single, internal object is nested within the exterior form, dividing the poché of dense programmatic volumes and the large, open volumes of the void. Internal subdivision does not include the pile, but rather, a secondary system of surfaces. As a result, the exterior shares a consistent edge with much of the interior, and the two are described through very similar formal languages. The bifurcation of the interior occurs along the edge of looming masses, a central core, or an offset of the skin that adheres closely to the envelope.

ROBERT CANNAVINO

THE CONTEXTUAL MONOLITH

This project investigates and questions the singular, monadic, and monolithic as an antidote to continuous differentiation and seriality now prevalent in contemporary architecture. On the surface, the monolith seems rhetorically singular; however, upon closer inspection of its ontology, it is clear that the monolith is paradoxically dyadic. It eschews exuberance, while asserting its presence. It is a reaction against the contemporary desire for the icon, yet is itself a mute icon. It exists in simultaneities—"solid and hollow, uniform and heterogeneous, impregnable and permeable, foreign and familiar."[1]

The monolith by its very nature is acontextual. "The simplicity and integrity of [the monolith's] geometry does not easily accommodate contextual inflections. In fact, their self-possessed posture seems to arrogantly dismiss such external influences."[2] In light of that fact, this project attempts to produce a monolith, that is very much *of a place*.

The city of Los Angeles functions as a place of projected and fictional realities, a "city with no name," a place without a singular identity. In a city with urban schizophrenia, one of the biggest challenges is designing a building in context. The May Company Building currently sits on the future site of the Academy Museum of Motion Pictures. Built in 1939, the department store, once described as the "western gateway to the Miracle Mile," was the icon of capital-driven urbanism, viewed from behind a windshield. Now, it sits vacant—monolithic in its inaccessibility.[3] There are plans to demolish the building to clear the site for the new museum. However, this design retains the May Company Building and grafts onto it, creating a paradoxically singular and dual structure.

Other contemporary projects that attach onto existing structures, such as the Caixa Forum, the Elbe Philharmonie, and the Hearst Tower, foreground the duality between the old and the new. This project, however, attempts to

---

01–03 Elevations, showing how the texture obscures the relationship between the old and new buildings

04 Section, indicating relationship of theater volumes to generative primitives

05 Diagram, showing monolith enveloping the existing building

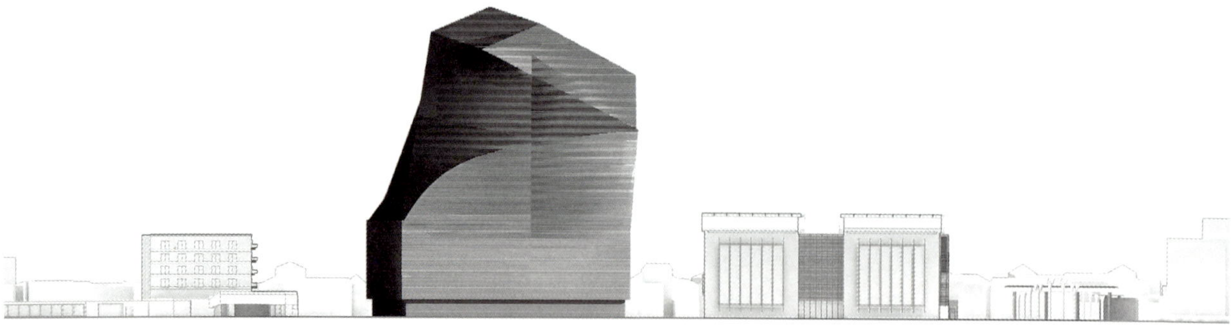

01

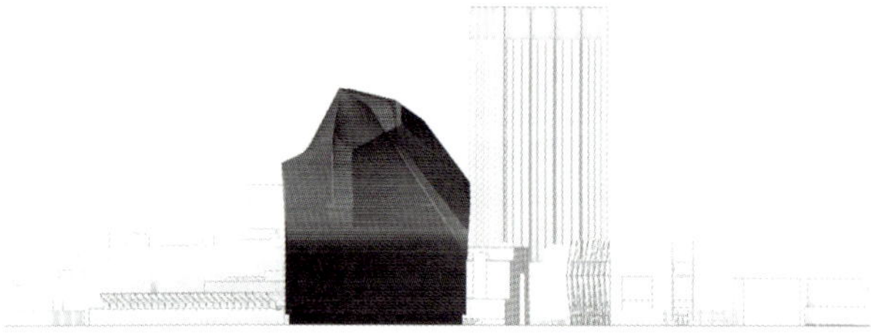

02

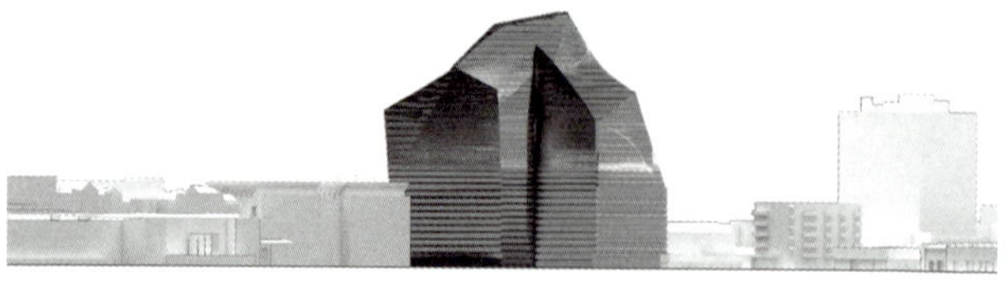

03

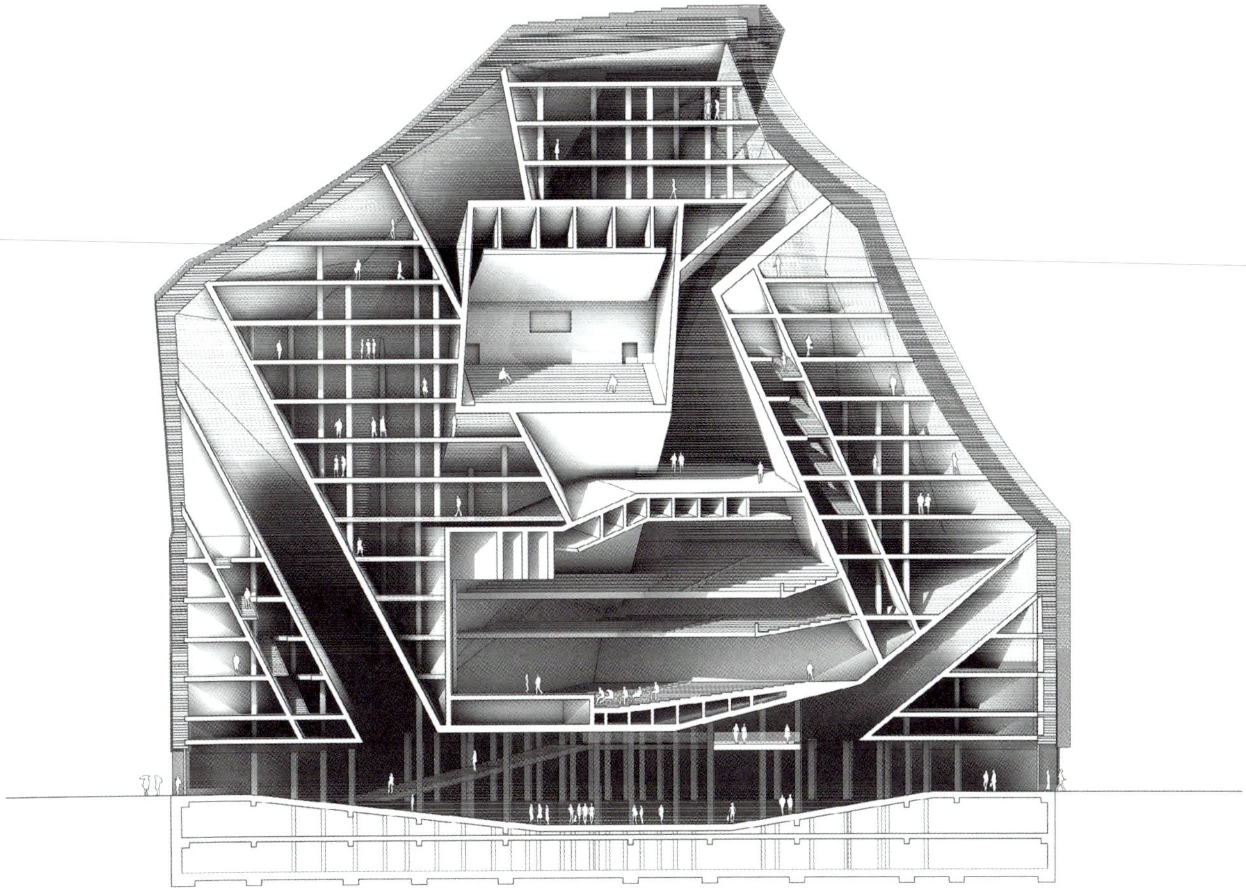

04

05

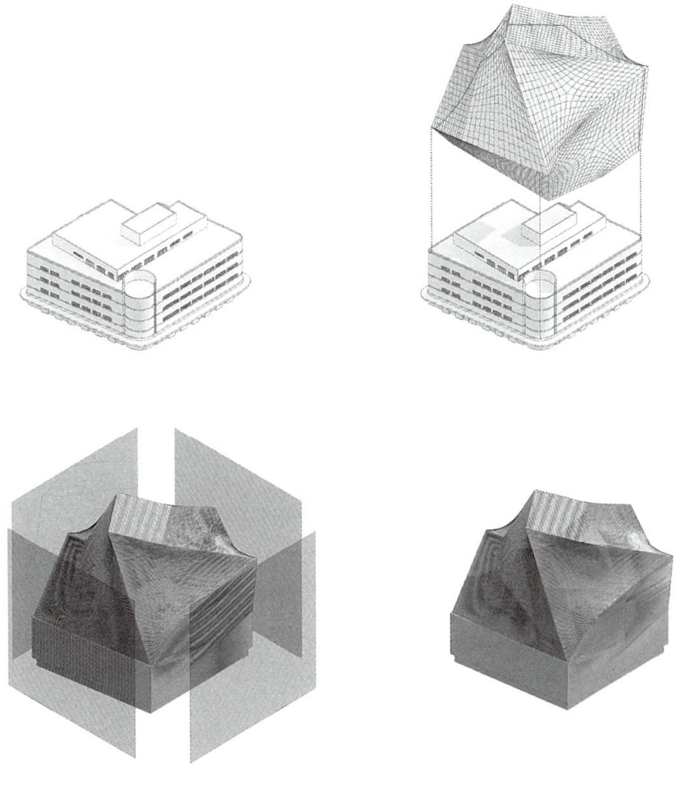

create a new whole by masking the difference between its two parts. It acts with aggressive contextuality, altering the original building to suit the monolith's formal desires. Operative cuts in the form attempt to conflate the reading of the two objects, at moments privileging a singularity, and, at other moments, attempting to create a duality. The cuts further reinforce the solidity of the form.

While the exterior of the building expresses the creation of a new whole, the interior destabilizes this whole. The solidity of the exterior is undermined by the interlocking, stacked primitive volumes on the interior. Any reading of difference between old and new dissolves inside. The primitive volumes fill the cavernous interior of the merged form, acting as the major public circulation between interior theaters and exterior skin. Simultaneously, the original structural columns extend from the existing building into the new form. These two systems produce a moiré of tectonic systems. This confined void surrounded by solidity conflates the distinction between subject and object, which are brought into such a close relationship to one another that limits are blurred.

Simultaneously thick and thin, the skin of the buildings is cut by a series of horizontal apertures. Applied orthographically to the four sides of the building, the openings are deployed in a pattern based on the shadows of the obverse side of the building, generating formal incongruity and topological misalignment. This pattern blends old and new and obscures the comprehension of the whole. From the exterior, these apertures read as shadows on the façade, while, on the interior, the truth of the skin's porousness is revealed.

1. Rodolfo Machado and Rodolphe el-Khoury, *Monolithic Architecture*

2. Ibid.

3. https://www.laconservancy.org/locations/may-company-wilshire

---

06 Final massing model in site context

07 Site plan, showing monolith in place of the existing building footprint

08 Unfolded elevation, illustrating the disjunction between texture and building form

06

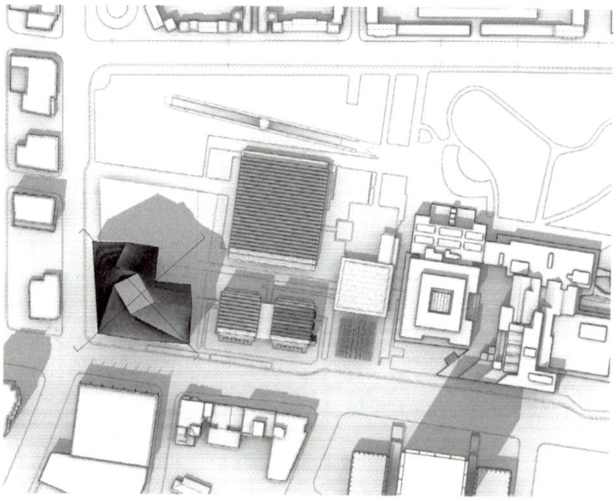

07

08

CRISTIAN ONCESCU

TOTEMIC PROJECTION

Architecture is not the only discipline whose output has grown progressively more homogenized in the past two decades. Cinema has also suffered from a misplaced nostalgia and a prevalence of parametricized processes. Both are increasingly homogenous and on the verge of no longer being affecting media. The establishment of an Academy Museum of Motion Pictures presents a unique opportunity to contemplate a new vision for film and the architectural icon, a vision that will make itself felt as a resistance to this leveling of culture and the spread of the generic, the automated, the easily distilled, and the seen-before.

This proposal is a vertical museum, a totemic monolith. The architectural monolith inherently embodies a difficult-to-resolve dualism, being at once solid and impenetrable, yet also hollow and inhabitable.[1] The totem as sculptural object, by contrast, is defined by a stable set of properties, including a clear orientation with a favored, frontal point of view, an in-the-round experience as a three-dimensional object, and a subtractive carving process that creates a hierarchical stacking of symbolic figures. In order to subvert the totem's aesthetic fixity, three strategies are employed. Form is abstracted and stripped of its cultural quotations to arrive at an object that is pure, blank signage, pointing only to itself and to the emergence of a new institutional form.[2] All points of view are made equally dominant in order to erase frontality and intensify in-the-round objectness. Its single-block nature is decreased through strategic carving of the mass while amplifying the "incongruity of mass to dimension, of façade to interior, and especially, of form to function."[3]

The museum's towering verticality distinguishes and dissociates it from the horizontality of the LACMA campus and the city of Los Angeles at large. The building presents

01 Elevations, showing totem-like qualities of monolith

02 Unrolled exterior skin, illustrating the disjunction between texture and form

01

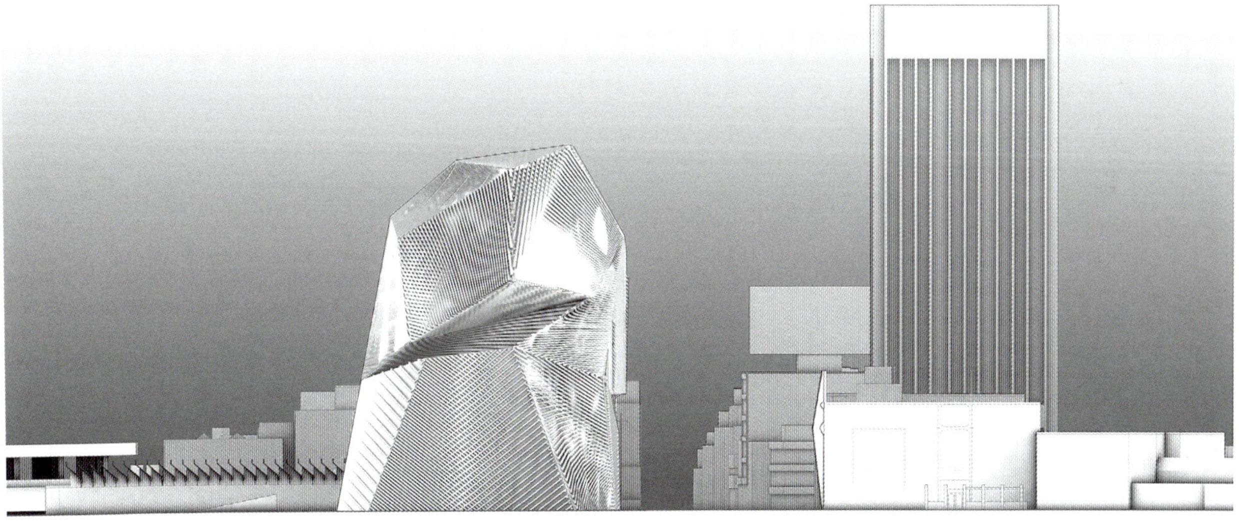

02

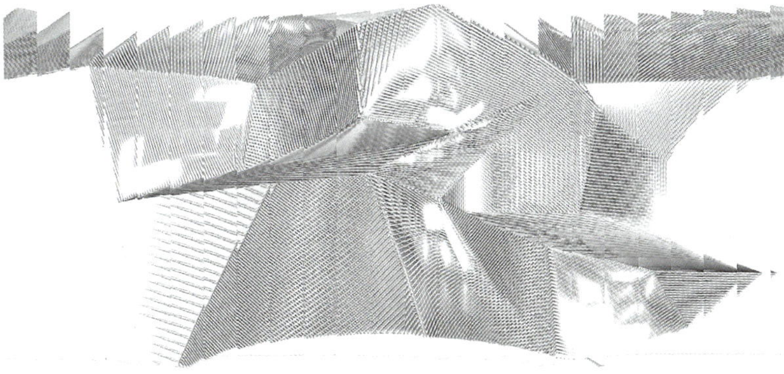

to its surroundings three equally dominant but muted sides, which are deformed by cuts through the mass. This non-hierarchical geometry does not reveal any interiority and presents an inconsistent, in-the-round, part-to-whole relationship. Further, this part-to-whole relationship is reinforced through a dematerializing micro-texture that layers another reading over the whole form. To further emphasize its paradoxical nature, the museum obscures any point of penetration by sinking the lobby level into a below-grade courtyard.

On the interior, monolithicity of a different kind creates a discrete and internalized world for film and multimedia presentations. The central void acts as an "interior exterior," delaying the visitor's entry into the exhibition program proper. This immersive space reads as a void carved into a solid mass or as an inverted totem. Completely devoid of natural light, this space allows a myriad of projected media to be displayed on the undulating, monolithic surface within. In contrast to Machado and el-Khoury's writing, which reduces the problem of monolithicity to an enclosing skin around non-monolithic objects, this project foregrounds the predominant geometric element present in the capture, projection, and distribution of film: the surface. Here, thickened surfaces of the skin contain the program, with galleries, auditoriums, and access points to the exterior terraces being located in the poché of the envelope. In keeping with the previous strategies, function is not privileged; rather, spaces are treated equally and ambiguously as unarticulated form.

1. Rodolfo Machado and Rodolphe el-Khoury, *Monolithic Architecture*

2. Jeffrey Kipnis, *Towards a New Architecture*

3. Roberto Mangabeira Unger, *The Better Futures of Architecture*

---

03 **Final section model, showing interplay between building texture and interior form**

04 **Final section model, showcasing how theater seating has no relationship to exterior**

05 **Section, showing how poché was used to create new relationships between interior and exterior form**

03

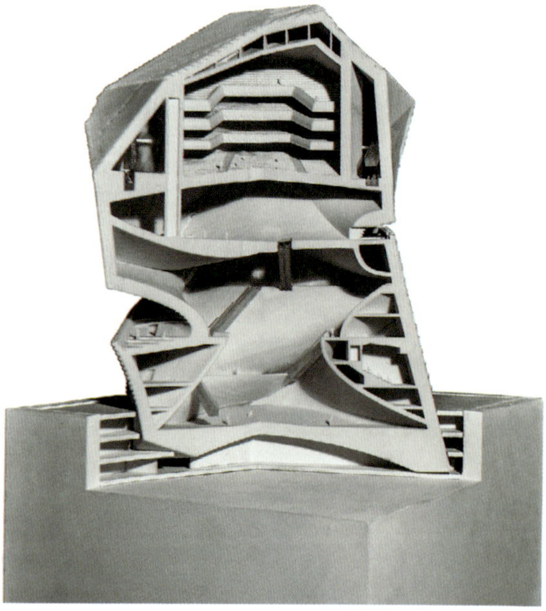

04

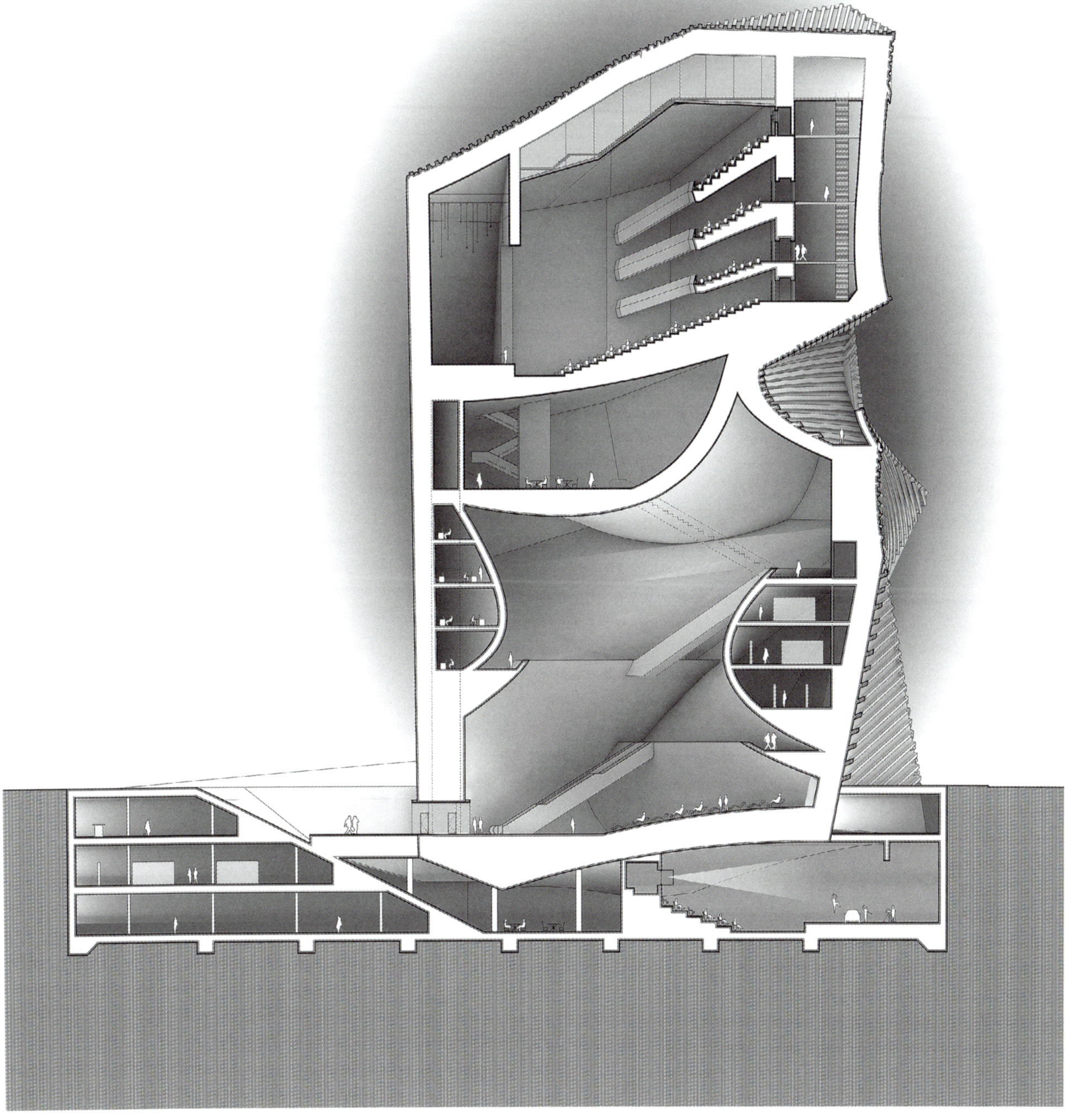

05

CHESSIN GERTLER

NEW BRUTALITY

This project seeks to envision a new monumental architecture. By generating a form fundamentally over-scaled for this location and by cropping only some of the faces of the mass along the major axes of the site, the project seeks to define monumentality by emphasizing "misfitting" within the project's surroundings. The building is wrapped by a texture that further emphasizes the muteness of its cropped faces. An abstract pattern was derived from a recombination of the original form's unrolled surfaces vertically projected over the exterior surfaces.

A variety of deformities are implied on the non-cropped faces, while the vertical, cropped faces are expressed by a series of banded protrusions and indentations. These protrusions and indentations house a mix of artificial light and apertures, adding another layer to the texture of the form.

01 Elevation, showing condition of monolith at sliced planes
02 Section, showing theater volumes pushing against exterior skin
03 Diagram, showing site strategy, form, and texture process
04–05 Final model, showing texture

01

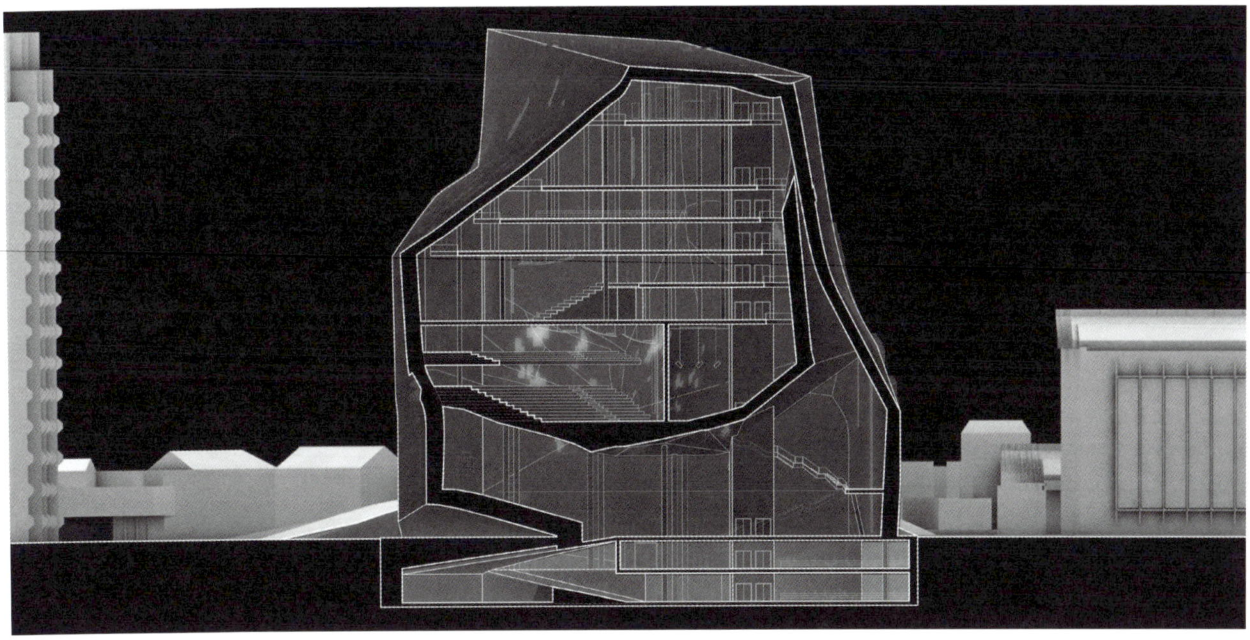

02

03

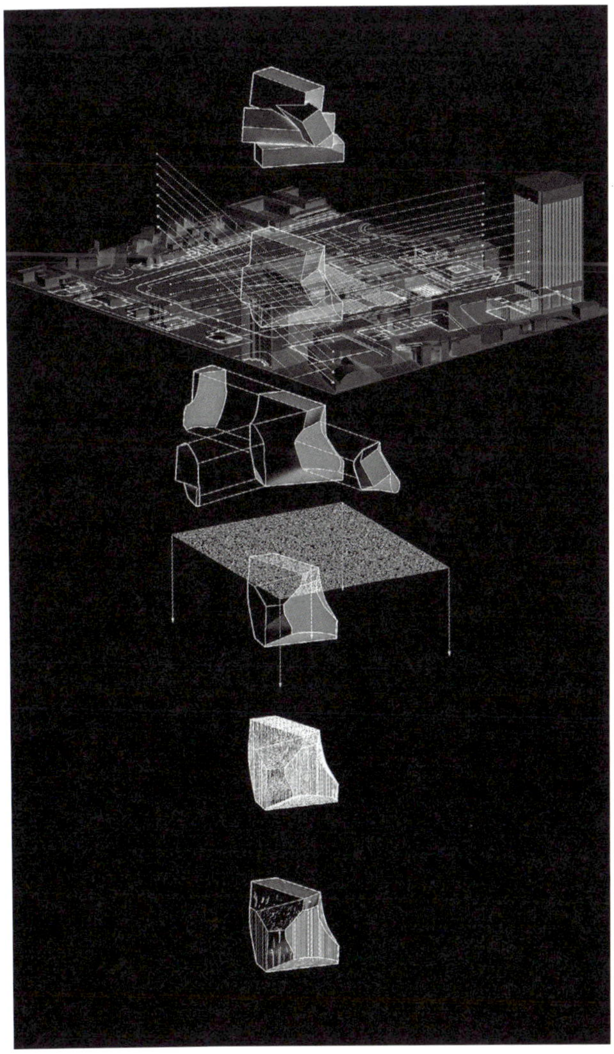

04

05

JONATHON MEIER

DISSONANT VOID

This project exploits dissonance as a means of floating between opposing elements: singular object and multiplicity, hard and soft geometry, solid and void, interior and exterior. Rather than juxtaposition, which may be seen as an overt contrast between two elements, dissonance may be described, in this case, as the coalescing of oppositions into a single limbo state in which the oppositions can neither be fully combined together nor fully extracted from one another.

The exterior appears to be composed of a series of cubes, both upright and rotating. As one moves around the building, that which appeared to be a cube quickly dissolves into soft geometry, and new cubes become visible. When one has fully circumnavigated the building, it becomes clear that there is no cube at all.

The building's apertures are as ephemeral as its cubic form. At times, their patterns line up with the cubic edges and, at other times, indiscriminately flow over them. The apertures read as if they were a texture. They are cut perpendicular to the curvature of each surface, which allows them to appear and disappear as one moves around the building. Each surface can be read, therefore, as either solid or porous, depending on one's location relative to the surface.

Masked by the texture of the apertures on the north façade, a large void peels inward and flows down into the building. The apertures from the exterior continue along the sides of the void. The surface eventually re-merges with the exterior on the south façade to create a strange sensation within the void, clouding one's sense of interior versus exterior.

---

01 Section, showing exterior void's independent relationship to interior theaters

02 Axonometric diagram, illustrating the interior void

03–05 Elevations, showing high-contrast texture wrapping around the monolith and obfuscating the void in building form

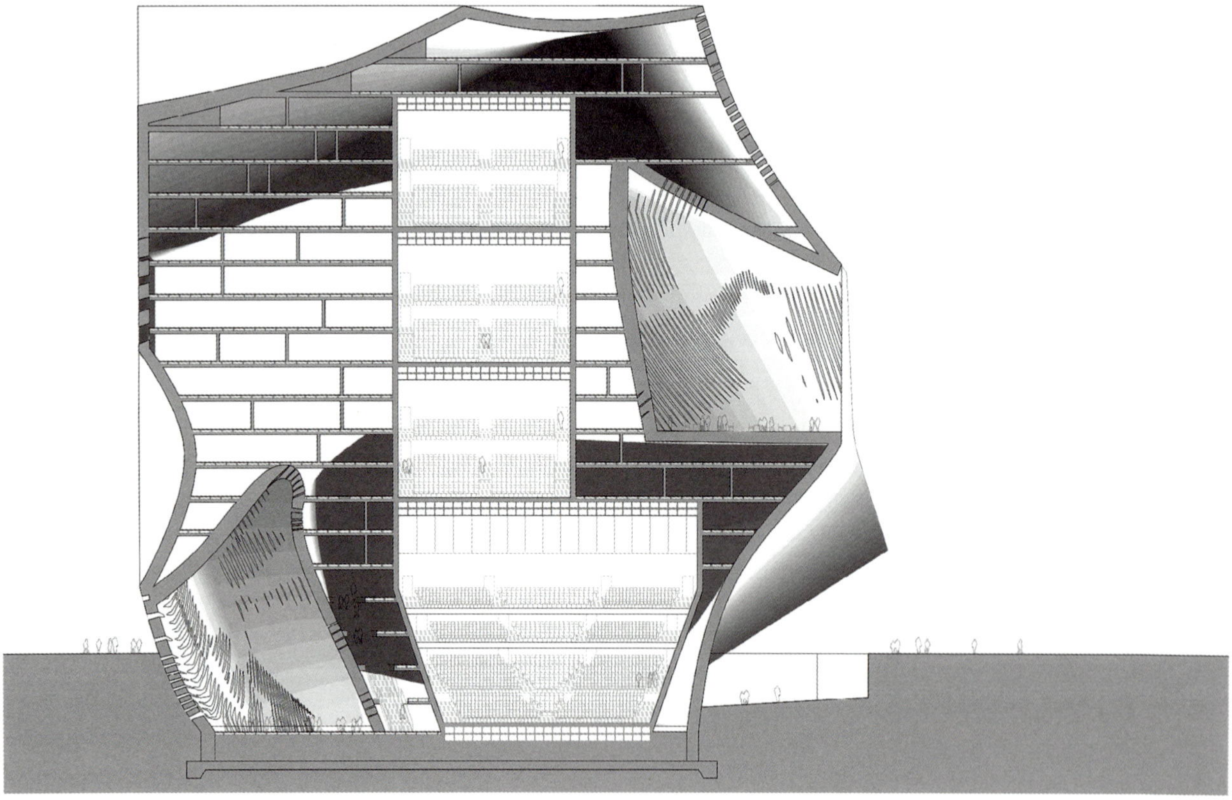

01

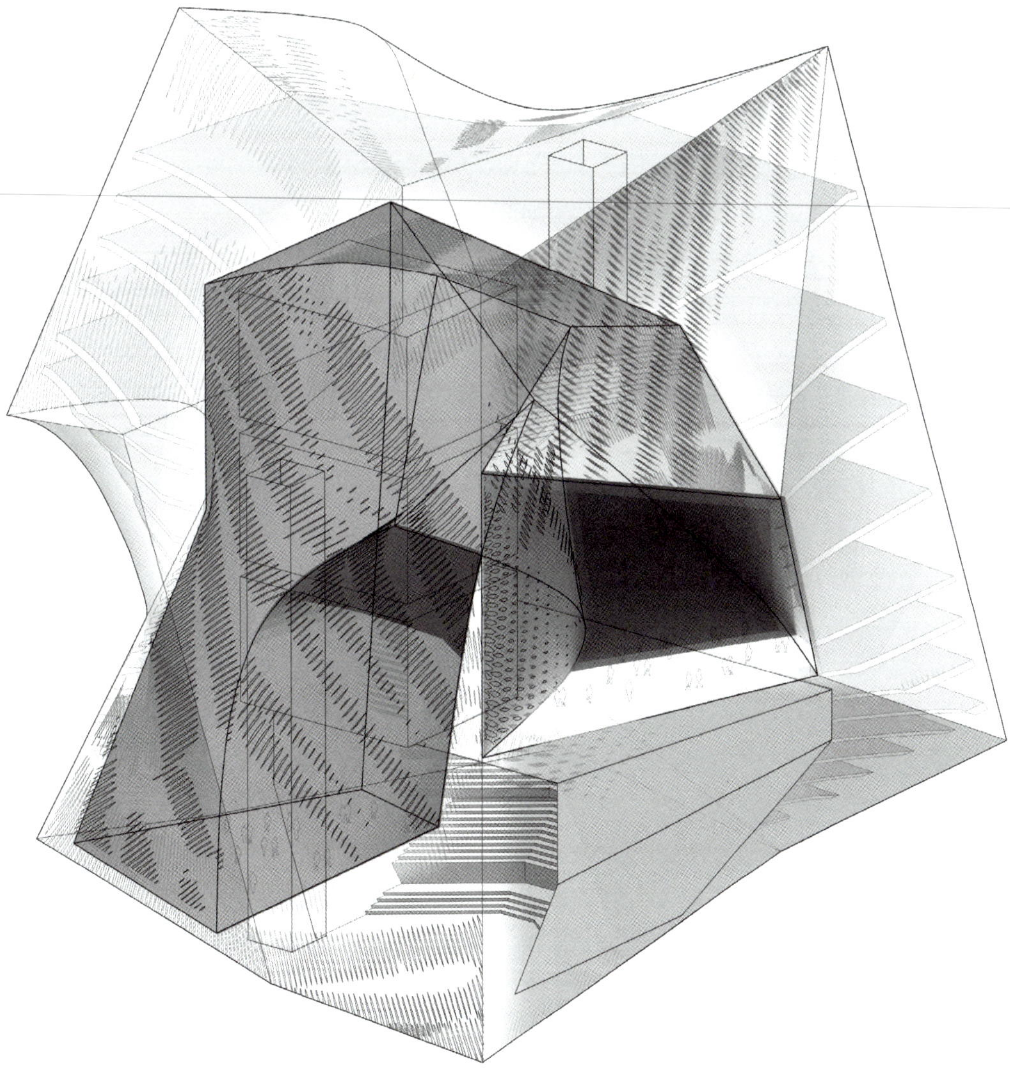

02

03

04

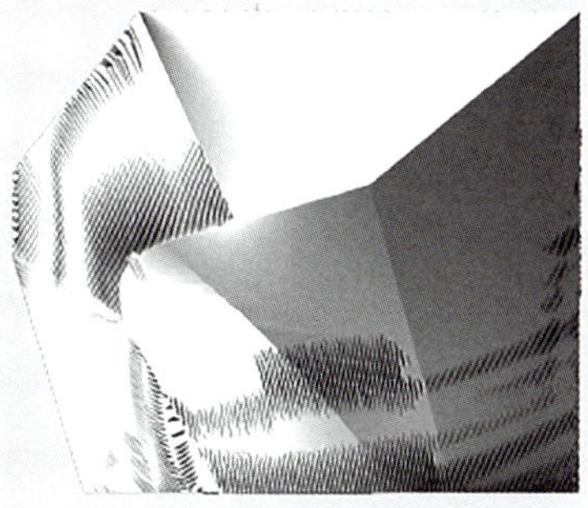

05

DAN WOOD

WORKING IN GABON

INTERVIEW

DAN WOOD

Dan Wood spoke about his work and approach with Nina Rappaport.

Nina Rappaport How did you and your partner, Amale Andraos, start WORKac and combine teaching with practice?

Dan Wood When we started WORKac, from our New York City apartment in 2003, we didn't know what our aesthetics were because, happily, we had been in this big brainwashing machine, working with Rem Koolhaas at OMA, in Rotterdam. At that time, we felt there were two directions we could take: teaching and doing competitions to build up a theoretical approach or being practitioners, which, given that, at the time, the recession seemed to be just about over, we decided to do. Our first five-year plan was to say yes to everything, and just take anything that came our way and discover our work—thus, the name of the firm. We had rejected the academic route, but, then, after a year or so, someone asked us to teach, and we had to say yes to that, too. After that, it became a very important part of our practice. It's like exercise: you have to stay on your feet and respond and yet make sure you are not projecting too much onto your students—you don't want to end up with twelve identical projects. We can also explore and think about things we are not commissioned to do. We did a seminar on ecological urbanism, for example, and we were able to research those ideas later in what became [the book] *49 Cities*. I am really interested in how you can hang onto the theoretical and experimental while also engaging in building. At Yale, we looked at "representational" architecture for the country of Gabon and how infrastructure and architecture can combine to create new institutions and a new national identity.

NR One of your interests is urban vegetable gardens and so-called productive landscapes, which follows on the long trajectory of community gardens: programs such as Operation Green Thumb, in New York City; the Brooklyn Grange, and vertical farms. How did you start looking at urban farming as an inspiration for your architectural design projects as well as your conceptual research?

DW A sudden revolution contributed to our thinking about food and architecture. First, it came out of our research for *49 Cities,* in which we looked at the history of urbanism and the ecological implications of these visionary cities. Many of our discoveries were made by looking at the projected relationship between the city and its surroundings and, also, around food production. The Garden City had a surrounding agricultural zone, for example, and Le Corbusier had urban farming components in Radiant City. Second, we happened to buy a copy of Michael Pollan's book *Omnivore's Dilemma* and became very interested in food and food systems. When we were invited, in 2008, to do an installation for the Young Architects Program at MoMA PS1, we realized that we could incorporate this research and these interests, putting together food and cities. We called the project P. F. 1, or Public Farm 1.

NR Producing food in the city was a new framework for you, so to speak. Had you yourselves ever planted a vegetable garden?

DW I grew up in the countryside. My parents were hippies, so we had a garden and pigs—and that was an influence, but I wasn't really directly engaged in it. Amale is much more of an urban person, so she didn't have any experience at all.

NR Do you see productive landscapes and gardens as a design tool, perhaps as a way to insert landscape into the city for sustainability or, rather, to integrate farming and healthy food into urban lifestyles?

DW There is excitement in the food world about urban farming, but, for us, it was a broader examination of the intersection between urban, rural, and the wild—and the give-and-take from one to the other as a kind of second nature. Many problems in the world have to do with the relationship between the man-made and the natural, and we hope that we can trigger a different way of thinking by using nature and natural systems and then making those systems visible.

NR The Edible Schoolyard project, initially conceived by Alice Waters, is a perfect blend of interests, both playful and educational, for your practice. How did you meet Waters and receive the project commission for the school in Brooklyn?

DW John Lyons, who sits on the board of the Chez Panisse Foundation, in California, but who lives in New York City, always wanted to do an Edible Schoolyard here. He was "Principal for a Day" at P. S. 216, where we were to build, eventually. He happened to see P. F. 1, and then we met Alice and went out to Berkeley to see her work. Our first project for Edible Schoolyard NYC took five years of planning and construction.

NR Why was it such a long organizational process? How did you integrate the various functions of the program?

DW They had to build the Edible Schoolyard NYC organization first and get the approvals from the Department of Education. The garden was completed first; we added a building that combines a greenhouse, a kitchen classroom, a small office for the organization, and the building systems. The roofs are joined together and collect rainwater. At the rear of the structure, the building systems are expressed as a series of sculptural elements, clad in sprayed blue rubber, that contain all the things that make the building work: a big cistern, a bathroom, the HVAC system, and a tool shed. You can see how one roof goes to the next and to the cistern volume and understand the water systems. It is really a micro-experiment of many of the things we have been thinking about.

NR It sounds like a good prototype for other schools.

DW It is a prototype, and Christine Quinn, the City Council speaker at the time, allocated funds on the condition that we do one in every borough. We started another one at East Harlem School P.S./M.S. 7, where we installed planters to begin the second Demonstration School. They have already started the kitchen classes. Edible Schoolyard NYC has an approved curriculum, so it's completely integrated with what the kids are studying—whether its history, math, science, or whatever. They see every kid in the school three times a month for the five years they are in elementary school.

NR You have expanded your commissions internationally through competitions, such as the one for the Assembly Hall for the 2015 African Union Summit, in Gabon. How are you combining ideas of sustainability and materiality while integrating local needs with new and appropriate construction technology?

DW We got that project by winning an invited competition, for which David Adjaye and Diller Scofidio + Renfro were participants, among others. The competition was an initiative of Ali Ondimba Bongo, the president of Gabon, who is trying to make the country into an emerging economy that focuses on green issues. His head of national parks, professor Lee White, is a one of his

---

01 Edible School Yard at P. S. 216
02 Public Farm 1 at MoMA PS1

02

03

right-hand people and previously worked for the Wildlife Conservation Society and lived in the jungle. So, we took those goals as our initial inspiration. Bongo is also a pan-Africanist, if I can say that, and is very interested in the future of Africa and the African Union. Having the African Union summit in Gabon puts Gabon on the world stage. We felt it should have a strong representational side to it, like a mini UN. Instead of looking to Gabon's past, we tapped into the positive side of Modernism in Africa, especially in Libreville. There are many fascinating buildings from around the time of Gabon's independence from France—and a few years later, too, when they discovered oil—that represent the super-optimistic ideas of what a country in Africa can or should be.

NR The cone-shaped organization of the building has a very strong formal quality that seems to be both symbolic, in terms of a gathering place, and functional, in terms of the sloped roof to move the rainwater down. How did you integrate the productive aspects of the building within the project?

DW The main auditorium is at the heart of the project, and there are three gardens surrounding it, each representing a different local ecology. One of them is an edible garden. There is the Inselberg, which is a very special type of mountain ecosystem, and, lastly, a rain forest garden. Because the building is on a hill, as you approach it from the city you can see the three gardens. It rains every day in Libreville, so, above the auditorium, rainwater can be collected, forming a water feature on the roof where the rain runs down the terraces. Then, the water becomes a waterfall in the rain forest garden and flows into the cisterns to be reused in a gray-water system.

NR The New Holland Island project, in Saint Petersburg, Russia—another project you were commissioned to do through an invited competition—is a cultural project housed within a former industrial complex, an idea you dubbed as a "city inside the city." How did you arrive at the idea to subtract from the historic building while adding something identifiable? In general, how do you combine the historical aspects with the desire to create something new, and what kind of tensions have resulted?

DW The project has been driven by a deep engagement with history, in that the warehouse buildings, built for the Russian navy, are very repetitive and quite dense. They were never really meant for human habitation; they were built to dry wood, and façades were added later. It is a delicate dance between how much you want to impact historic structures visually and what you choose to preserve. Since they are such robust structures, we realized we could cut big holes into them. Norman Foster had designed an earlier project for the island which was not built but for which they tore down a huge number of buildings; basically everything from after the nineteenth century, including the radio station where Lenin gave a significant speech during the Russian Revolution, the laboratory where Dmitri Mendeleev discovered the periodic table of elements, and the site of the first Russian submarine testing grounds. Our design, in contrast, combines preservation, public space, and new construction.

NR How has your work in Gabon and St. Petersburg influenced your current projects and what are you most intrigued with at the moment?

DW So, if P. F. 1 was the end of our first "five-year plan," in 2008, the end of our second five year plan came in 2012, when we finished the New Holland Island master plan and won the competition for the Gabon project. These two projects are, in many ways, the culmination of all the research and thinking we had done post-PS1 on the relationship between cities and nature, and the start of a whole range of new projects focused much more intently on the scale of architecture. New Holland's museum building is actually a physical hinge between the city and landscape, presenting a civic face to the city and a landscaped, occupiable roof to the park. Similarly, the Gabon building takes many of our urban ideas about representation, infrastructure, the incorporation of nature, and circulation as inspiration for its design. We are more focused now on architecture—and finding ways to combine our programmatic experimentations from the first five years and our urban obsessions from the second with new form, detail, and material investigations. Our parking garage façade in Miami, for example, contains—within only a four-foot-deep space—everything required for a city: circulation, art galleries, an auditorium, bars, gardens, fountains, a library, playgrounds, a DJ booth, and a listening lounge. At the same time, it is a really engaging and highly "designed" façade of perforated metal and expressive cutouts. We have also recently completed a few competitions in which we have taken these new geometries and spatial experiences even further. It's still not one hundred percent clear where we are going, but needless to say, Amale and I are looking forward to 2017!

---

03 Rendering of Assemblée Radieuse Conference Center in Gabon

KEEP *RUNNING*

DAN WOOD

In 2012, we received an email from President Ali Bongo of the Republic of Gabon inviting WORKac to participate in a paid competition for a new congress hall in Libreville. It had been sent to a dozen Pritzker Prize winners and a smaller group of "up-and-coming" architects. Signed by the president and including a smiling photograph of him, the attached letter gave detailed instructions for providing bank account information in order to receive payment. Needless to say, it was a very suspicious email.

All the Pritzker Prize winners declined. All the up-and-comers accepted, including David Adjaye, Diller Scofidio + Renfro, PPMS Arquitetos Associados, Sou Fujimoto, and WORKac.

Project

The new congress hall is to host the biannual meeting of the heads of state from the African Union. At other times, the facility will be a diplomatic meeting center, hosting government and NGO gatherings and discussions and sponsoring debate and exchange.

The president's letter of introduction stressed that the building should announce Gabon's emergence on the world stage, in order to take advantage of the media attention that comes with the African Union event. Therefore, the design brief asked that, in some way, the building represent the country itself, focusing on the president's economic vision of moving the country away from an oil-based economy to a service economy, encouraging tourism, and discovering new forms of industry.

Moreover, the president's personal commitment to ecology and the environment is deep. His right-hand man is Lee White, the minister of national parks and, previously, an ecologist with the World Wildlife Federation who spent decades living in the Gabonese rain forest. The president's vision for the country's transformation was called Gabon Vert, or "Green Gabon."

Climate

Gabon is located just below Africa's western bulge. Its capital city, Libreville, is only twenty-five miles north of the equator, which bisects the country. The sun rises at 6 a.m. and sets at 6 p.m. every day. There is no difference between northern exposure and southern exposure. Sunrises and sunsets are amazingly quick: minutes after it starts to get dark, it is dark. The average daytime high temperature is 85 degrees Fahrenheit, the average nighttime low is 75 degrees. There is hardly any wind to speak of, no hurricanes, and no earthquakes. It just rains, really hard and almost every day.

Country

Gabon is almost entirely uninhabited rain forest and has some of the world's most incredible—and undiscovered—landscapes, from jungle and savannas to beaches, mountains, and waterfalls. Wildlife abounds. Gabon now boasts the largest remaining population of forest elephants, although this is due less to the success of its very aggressive anti-poaching and anti-ivory trade efforts and more to the complete failure of such efforts in other countries that, previously, had much higher elephant counts.

Half of the two million Gabonese population lives in Libreville, the coastal capital, and the majority of the rest live within a handful of smaller cities, leaving the interior unpopulated. Despite this, every year, fewer than one hundred tourists visit the country due to the high costs of travel and accommodation. The oil economy drives up the hotel and restaurant prices, making Libreville one of the most expensive cities in the world. Further, the country suffers from a lack of any inland infrastructure, including roads, hotels, and airports.

Omar Bongo

Ali Bongo's father, Omar Bongo, ruled Gabon for forty-one years and is, to date, Africa's longest-serving leader. When the elder Bongo died, in 2009, the country moved to a more democratic voting process, and Ali Bongo won the next presidential election. The vote was contested but, after a recount, ruled fair by the country's supreme court.

In 2002, Omar Bongo created a series of national parks to preserve Gabon's rich rain forests and natural resources, working with the Wildlife Conservation Society to turn more than 11 percent of the entire country into protected parkland. Only Costa Rica has a higher percentage. President Ali Bongo has continued this legacy, declaring almost 25 percent of Gabon's territorial waters as a protected marine park and working to promote ecotourism, safeguard Gabon's African forest elephants, and fight against the global ivory trade.

Gabonese History

Similar to its temperate equatorial climate, Gabon's history is fairly even-keeled, with a bloodless independence from France, in 1967, followed by the discovery of offshore oil several years later. Under the long-running rule of Omar Bongo, civil order was maintained and the country established a higher-than-average GDP and literacy rate and an improved standard of health care and quality of life. The 2009 elections and continued disputes by the opposition sparked, in 2011, small protests, which were quickly put down by the government. In 2012, the government charged the leader of the opposition with treason and jailed him. Currently, the country is debating a claim that Ali Bongo is, in fact, a secretly adopted Nigerian Biafran and, therefore, ineligible to be president.

Architectural History

Post-independence, Gabon has seemingly always embraced alternative forms of Modernism for their significant buildings and urban planning projects. In the late 1950s, the Colonial-style buildings were replaced by bold forms inspired by the Tropical Modernism movement. These buildings generally follow the type of work detailed in the influential 1956 book *Tropical Architecture in the Humid Zone* by architects Maxwell Fry and Jane Drew, who were based in Ghana. The movement is characterized by buildings that employ operable windows, *brise-soleil*, and other shading devices tailored to orientation, lots of

---

01–02 Buildings in the old center of Libreville
03 Musée des Arts et Traditions, completed in 1975
04 Ministry of Petroleum and Energy, completed in the 1990s
05 Rond-Point de la Démocratie, a statue marking the entrance to the Cité de la Démocratie
06 Cité de la Démocratie conference center, Energoprojekt, completed in 1977

balconies, wide openings between inside and outside, and lush landscaping, among other features. It is this legacy of "optimistic" Modernism that struck us most on our initial visits to Libreville—these buildings seem to pulsate with idealism and a vision of a "new" Africa.

Our research later directed us to Marcello D'Olivo, an Italian architect who spent most of his career working in Gabon, especially in Libreville. D'Olivo was a contemporary of Paolo Soleri and a signatory to Bruno Zevi's 1945 *Organicist Manifesto*. Relocating to Gabon, in 1965, he designed Libreville's master plan, featuring curving roads and circular roundabouts inspired by natural forms and the local topography. He built, in 1966, a stadium and practice facility that featured swooping organic forms and circular organizations. D'Olivo's legacy still looms large when traveling around the city, and his ideas about an architecture and urbanism that more closely embrace nature were influential on our thinking for the conference-center project.

The last significant alternative Modernist strain in Gabon can be seen in the country's commitment, during the Cold War in the 1970s and 1980s, to the Yugoslavian-initiated Non-Aligned Movement. Yugoslavia's support for African nations came in the form of, primarily, infrastructural and building projects that were designed, managed, and constructed by the giant, state-run construction firm Energoprojekt, whose architecture and engineering arm was founded by Milica Šterić. Šterić was a female architect who had worked, in 1957, under Jaap Bakema in the Netherlands and was a firm adherent to the Team 10 ideals that Bakema had helped to develop as a founding member of that group.

Site

In 1976, Omar Bongo enlisted Energoprojekt to undertake a massive redevelopment of the city. Over the course of two years, they built Libreville's main north-south connector road, the Boulevard Triomphal—along which most government buildings are located—and its city hall. They also developed and built the Cité de la Democratie ("City of Democracy"), an enormous, hilly, green diplomatic park at the northern edge of Libreville. Larger than New York City's Central Park, the complex was built as a collection for international diplomacy and included the old conference center, a banquet hall and theater, spaces for the United Nations, and some military facilities, as well as residential villas for visiting diplomats. Buildings were constructed, following standard plans, entirely from Yugoslavian materials, fixtures, and equipment, which were shipped to Libreville. Exact copies of the Cité de la Democratie conference center, for example, still exist in Uganda and Nigeria.

Ali Bongo's idea, in 2012, was to modernize the entire Cité de la Democratie, demolishing most of the old conference center and almost all of Energoprojekt's other buildings. The competition for the new conference center stipulated that, to save time, the building reuse as much of the old conference center's structure as possible. This mandate meant that the new building would be sited on one of the highest hills in the city, clearly visible when looking up from the outskirts.

Work Climate

The new conference center, for which we were competing, was just one of dozens of building projects and infrastructural improvements initiated by President Ali Bongo after assuming office in 2009. Other projects included a huge, New Urbanist-style low-income housing development in Agondjé, a small town on the other side of Libreville; new stadiums for the Africa Cup, in 2010; and a Chinese-funded land reclamation project to create a new Central Business District in a former harbor in the middle of downtown, as well as new highways and schools. For the Cité de la Democratie, a new, Gary Player-designed golf course was proposed, along with a presidential events center, a renovation of the conference center's neighboring banquet hall, and a new outdoor amphitheater, awarded, in 2013, to New York City architects Aranda Lasche.

To manage all these projects, the president hired, in 2009, the United States-based construction and engineering giant Bechtel to create and staff a new government agency, the Agence National des Grands Travaux (ANGT), which initiated the international competition for the new conference center and managed the design process and the beginning of construction.

Design Concept

Our idea for the competition design was to channel the spirit of optimism we saw in the work of the Tropical Modernists and Marcello D'Olivo. To answer the competition brief's call for a building that represents the country of Gabon, we set out to create a building that would harness the representative power of the land itself—its amazing natural features and climate—rather than relying on historicist clichés or nostalgia.

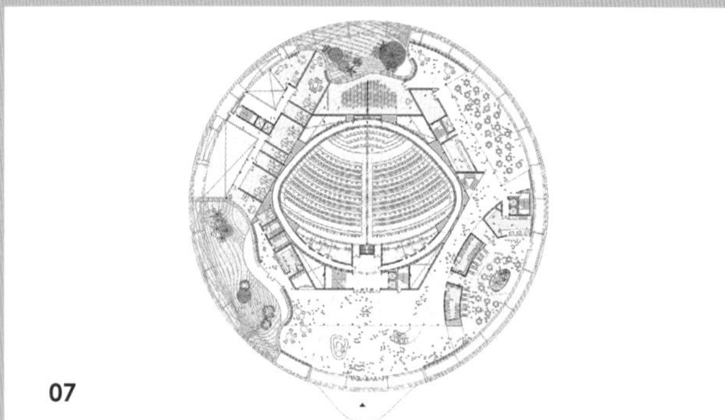

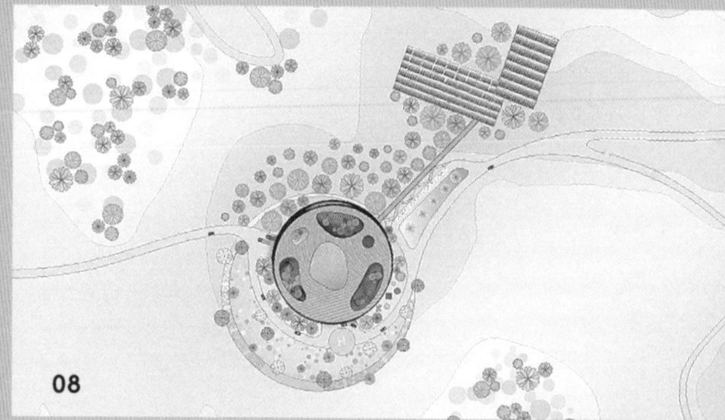

We began with a circle, with the main, 1,000-seat auditorium at its center. Around the perimeter, we carved from the mass of the building three gardens, each representing a particular Gabon ecosystem. These gardens also organize the secondary program of smaller auditoriums, a cafeteria, restaurants, and so on. By extruding the circle as a cone and tilting the roof, the gardens are visible from the city below. The roof, therefore, becomes the building's most important façade.

In Libreville, stormwater and sewage are mixed together and emptied directly into one of the seven rivers that flow into the Gulf of Guinea. Because it is on a bay, the urban coast is quite polluted. For our building, instead of channeling the rainwater to the sewers and out to the sea, it is collected in a cistern and reused as a gray-water system for toilets and irrigation. More than just a demonstration project of best practices for water management in the city, our building uses these sustainable systems to create unique experiences that are central to the design.

In the center of the roof, a series of steps in the shape of the auditorium below creates a water feature of rainwater cascading down to a shallow pool. From there, the water passes through a weir and becomes a waterfall in the "rain forest" garden, collecting in a deeper pool that directly drains into a cistern in the basement. Similarly, throughout the site, a series of stormwater gardens—each featuring different native plants, walkways, and eating areas—control runoff while creating special moments in the landscape.

Sustainable systems, the ecology, and the program are, therefore, all exploited to create visible and experiential representations of the country throughout the building. This deeper sense of transparency is extended to the façade. In order to have large openings, the building is clad in fixed louvers, which are made from a golden African limestone and shade the building. These louvers are set ten feet away from the building's weather wall. Between the two surfaces, we introduced a continuous promenade that winds up, down, and around the structure, providing views and access into the gardens. We integrated, at fifty-feet intervals, benches into the wall of the building and, for a future installation, worked with Heidi Zuckerman Jacobson, the director of the Aspen Museum, on a series of artworks by contemporary African artists. The idea is that this space can function as an informal meeting space. At the end of a day of discussions, you can grab your fellow head-of-state, ally, or enemy and continue the conversation as you wind your way around the building and visit the gardens.

The same golden limestone is used to clad the roof. Beneath this, a three-foot space is used to accommodate any required roof penetrations, resulting in a very uniform surface of stone panels. The organic forms of the garden walls are clad with the same stone, cut into shingles to reduce piece count and simplify construction of these complex shapes.

Planning to keep the structure of Energoprojekt's conference center, we used its hexagonal perimeter structure to create space around the central auditorium to accommodate egress stairs, mechanical shafts, restrooms, and other ancillary spaces. As the design became more detailed and cost estimates were completed, it became obvious that keeping the original concrete structure was unfeasible. The schedule, however, allowed no time for major redesign, and the hexagonal shape of the old

07 Floor plan of conference-center ground floor, showing how the original conference center's structural grid effected the interior organization

08 Site plan, showing the project in context with the Aranda Lache proposal

conference center was retained. We had grown to like it, as well as the idea that at least a memory of the Energoprojekt building would remain.

The wall of this hexagon that faces the public lobbies and circulation spaces was designed as perforated metal with lighting behind. The complex, curved forms of the garden walls create a visual counterfoil to this "public" wall. Covered in reflective brass disks, the garden walls' curved surfaces reflect the light that emanates from this wall.

Each of the three smaller auditoria are associated with a specific garden. The Orchard Auditorium is located beneath the Orchard Garden, containing newly rediscovered edible forest plants and nut trees, many of which have never been cultivated. The curved underbelly of the garden forms its ceiling, and a graphic pattern of acoustic perforations on the rear wall evokes the roots of the plants above. The Rain Forest Auditorium has a ceiling of metal panels, which are configured to evoke the leaves of the forest, with glass tubes around the perimeter suggesting tree trunks and allowing for lighting and circulation behind.

The largest auditorium, the 350-seat Inselberg Auditorium, is associated with a garden that is planted to replicate one of Gabon's most unusual ecosystems. "Inselbergs" are isolated mountains that rise from a level plain—in this case, the rain forest. They are typically formed of resistant rocks that are left as less-resistant rocks are eroded away; in Gabon, they have a particular rocky landscape, with geological formations that resemble rounded "bowls" dotting the ground, punctuated with brightly colored flowers. As the most technical of the three, this auditorium has a sleek stone floor, felt walls, and a gray palette, with moments of intense color in the seating.

Process

Upon winning the competition and negotiating a contract with ANGT, we formed an immense team of talented consultants to carry out the project. Epstein, whose New York City office had just completed executive architect services for the renovation of that city's Jacob K. Javits Convention Center, became our joint-venture partner. With no local architects having the staff or experience to assist with such a fast-track project, we relied on Epstein to assist with coordination and management and help us create the construction documents. We formed a completely blended team in which both offices contributed equally. As Epstein was looking for new office space, we were able to have everyone on a conveniently available empty floor above our office. ANGT also sent a representative to work with us daily, and we initiated weekly calls and trips to Gabon every few months. Silman was our structural engineer, and Arup provided MEP engineering, acoustics, and theatrical consulting. FRONT was retained directly by ANGT as the façade consultant for the project. Due to the lack of local expertise, FRONT was retained to develop details almost to the shop-drawing level, allowing more competitive bidding on the cladding and interior glass. Nathan Browning of Island Planning Corporation worked with local horticulturists and experts to begin gathering and growing plants for the gardens. Mark Thomann worked as part of WORKac's New York City team on the landscape design.

The fast-track schedule meant that, following the construction schedule, packages of different work scopes were sent out in sequence as they were completed. Early work, such as demolition and foundations, and long-lead items, such as structural steel, went out first, before the interiors were completely defined or drawn. In fact, we did not even have our first design presentation with the president until nine months after we started the project and had already finalized the structural-steel design!

Travel

To fly to Libreville, you have to pass through either Paris or Frankfurt. It is an overnight flight to Europe on the way there and an overnight flight from Libreville on the way back. The leg between Europe and Libreville is almost entirely over the Sahara Desert—there is just sand in every direction, for hour after hour. When the scenery changes to the deep green of the rain forest, the plane quickly lands, and you are in Libreville. The humid heat hits you as soon as you exit the plane, and the airport is barely air-conditioned. There always seem to be women in brightly colored African cloth greeting the plane, holding small signs for different oil executives, and the variation in the uniforms of the various security forces and military personnel at the airport is impressive. Almost everyone to whom you hand your passport or your visa letter or your vaccination paperwork seems to be wearing a different, exuberant epaulet.

Libreville is uneventful and expensive. Dinners routinely cost upward of $100 per person. Hotels are $500 per night and are wet, dirty, and smelly. We eventually discovered the Hotel du Phare, a kind of resort at the edge of the city. The rooms were full of sand, but only because the hotel is

09

10

directly on the beach, which was beautiful, if you looked past all the washed-up garbage. Sunsets were amazing, and swimming was forbidden.

We made other trips. Early in the process, we went to Italy to meet with the stone purveyors in Forte Di Marmi and select the limestone. The quarry in Africa would need to close for an entire year solely to provide all the stone for the building. We later returned to view two mock-ups of the louver wall. We went to Istanbul several times once the Turkish contractor, Enka, was selected. In order to have the most beautiful waterfall, we created a one-third mock-up of the waterfall—at a stoneyard near Woodstock, New York, that specializes in water features—to test the flow, angle, and profile of the weir that would channel the water.

Presidential Presentation

In August 2013, we were told that the president would be in town for the UN General Session and would like to review the project. We immediately began to plan for his visit to our office, which is located in three interconnected, old tenement buildings with only an aging, hand-operated freight elevator. Since we were sure he and his entourage were not going to take the stairs, we completely transformed this elevator, adding a red felt carpet, backlit polycarbonate walls, and new lighting. We painted the outside of our building and set up an elaborate, choreographed presentation of our drawings, models, material samples, and mock-ups. The centerpiece was two 1:24 scale models, each more than three feet in diameter and showing the exterior and interior of the building.

Everyone dressed up, especially Kenny Petricig, our office manager, who was charged with operating the elevator. He bought his first tie in twenty years for the meeting. Staff from ANGT arrived early and were milling around like Secret Service agents. We checked and double-checked all the material and went through the sequence. Food arrived.

About thirty minutes before the meeting was supposed to commence, we received a phone call. The president could not come down to us. Could we meet, instead, in his hotel near the UN? He had only one hour to spare, so we could not change the meeting time.

Car services were called, and SUVs started arriving. Teams from the office boxed materials and carried models out to the waiting cars. Within ten minutes, we were able to get everything out the door and into the SUVs. We got on the road, and everything was carried into the president's hotel, past surprised hotel guests and diplomats who were just settling in for cocktails after the day's sessions.

I was stopped at the door to the suite and told I needed a tie if I was to meet the president. Looking around, I spied Kenny putting the last box down—I had my tie.

The president was appreciative, warm, and funny as he reviewed everything in the very crowded hotel suite. We posed together for pictures, and he asked if we could leave everything there, as he was going to meet with the president of Nigeria and the king of Morocco later and wanted to show them the material. (We, of course, agreed.)

When we called the hotel the next day to arrange a pick-up, we were informed that the president and his entourage had left early that morning and that the rooms were empty. Completely empty. We never saw any of the models, mock-ups, or samples again, but, several months later, we heard that the two large models had been installed in one of the president's main offices.

Last visit

My last visit to Libreville was with our Yale students, in February 2014. The class had done amazing research on the history of the city and its architecture, filling in many of the gaps in our knowledge and uncovering stories and projects that most architects and urban planners in Libreville were seemingly unaware of. We saw many parts of the city I had never been to before and met with local architects and historians. Lee White, the president's director of the Gabonese National Parks Service, gave a presentation on the national parks, and his wife, the botanist and illustrator Kate White, took us on a hike deep into the closest rain forest. At one point, she bounded off the trail and came back with a huge bunch of red fruit. "Eat them," she commanded. We did, without hesitation, despite all the university's warnings. They tasted like a delicious combination of blood orange and mango. The fruit, apparently, has no name.

We found hidden architectural gems buried under additions and signage. We walked the entire length of the Boulevard Triumphal and almost got our cameras confiscated. We presented our research to ANGT and heard

09 Interior rendering of promenade between screen and weather enclosure

10 Interior rendering of main auditorium

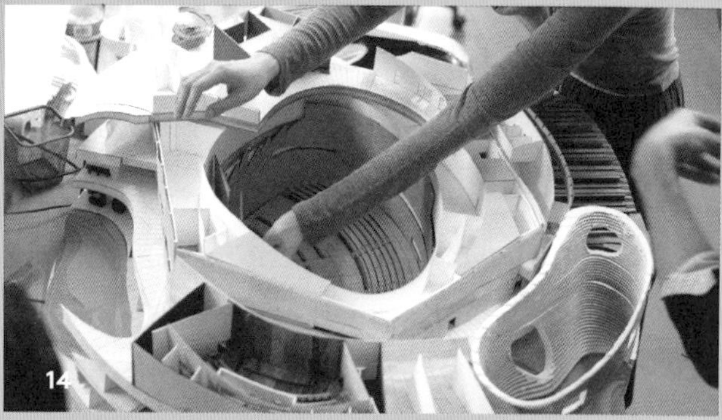

about all its projects. We toured a plywood factory. We took a boat across the bay to amazingly clean beaches with almost no people.

We toured the site of the new conference center. Enka had built a canteen, offices, a carpentry shop, and a weigh station, which was necessary to determine, for LEED compliance, the amount of material entering and leaving the site. Almost four hundred people were working at the site, clearing away parts of the demolished old conference center and preparing for the piles.

It turns out the project never made it much further than that. The site was cleared a few weeks later, and the piles were all drilled and poured by the spring. Foundation shop drawings were finalized, but financing ran out once the final budget numbers came in and new loans and grants had to be negotiated. At one point, my partner, Amale Andraos, flew to Istanbul to see whether we could qualify for a large loan from the Turkish Export-Import Bank by providing 75 percent of the project entirely from Turkish sources. We thought we probably could, if the steel and stone had not already been purchased and fabricated.

At root, there were political issues, as well. With an upcoming election in 2016, it became more and more difficult for the president to concentrate attention and money on projects that would not be completed before then. People were demanding to see progress. Today, the project has been placed on hold, the team disassembled, and the drawings and models archived. There is still an ANGT logo sticker on our upstairs conference room, and the replacement models for the ones that the president absconded with are still on display. We continue to stay in contact with ANGT with phone calls every few months, looking for ways to get the project moving again. The election has been postponed, but we have hope that, if Ali Bongo is reelected and the price of oil rises again, the project will be put back on track.

Looking back on that last trip with the students, my favorite memory is our Yale Architecture Gabon Running Club. Most of the students were great runners, and many joined me for early morning runs along the corniche or the beach. In Gabon, we discovered there is a tradition that is enacted when two runners approach each other: when you are about twelve to fifteen feet away from each other, you make eye contact and clap your hands a few times in encouragement to your fellow jogger. It's a great feeling.

"Keep running," the other runner seems to to say. "You'll make it."

11–13 Images from day of presidential presentation

14–16 Photos of model, showcasing the exterior façade

15

16

BOULEVARD TRIOMPHAL:

ECOLOGICAL INFRASTRUCTURE, *ARCHITECTURE,* MODERNIZATION, *AND THE IMAGE* OF THE CITY

Gabon is a small country in West Africa with big ambitions. While the country is primarily uninhabited rain forest with breathtaking natural beauty and impressive natural resources, almost three-quarters of the population lives in the capital, Libreville. Following the country's liberation from France, in the 1950s, and the discovery of oil off its coast, in the 1960s, Libreville embarked upon its first wave of urbanization and development, with eco-urbanist Marcello Di Olivio's master plan for the city, new infrastructure, and a number of buildings inspired by Maxwell Fry and Jane Drew's "Tropical Modernism." Initiated by President Ali Bongo Ondimba, the city's second wave of urbanization and development has the goal of moving the country into the ranks of emerging economies in a visionary program he has called "Gabon Emergent," an initiative that focuses on industrialization, services, and green jobs and development.

This studio looked at the Boulevard Triomphal, one of the two major axes created by Di Olivio's Libreville master plan, as the locus of a new, forward-looking image for the city. Leading inland from the sea coast into the center of the city, the boulevard is the location of major public buildings, including the parliament, government ministries, and many embassies. We looked at how the introduction of sustainable infrastructure could both transform the boulevard and create the opportunity for new representative public architecture, thus providing a physical manifestation of the country's goals and a model for a progressive, twenty-first-century Africa.

The class researched African Modernism, focusing on Libreville's buildings and urban planning, as well as more detailed investigations into the country's history and recent development, creating a booklet that we took with us to Libreville. Once in the capital city, we were hosted by the Agence National des Grands Travaux (ANGT), which currently is carrying out more than seventy large-scale infrastructural and architectural projects throughout the country. We met with local experts, toured the city and the surrounding rain forest, documented and researched the site, and presented our findings to the ANGT at the end of the trip.

Upon returning to New Haven, we first developed a master plan for the boulevard, focusing on the creation of sustainable water, waste, energy, transportation, and food infrastructure. The studio also explored new hybrid forms of public space to re-imagine the twenty-first-century African city.

For the remainder of the semester, the students developed their individual projects for new public buildings, civic institutions, or complexes along the boulevard, seeking to represent the possible futures of the country as it moves beyond a petroleum-based economy. Channeling the spirit of Tropical Modernism, the studio sought out a new architectural language and new means of representation, moving beyond clichés and nostalgia for an imagined native past and looking toward a new global identity for Gabon—and Africa—as the country reinvents itself.

Assignments

Assignment I: African and Gabonese Modernism

During the first three weeks of the studio, we embarked upon an intense effort to research and define Gabonese Modernism and place it within the wider context of African Modernism and the Modern movement in general. Working in groups, students researched the following topics and concepts and created a series of booklets that were presented on our trip to Gabon.

Book A: Gabon, Libreville, and Africa Basics

- Basic drawings and diagrams, showing size, location, and regions, among other factors, of Africa, Gabon, and Libreville. The goal was to try to discover—and present visually—elements that make Gabon unique or that can help to better "understand" the country.
- Timeline of Gabonese history with a comparison timeline of modern African history.
- Focus on the president's Gabon Vert ("Green Gabon") plan, looking at elements such as natural resources, the national parks system, the climate, and green infrastructure opportunities.
- Focus on the Gabon Emergent ("Emerging Gabon") plan, looking at the economics of the country, both currently and under the president's programs. The studio focused on resources, industries, free-trade zones, ecotourism, and emerging services, among other factors.
- Focus on oil and its economic and social impacts throughout Gabon's history, as well as oil's impact on national infrastructure and development, diagramming comparisons to other resources and industries.
- For each of the above, provide a comparison between Gabon and other African countries in order to contextualize and compare findings.

Book B: African and Gabonese Modernism

Basic information on Libreville urbanism
Timeline of significant architecture and urbanism in Gabon
Comparison timeline of African Modernism, including seminal moments in African Modernism
Focus on Marcello D'Olivo, researching his biography and seminal works; urban planning for Libreville; buildings in Libreville, Gabon, and other work in Africa; and collecting images, drawings, books, and other relevant material.
Focus on Energoprojeckt, the architecture and construction arm of Yugoslavia's state oil company. This company's projects include Cité de la Democratie, the Boulevard Triomphal, and parliament. Compare Energoprojekt's work in other African countries with its work in Gabon; investigate relationship with Team 10.
Research into Africa's relationship with Western Modernism; look at Le Corbusier, "Tropical Modernism," Prouve, Doxiadis, and so on, and find all relevant links to Africa.
From the lists established above, focus on supposed relationship with the "local" and how interpretation of this has changed throughout time.
Diagrams and drawings that show relationships between time, scale, degree of ambition, program, and so on, for African and Gabonese modernism.

Book C: Building Taxonomy

Basic information on important and iconic buildings in similar tropical climates around the world and in Africa and Gabon, including images, drawings, program, size, date built, architect, and so on.

Assignment II: Master Plan

A. Site Analysis
We focused on Libreville's infrastructure, documenting the current state of both formal and informal infrastructures that exist and service the city. We also looked at potential infrastructure for the city, interacting with local ANGT experts to understand the agency's plans and looking to define what a new, more sustainable Gabonese infrastructure could be. Students investigated both Libreville's formal and informal infrastructure; researched and documented sustainable alternatives to traditional infrastructural systems for waste-recycling, water, energy, transportation, and food; and cataloged new technologies and approaches to infrastructure. Combined with information gleaned from discussions with the ANGT, students were asked to create a conceptual design for new sustainable infrastructure along the Boulevard Triomphal. Projects were challenged to imagine how these new forms of infrastructure could create new public spaces or experiences, organize the boulevard in a new way, and create a new identity for the city and country—an identity that builds on the city's past and present.

B. Master Plan
Working together as a class, we took the ideas developed in Libreville for each of the specific infrastructures and combined them, in a kind of Cadavre Exquisse, to create a master plan for the new Boulevard Triomphal. Each student used research, observations, and detailed cataloguing of the boulevard to create a site and context for their individual projects. Students were asked to employ the new sustainable infrastructure to create public spaces and experiences and link a series of sites for the projects. In the end, the Boulevard Triomphal master plan was presented as a physical site model, which, as a whole, showcased each individual project.

STUDIO WORK

01 RAIN FOREST *AS RESOURCE*

One of Gabon's greatest natural resources is its rain forest. Covering 80 percent of its land, Gabon's rain forest is key to preserving some of the world's most unique species, as it contains eight thousand known plant species as well as two hundred mammal and six hundred bird species. Currently, Gabon's economy is dependent on wood, manganese, and oil, which, alone, consists of 70 percent of the country's exports. However, the government realizes that oil has a limited life span and is looking at other resources as sustainable alternatives for the economy. For example, the government is looking to shift to a tourism-based economy, centered on the rain forest, by investing in education and infrastructure to boost the country's service industries.

Despite the vastness of the rain forest, the majority of Gabon's citizens live in cities, removed from the country's main landscape. The following projects bring the rain forest into Libreville's urban center, thus bringing it to the forefront of the public's eye. The projects address the variety of potentials the rain forest has to offer, whether it be economic growth or preservation and coexistence with of one of the planet's most unusual habitats.

BRYAN MADDOCK

THE MINISTRY OF PARKS

Gabon contains some of the most incredible, untouched natural ecosystems on the planet. Because of the scarcity of tourists and a lack of infrastructure to support ecotourism within the country, very few people know about, much less have experienced, these parks. Dedicated in 2002, Gabon's thirteen national parks cover 10 percent of the country. Gabon is trying to modernize while preserving some of the last remaining rain forest habitats on the planet. For example, 85 percent of the population of African forest elephants now reside within Gabon's borders and national parks due to poaching throughout the continent. To organize, research, and enforce the protection of the rain forest, the National Agency for National Parks (ANPN) was formed in 2002. Led by managing director Lee White, ANPN is responsible for the implementation of government policy for the national parks. That policy comprises the protection of parks and natural resources through policy and procedures, development of the park network via research and management, and enhancement of the parks through information, education, and tourism.

With the increasing pressure to develop alternatives to oil production, Gabon has bet on ecotourism and sustainable-resource management. The future of the economy is dependent on the widespread acceptance of the ANPN as a force for good.

Just as a government ministry mediates between the government and the citizenry, so this project's Ministry of Parks building mediates between a system of parks and established neighborhoods. The building serves as the link between the two and will remain a useful part of the built fabric, instead of a privatized workplace that is typical of ministries in Libreville. The site is along the Bord de Mer, a major vehicular road that follows the coast, from the airport to the oldest part of Libreville. The new port, under construction to the south of the boulevard, will be disconnected from the rest of the city unless a link is made over the road. The project's proposed building straddles this edge. The final form establishes a lifted pedestrian surface of bridges above the busy boulevard while linking programs and transportation in a tripartite procession above newly established parks. The project acts as a link to connect, to the north, the city's busiest nightlife district

01 Final model, showing aerial view and the project context

01

and a revitalized neighborhood park, and, to the south, the largest beachfront in the city; it also establishes the city's first large public plaza and recreation fields, adjacent to the new building. The program sits on a knuckle of controversial forces (the public beach, the country's primary road, the new China-led port development, and the end of the government zone) and presents itself as a manifestation of the mutual integration of these forces.

There are cores at two corners of the building and a bridge that connects across the Bord de Mer. Public interior circulation is triangulated around the center, while the employees' circulation steps vertically along the tower for their daily routines. Botanical gardens and helipads step up the layers of the building, which is an extension of the transportation network and a plant nursery for the new park system. The sectional shifting of programs allows the corners to serve as a lobby for the three independent occupants within the building—ANPN, parks research, and the community center. Helicopters are currently the best means of visiting the remote national parks and monitoring the elephant population, and, when available, the helipads will be leased for tourism. Unlike the traditional government ministry building, the private functions of the

02

03

04

ANPN are sandwiched by the public functions, allowing the public to visit and talk to those protecting their national parks. Gardens are used throughout the building as a laboratory for raising rain forest plants within the city while offering opportunities to educate children and adults about the rain forest. Stacked, tiered auditoriums face the parks and the sea. Events will be visible from the new park below, and accessibility is guaranteed via the public staircase on the interior of the building. Above the road and linking the parks with diverse functions, the Ministry of Parks building is representative of a necessary shift in the power of parks, tourism, and culture as the political and social foundations for a new national identity.

02 View of the final model, featuring the conference and office areas in the tower and their relationship to the vertical circulation

03 Site plan, showing how the building connects the nightlife district and neighborhood park to the north and the beachfront to the south and establishes, adjacent to the building, the city's first large public plaza and recreation fields

04 Unrolled section, showing the circulation between each of the three sides of the building

05 Early study models, showing different strategies for bridging across the Bord de Mer

06 View of the final model, showing the main lobby

05

06

ROBERT CANNAVINO

ANPN HEADQUARTERS

This project establishes a new headquarters for the Agence Nationale des Parcs Nationaux (ANPN) within the center of Libreville, as well as a new identity for the institution as a critical force in shaping the future of the country. Gabon's forests cover 80 percent of the country and are home to over 8,000 known plant species, as well as 300 mammal and 600 bird species. The government recognized the importance of this biodiversity and, in 2002, created thirteen national parks, protecting 10 percent of the nation's forests. ANPN was created to act as protector and steward of these forests.

The proposed design for the ANPN headquarters sits at the intersection of the three important areas of the city: the thoroughfare of ministries along the Boulevard Triomphal, the commercial center at Port Mole, and the economic and tourist center in downtown Libreville. The design for the new ministry building highlights the major goals and strategies of the ANPN: education, conservation, and protection. One of the most powerful tools against illegal logging and poaching is the dissemination of knowledge and collaboration with the public to protect these lands. However, the thirteen national parks are located in remote regions of the country, with limited and complicated means of access. Instead of bringing the people to nature, the design brings nature to the people.

The building is set within a proposed reforested park—the first major public park and space in downtown Libreville—which sits next to a rehabilitated stream as well as a new nursery for reseeding portions of the national parks. Amid this verdant Eden, the ANPN building is surrounded by the resources it is charged with protecting. The park is designed as a large-scale nursery and proving ground for ANPN. This park creates a new public realm and public consciousness about a remote problem.

The building is designed as a tower of stacked programs, wrapped by a continuous, outdoor public pathway. This spiraling pathway penetrates the tower's mass and carves

01

out exterior spaces for viewing, education, and public engagement. These public zones align with the significant sectional strata of the rain forest so that the public can interact and experience the diversity within the forest. The public procession culminates at the top with commanding panoramic views of Libreville, a reminder of the individual's power to see new horizons and the necessity for protecting such important assets.

Entwined with this path are ANPN's conservation and operation centers, including a botanical research laboratory and a nursery for rehabilitating logged portions of the forest. In support of ANPN's efforts to protect the forests, the ANPN building incorporates landing pads for surveillance drones and workshop for the fabrication of small-scale research stations. These research stations are deployed into remote regions of the rain forest, territorializing and protecting areas often left untended. There are also a series of meeting rooms specifically designed to bring together important decision-makers and stakeholders in the nation's forests, including representatives from the timber industry, conservation organizations, and the Ministry of Forestry. All these programmatic elements are directly visible and accessible from the public pathway, in an effort to engender a sense of governmental transparency.

The new ANPN building acts as a beacon of change for the people of Gabon. Through the design of a facility which involves and educates the public on the country's most important asset, the ANPN becomes a force for positive change.

01 Sections and elevation, illustrating how the different levels of the building relate to the proposed context

02 Axonometric diagrams, illustrating the form as a response to the layers of the rain forest, the creation of a continuous vertical public pathway, and the programmatic necessities for the agency

02

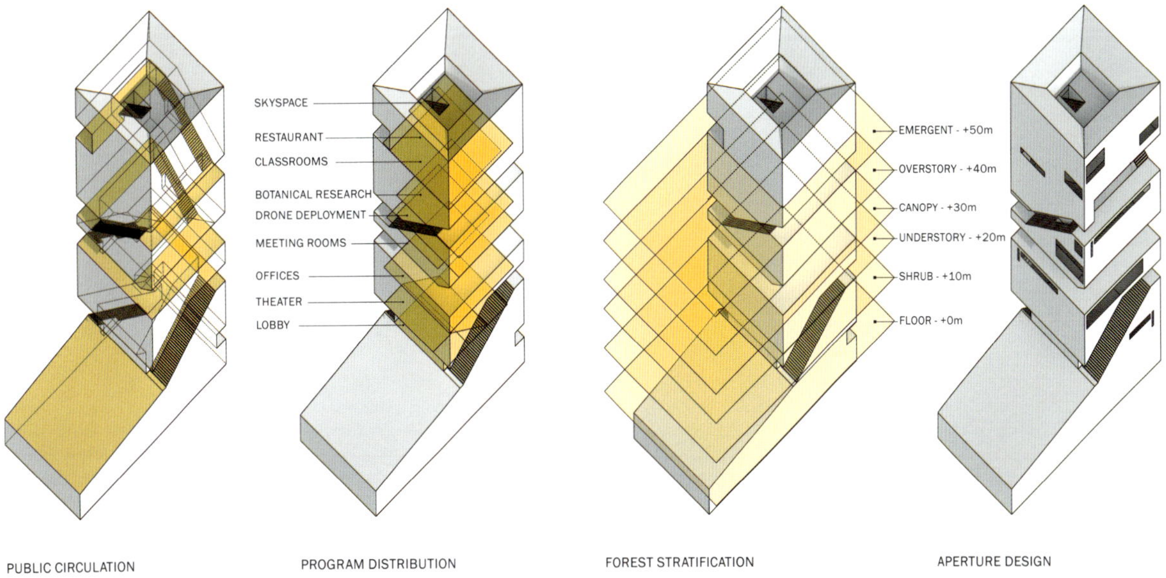

ROBERT CANNAVINO

03 Site plan, showcasing proposed building and park landscape within the city
04 Final model, showing how the exterior circulation carves out the building's form
05 Exterior rendering of the building within the landscape

03

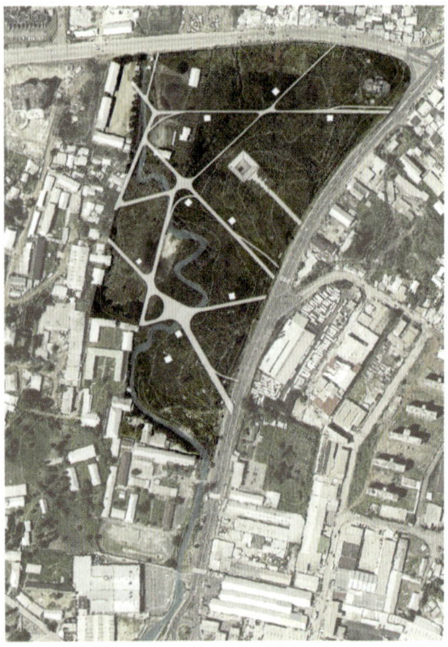

04

05

RUSHYAN YEN

FEEDING GABON: NATIONAL AGROFORESTRY CENTER

Gabon is a small country in West Africa that has benefited greatly from its oil reserves, allowing it to boast a GDP three times the Sub-Saharan average. Yet this reliance on oil has crippled the agricultural sector, which accounts for just five percent of the economy. This means that more than 80 percent of the food in Gabon is imported from abroad, resulting in a massive food insecurity issue. This problem is intensified by the country's declining oil reserves, which are estimated to run out within twenty years. The country must find a way to feed its people while creating new ways to sustain its economy.

Covering more than 80 percent of the country, Gabon's dense tropical forests are a major resource that could solve the country's problems. With the goal of becoming the first carbon-neutral country in the world, Gabon recently set aside 10 percent of its land for national parks, a ratio of protected territory second only to Costa Rica. Yet, in spite of these efforts, Gabon's rain forests and wildlife remain threatened by urban sprawl, poaching, biofuel production, mining and oil drilling, and habitat fragmentation. While recent initiatives to increase the country's food security are much needed, the proposed increase in agricultural production would add further strain to Gabon's rain forest ecosystem.

01 Final model, an aerial view showing the building and proposed landscape

01

RUSHYAN YEN

Agroforestry is an innovative technology that combines trees with agricultural crops and animals, benefitting plants, animals, people, and the environment. One example of agroforestry is forest farming, which proposes to modify but maintain the forest's canopy to allow proper sunlight to reach crops grown on the forest's floor. It provides a way to address Gabon's food insecurity, resource conservation, and habitat restoration while building the country's economic capacity.

This proposal for a National Agroforestry Center, located in the nation's capital city and connected to Omar Bongo University, aims to be the center of this effort to promote economic and food security. Research labs and classrooms encircling an open atrium allow scientists and students access to all levels of the rain forest ecosystem. Public facilities, such as the library, auditoriums, farmer's market, and restaurant, provide welcoming spaces for visitors and locals to learn and participate in the effort to promote agriculture and conservation while fostering the economy. The center's location at the head of Libreville's river provides an opportunity to clean and filter the city's water, offering an added social and environmental value.

---

02 Section, showcasing the relationship between the central, open atrium and the surrounding research labs and classrooms

03 Floor plans, depicting how the different programmatic elements are associated with different layers of the rain forest canopy

04 Site plan, showing the building situated along the river and in relationship to Omar Bongo University

02

03

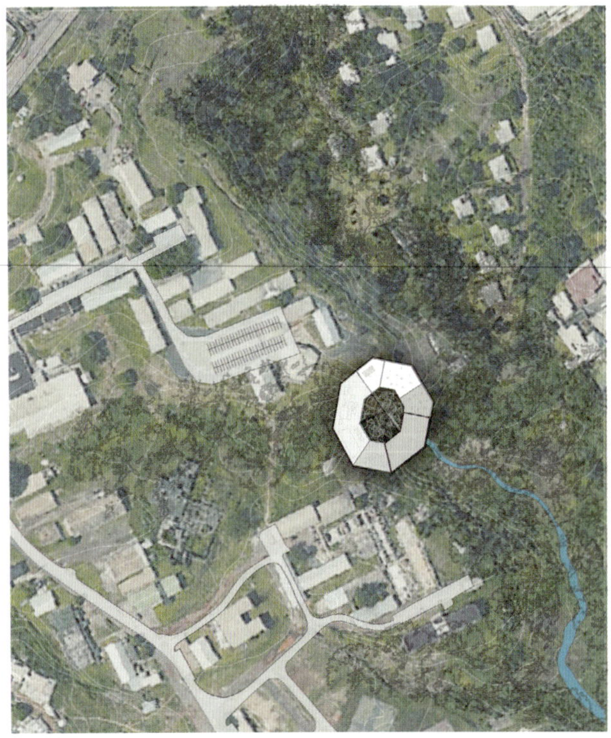

04

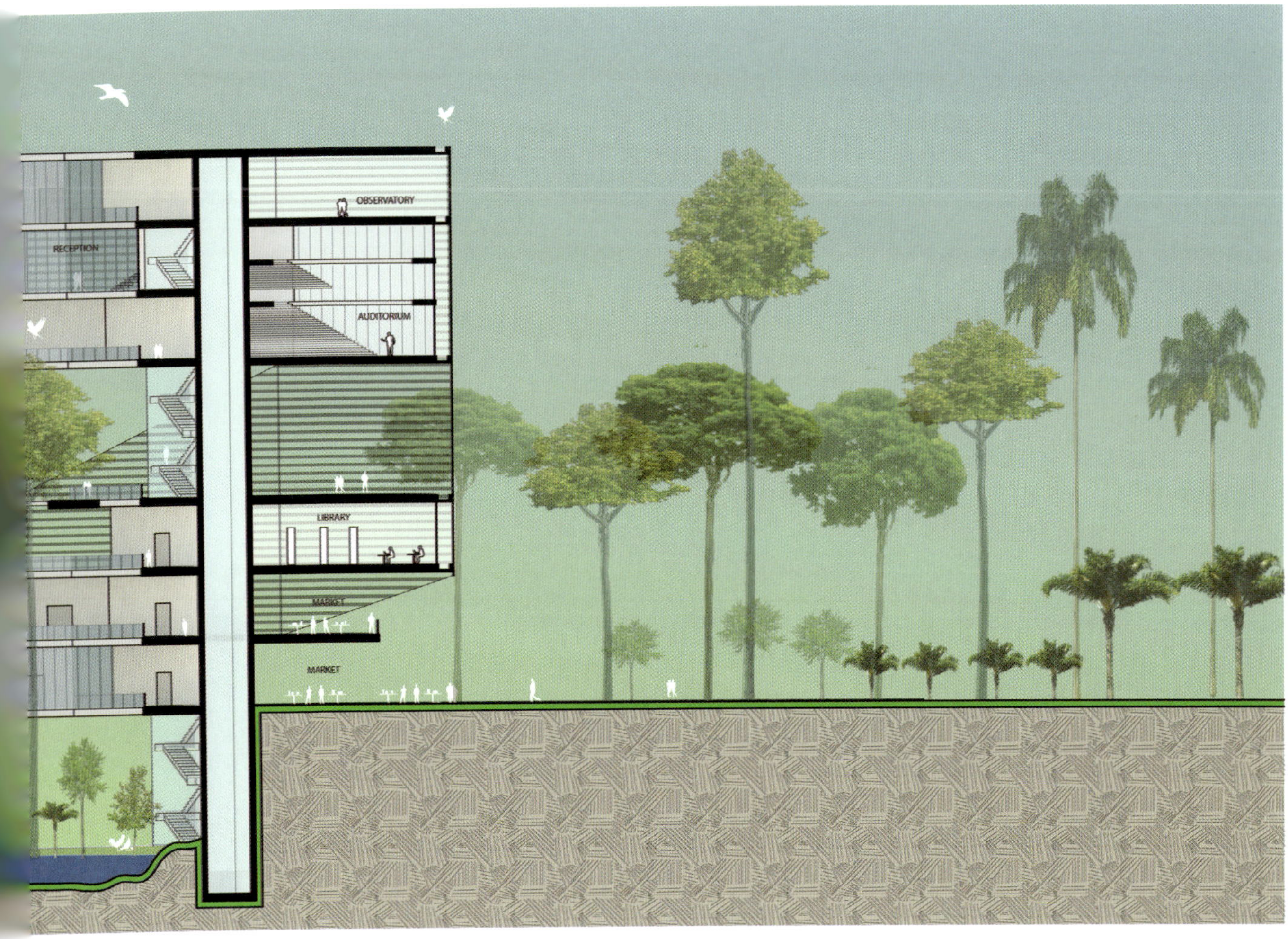

ANN MORROW JOHNSON

HOTEL EDEN

Drawing on Gabon's emerging ecotourism economy, Hotel Eden provides a resting point for travelers en route to the country's lush rain forests.

The organic form of this proposal takes advantage of Libreville's consistently mild but wet climate on the equator. The bulbous forms provide the open-air lobby with coverage from the sun and daily rain showers while facing out over the water, allowing each of the rooms access to waterfront views and a breeze from the prevailing wind.

The form, reminiscent of local rain forest flora, also presents a striking profile along the water's edge and Port Mole. The iconic hotel serves as a landmark for the city and an announcement of the next step in Libreville's development.

---

01 Floor plans, showing key public floors and hotel-room layouts
02 Section, illustrating the intersection of the two bulbous forms and elevated courtyards
03 Final model detail, featuring the exterior open-air lobby
04 Site plan, showcasing beachfront orientation
05 Final model, showing the view as a guest approaches the hotel
06 Final model, showing beachfront elevation

01

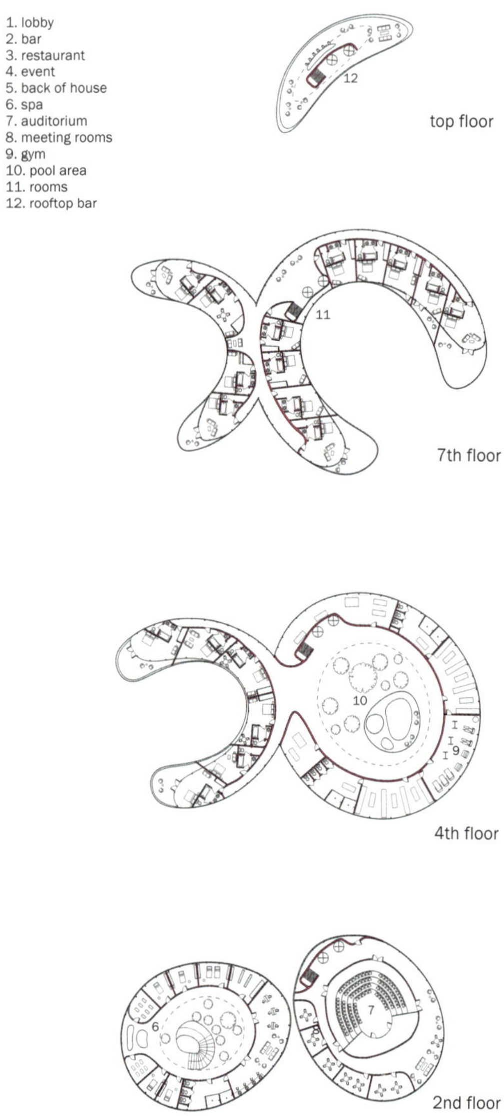

02

03

04

05

06

02 GOVERNMENT/ *PUBLIC INTERFACE*

The Boulevard Triomphal is a vehicular thoroughfare alongside which all the government ministries are headquartered and isolated from the general public. The monumental buildings showcase the nation's recent wealth but are physically detached from the general public they are supposed to serve. The following projects attempt to form buildings that engage the general public specifically through new ministries that address the growing infrastructural needs of the nation, challenging the typical building typology in Libreville.

EVAN WISKUP

MINISTRY OF OPEN SPACE

This project represents a new attitude toward outside space in Gabon. The central African country has recently taken tremendous steps to preserve its surrounding zones of pristine ecological diversity. Within the small country of Gabon is a wide variety of climates, including rain forests, beaches, and grasslands. The current president of Gabon has made unprecedented steps toward preserving 10 percent of the overall land in the form of national parks. However, more than 85 percent of the population of Gabon lives in urban centers. This project looks to address both landscapes, establishing a ministry to maintain the open spaces both within and outside of cities by merging the existing National Parks Services with a new Ministry of Open Space. This innovative, unprecedented government agency would serve as a cornerstone of the future of Gabon and project to the world a commitment to the preservation and celebration of all the lands of Gabon, both urban and rural.

This project serves as an exhibition of this new attitude. The Ministry of Open Space's headquarters redefines the relationship between inside and outside by collaging interior and exterior programs. Individuals meander through a schizophrenic array of climactic and programmatic experiences. This project presents the superpositioning of interior and exterior through a radical redefinition of the sectional parti.

01–02 **Sections, illustrating the building's parti and relationship to the landscape and vehicular road**

01

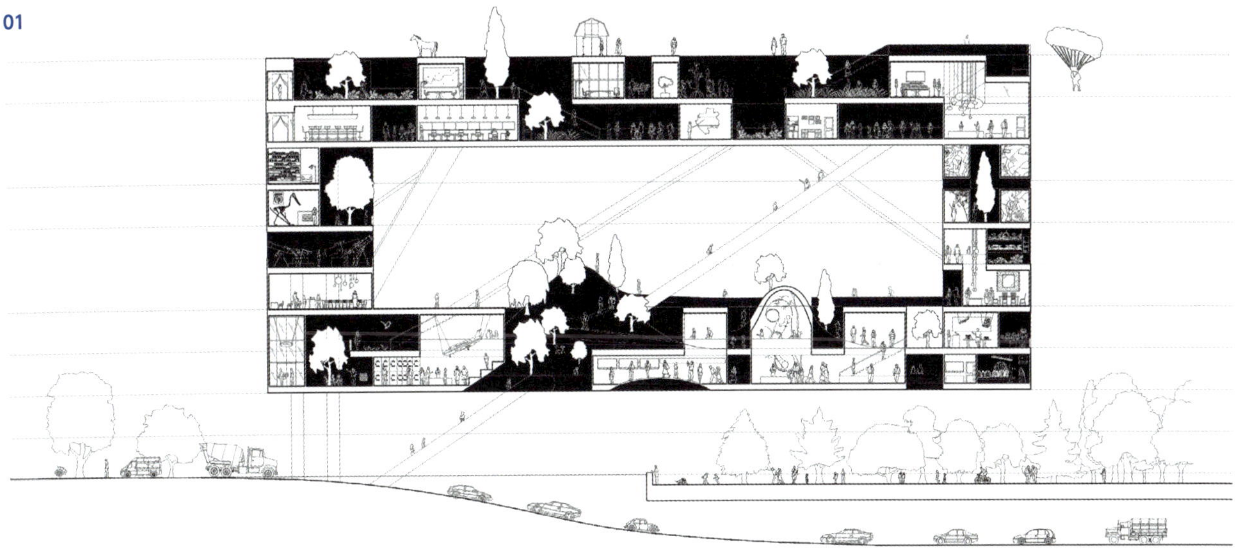

02

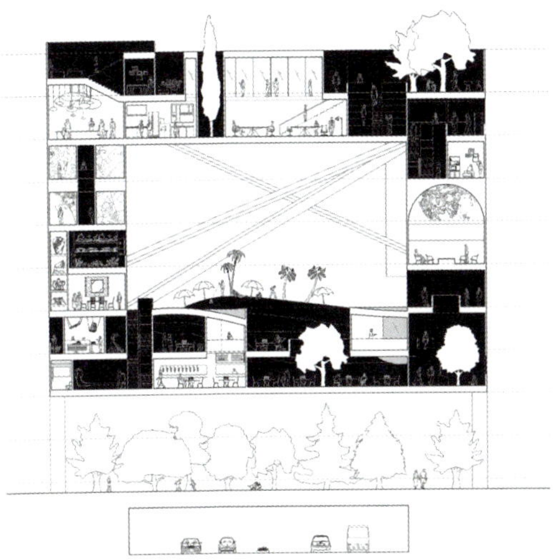

EVAN WISKUP

By embracing the multi-scalar opportunity afforded by the notion of "open space," the building's porosity is defined at a variety of scales. At the scale of its urban siting, the building cantilevers above an existing thoroughfare over a new forest parkland. By situating the building between the street and park, the project symbolically bridges open space in the city and in the national parks.

The building itself is a hollow cube that forms an open framework for Gabon's, varying climatic zones to be represented within the open areas created by the frame. Within the building, open space cuts through interior spaces, creating an unusual 1:1 relationship between the area of open space and the area of enclosed space. Visitors can jump from one side of the ministry to the other using the shortcuts provided by catwalks, which cut across the hollow cube while being suspended in the interstitial space between city and park and between urban and rural.

The sky, as the greatest complement to open space, is applied as an image against the façade of the building. This gesture acts as both a conceptual reinforcement to the potential of the laboratory of open spaces created within the new ministry building but, also, as a camouflage that allows the building to blend into the surrounding sky.

03 Floor plans, showing main floors hovering over the site
04–05 Final model, showing interior spatial organization in relation to exterior form and site
06 Rendering of proposed landscape over the Boulevard Triomphal and through the building's central void
07 Exterior rendering, showing the building through landscape

03

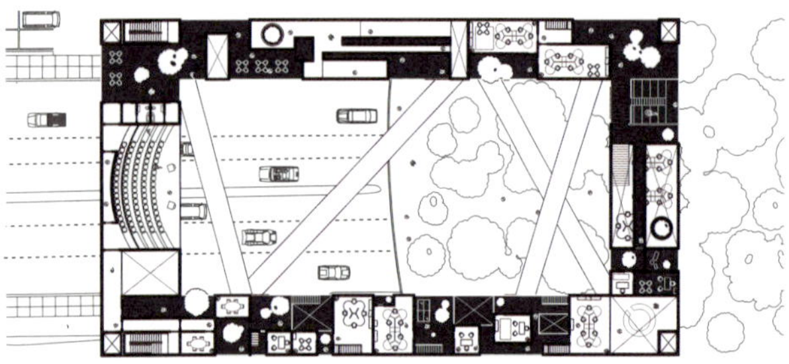

04

05

06

07

WILLIAM SHERIDAN

LA ROTUNDE

In a city in which almost half of Gabon's 1.5 million people call home, Libreville faces a number of challenges due to its rapid growth. ANGT, a quasi-public national agency created by the president of Gabon, is operated and staffed as a subsidiary of Bechtel, one of the world's largest construction and engineering companies. Libreville currently suffers from severe traffic and congestion. As part of the so-called Gabon Emergent major-works program, ANGT is planning to expand the country's transportation infrastructure to address this growing problem. ANGT is working to twin National Route One, a major trunk road extending inland from the city. The plan to expand the road requires the razing of the homes, businesses, and informal markets that have coalesced along this corridor. In one case, located at the center of a roundabout, a vibrant market on the way to Nkok—the site of the future airport and on the way to Gabon's new special economic zone for the timber trade—is to be shut down to make way for the new road. This approach is representative of the ANGT's traditional thinking regarding infrastructural development: expand capacity through major projects to accommodate rising demand. But such a plan comes with significant costs. For example, while only 10 percent of the population owns a car, as that percentage expands, it will be increasingly difficult for ANGT's expansionary effort to keep up with demand.

A deeper and more comprehensive understanding of the urban composition of Libreville might suggest alternative ways to improve its transportation infrastructure. For instance, Libreville already has a robust, if chaotic, taxi and bus system. Rather than simply expanding the roads as more Gabonese use automobiles to move around the city, why not re-imagine the existing taxi system so that it can function more effectively?

The current system is woefully inefficient. First, you must flag down a cab, which is almost always nearly full, and then inquire where it is headed. If it happens to be going in the same direction as you are, you hop on; if not, you let it continue on its way and try to flag down another. Of course, this system causes delays for everyone, with taxis constantly starting and stopping without necessarily picking up additional passengers.

This project begins by selecting a prime site on the Boulevard Triomphal. The Place de la Paix is a roundabout at which the boulevard meets the city's ring road before continuing on to the Cité de la Democratie. This location would be transformed into a central hub for the entire city and provide easy access to most destinations. In fact, it is already a popular location for people to flag down a taxi. The site would function as the main point of transfer for most trips. Curbside transfers would occur on the periphery of the rotary, where simple signage would clearly announce destinations throughout the city, allowing for much more efficient commuting.

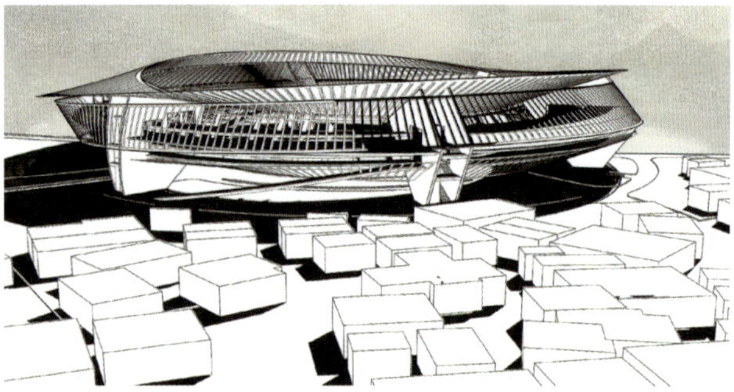

01

02

The building itself would help to facilitate pedestrian movement around the rotary by providing a continuous circulation path above street level. It also would establish a stronger connection between the Boulevard Triomphal and the developing civic and cultural campus of the Cité de la Democratie. Currently, the boulevard is not a particularly convivial place for pedestrians. A wide civic avenue, with cars travelling at high speed and no sidewalks, now provides the spine for a series of isolated enclaves—that is, institutional buildings fenced off to the general public. Typical of modern urban planning, the city segregates its urban programs so as to avoid interference and promote efficiency. Yet, the most exciting urban spaces in Libreville tend to be messy agglomerations of program in Centreville.

This new taxi hub, wrapped with a market that can leverage the influx of commuters to the site, marks a first step in recoding the urbanism along the boulevard, transforming it into a bustling pedestrian thoroughfare. Six cores, each touching down in different sectors of the rotary, support the circulatory rings above. On the ground level, an open market with enclosed refrigeration facilities interfaces with the existing informal settlement to the south of the rotary. Facilities for the new, expanded taxi system—a gas station and a taxi tea stand, with parking, where drivers can take breaks—also wrap the rotary at the ground level. A new welcome center for the Cité de la Democratie is located on the ground level, as well. Two long ramps for vehicles allow for easy access to the two levels above, which provide further open-air market space. Conditioned spaces selectively wrap the perimeters of the market, housing a control center and the new taxi system's headquarters, a new department of motor vehicles, and new public bathing facilities. The DMV, which will help to regulate the city's growing population of drivers, is prominently and conveniently located at a node of concentration for urban transportation and integrated with the market program. The public bathing facilities are intended to support the nearby informal community, which lacks sufficient access to water and sanitation. At the same time, the public bathing facility is open to all of Libreville, transforming the building into an integral part of commuters' daily routines.

The integration of infrastructure and public space promised by this confluence of programs around a new, busy transportation hub proposes nothing short of a new urban idea for the city. The Place de la Paix has long been an important site for civic protest. Now, despite relatively little program explicitly dedicated to civic functions, the site is transformed into a newly visible and, therefore, powerful civic space.

The building's circular form, while obviously a response to the site itself, is also a deliberate reference to the legacy of the organicist architect Marcello D'Olivo, who was responsible

01 Perspective view from an informal community

02 Building section, showing the relationship between floor levels and exterior skin

03 Exterior rendering from inside the roundabout

03

for the city's first urban plan and whose buildings were once scattered throughout the city. Many of these buildings have been demolished by the ANGT in its efforts to modernize the city. By drawing on his formal approach, in which the circle operates as a fundamental element, this project preserves what remains of D'Olivo's work.

Finally, the project strives to take advantage of, yet temper, Gabon's hot, tropical climate. Following the design principles for tropical climates set out by Maxwell Fry and Jane Drew, a series of canopies provides shelter from the sun and the country's daily showers. These ring-shaped canopies are separated by section but overlap in plan so that they keep the sun and rain out while allowing for a stack effect that keeps air moving throughout the building. The canopies themselves are intended to act as an iconic presence for the city, but, despite their formal exuberance, they are constructed relatively simply, as they are derived from ruled surfaces. Timber slats are arrayed parametrically to control each canopy's opacity relative to its solar orientation, and a simple transparent plastic membrane allows the system to shed water, which is collected and reused by the building's public baths.

The modern buildings along the boulevard tend to exaggerate many of the design principles set out by Fry and Drew so that they cease to perform according to the functional rubrics of tropical architecture and, instead, operate on a purely symbolic level, projecting a sense of Gabonese identity. This building attempts to do both at once, offering a new but quintessentially Gabonese architecture that also performs well environmentally.

04

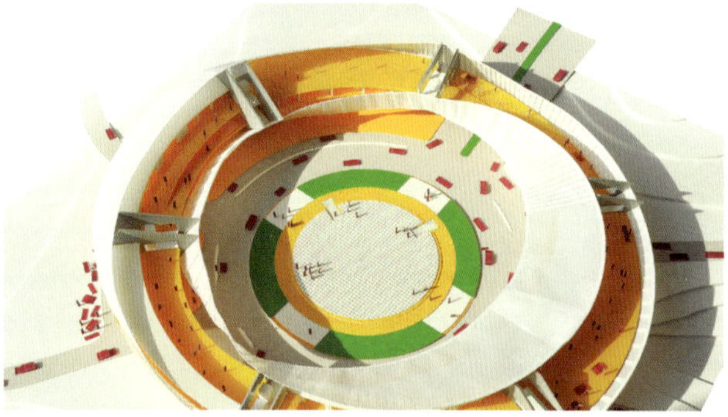

05

04 Final model, showing a bird's-eye view

05 Final model, showing an aerial view of the ramp to the second market level

06 Unrolled section, showing the building as a continuous loop and how the structural piers connect each level and the ground plane

07 Ground-floor plan, illustrating how the building functions as an infrastructural hub

06

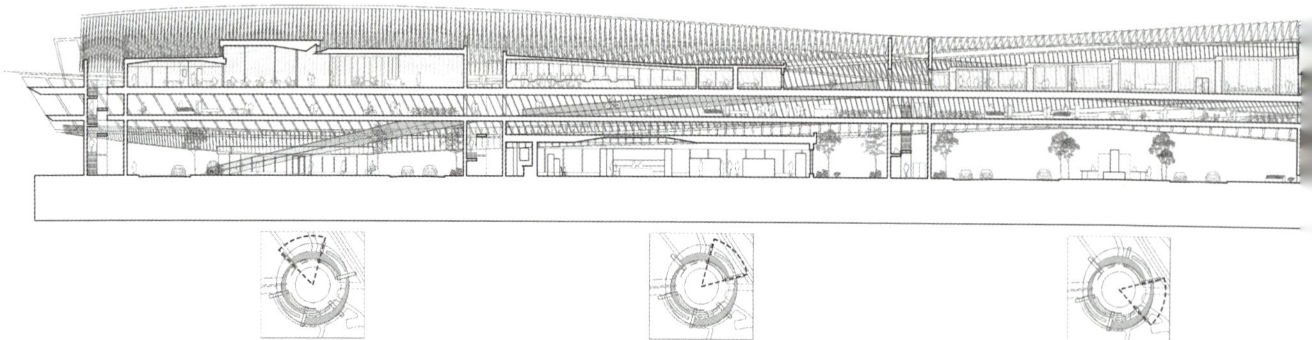

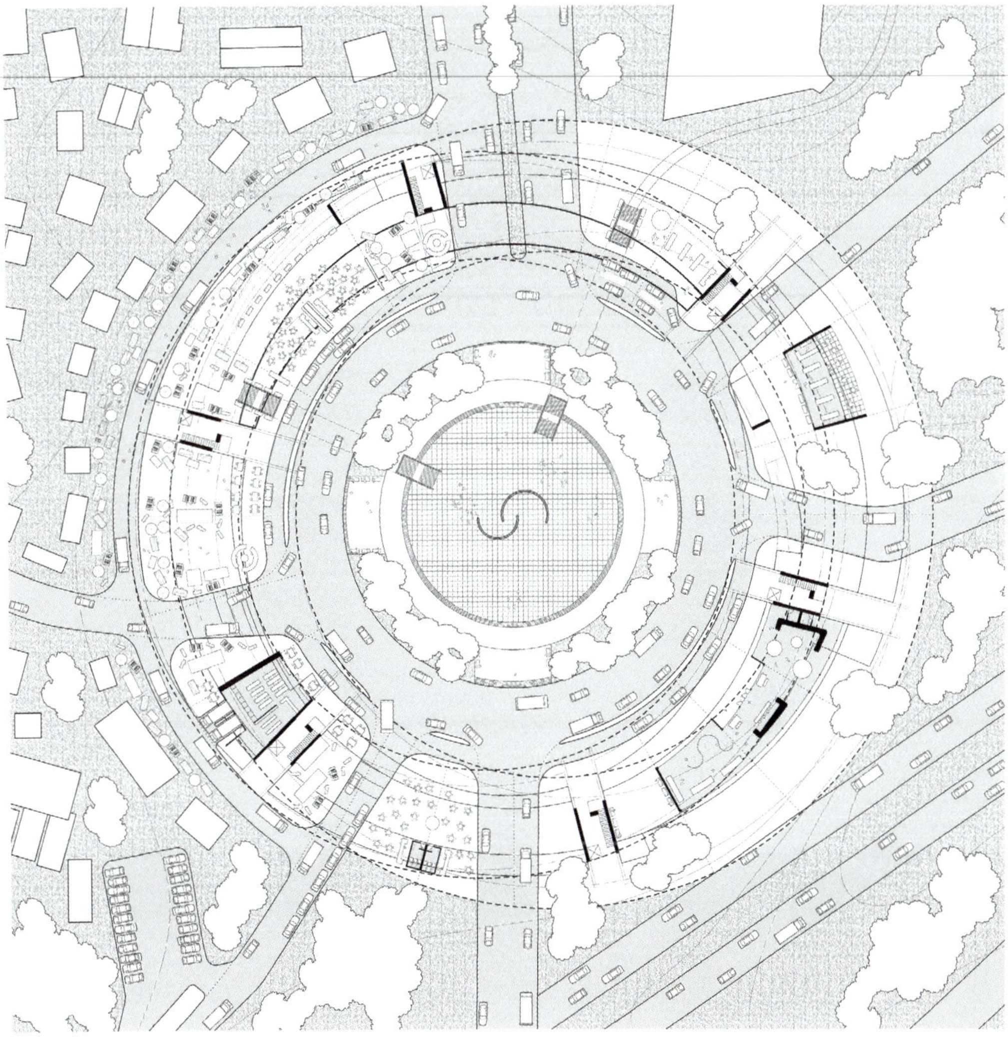

07

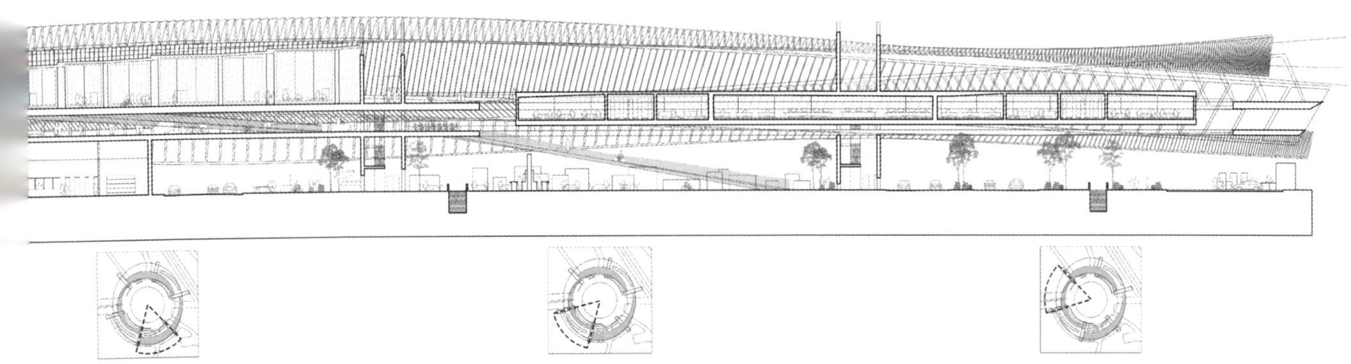

ADAM WAGONER

GABON BLEU

Gabon, located on the equator, is 80 percent covered in rain forests. However, the country lacks the infrastructure to capitalize on its abundant water resources. With no real country-wide sewer system, 67 percent of Gabonese lack modern sanitation facilities, and 12 percent lack access to clean drinking water. Gabon needs a new direction for how it manages water infrastructure. This system should not be merely a continuation of the standard Western model of isolated infrastructure; ideally, it should become visibly integrated into the area's ecology and the city's urban infrastructure.

The purpose of this intervention is to foreground these pressing water and sanitation problems within Gabon. The site for this project, the capital city of Libreville, is located at the bottom of a large watershed area that allows for easy access to the commercial and governmental buildings along the Boulevard Triomphal, the surrounding neighborhoods, and the country's main university.

This project proposes a water-treatment plant and community center that, together, will not only provide clean drinking water but also be an asset in other ways for the adjacent neighborhoods. It proposes combining the utilitarian functions of water purification with social programs—such as laundromats, pools, restrooms, car washes, cafeterias, bars, meeting rooms, media labs, auditoriums, and galleries—that can feed off the by-products of the plant's processes. Arranged as a stacked system, the new water treatment plant and community center would become Gabon's tallest structure, establishing itself as an unavoidably visible statement about the importance and potential of water and water management for the future of Gabon as a developed country.

---

01 Axonometric diagrams, one showing the vertical flow of water and the other showing the circulation of people through the different programs nested in the building

02 Final model, showing the interlocking of water treatment and community center spaces

03–04 Details of final model, showing large, exterior spaces

01

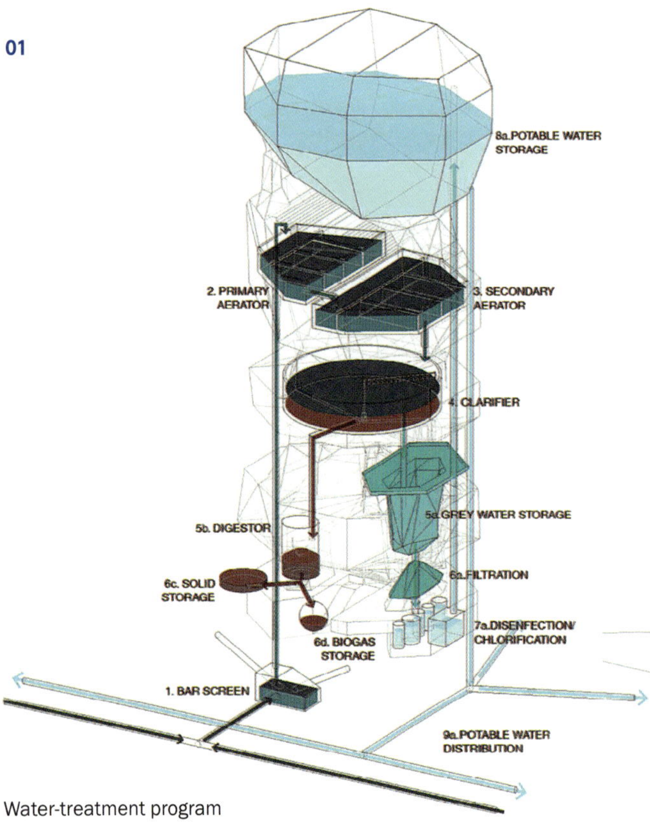

Water-treatment program

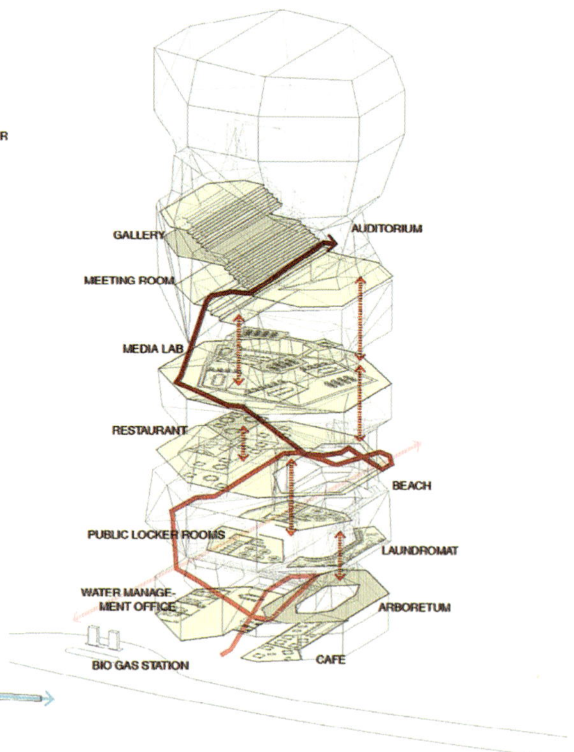

Community-center program

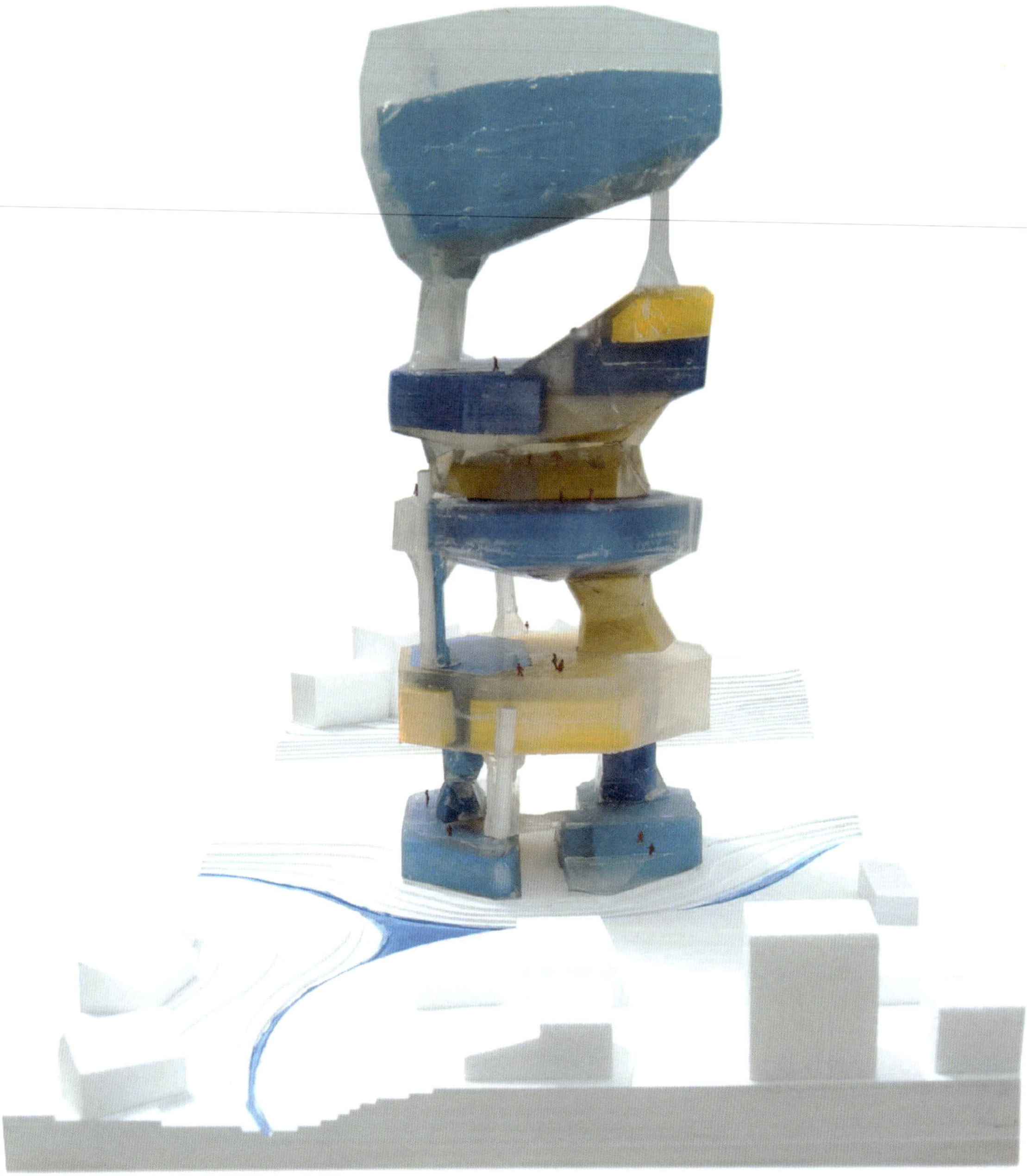

02

03

04

05

06

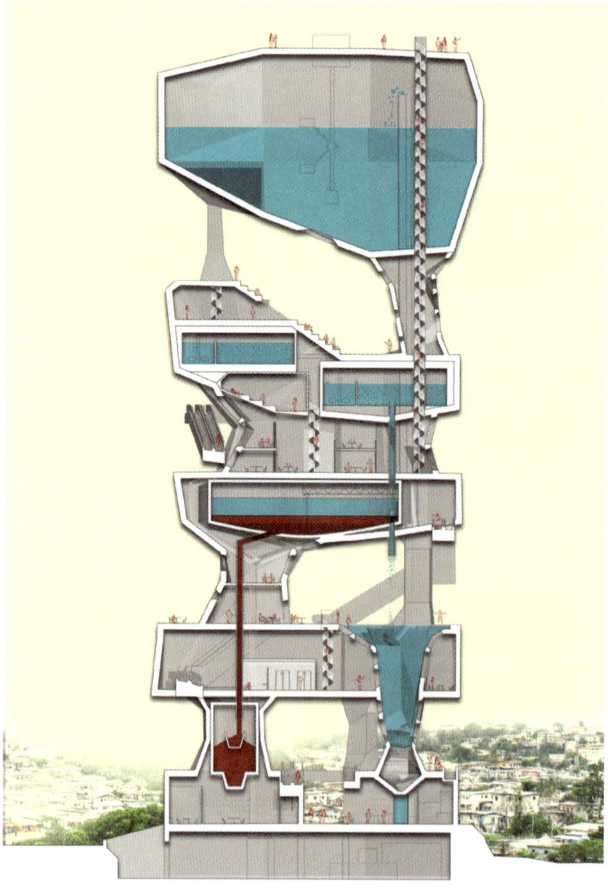

07

throughout the building

05 Exterior rendering, showing the building form within the context

06 Final model

07 Section, illustrating the relationship between water-treatment and community-center spaces

HENRY CHAN

HÔTEL DE VILLE

The Boulevard Triomphal is the location of most government agencies in Libreville; the two sides are fortified with urban ornaments that showcase power, wealth, order, progress, and optimism. Broad-stroke security details are in place to protect government employees; to further mitigate the congregation of ad hoc street-market activities, corner-to-corner fences have been erected around each agency. Among them is Libreville's city hall, the identity of which is, likewise, symbolically authoritarian in nature, preventing any physical connections with the general public. As the locus of a new, forward-looking image for the city, Hotel de Ville represents a unique opportunity for a new public architecture and, by extension, provides a physical manifestation of the country's goals and a model for a progressive, twenty-first-century Africa.

The new proposed city hall aims to create a hybrid form of public space by increasing interactions between civil servants and their constituents. It is envisioned as a vibrant civic hub that mediates between the public and the government while presenting an optimistic future. The project aims to bridge the polarity of the city and the people, between the high-speed vehicular and low-speed pedestrian traffic. A Nolli-esque figure-ground study focusing on the barrier between the city and nature reveals a counterproductive delineation, as the site is located on the edge of the seemingly impenetrable wall that encases the existing city hall's grounds. As a portal that traverses and unites the three volumes of work spaces, the proposed project will remain a useful part of the built fabric, instead of a privatized workplace.

The building massing is divided into three functional blocks: city council, administration, and wedding hall. The nested space created by these volumes forms the public space that connects with the streetscape that faces the boulevard. The tripartite structure props up the mayor's "bullpen," an open office in which employees of different departments sit side by side. Its double-height volume tapers up to the razor-edge of the roof, providing solar protection for the pedestrian plaza below.

01 Collage of the city fabric over the elevation of the current city hall

01

HENRY CHAN

All the program elements are brought together into a single mass and made to be as compact as possible, maximizing efficiency while conserving open space and creating shaded public space. Taking advantage of the site's raised topography, the three administrative volumes are connected and accessed by a single below-grade common lobby, which acts as a submerged plinth and stage. On one side, the lobby provides views to the boulevard and the city at large and, on the other, to the settlements and the natural landscape beyond. The inward-facing walls of each of the three volumes are glazed from floor to ceiling and sheathed in a porous mesh, making transparent, from the inside and the outside, all of city hall's activities and creating a visually dynamic environment for both participants and passers-by. A boulevard-facing grand staircase forms the main entry and culminates in a magnificent view of the city.

Comparatively informal and park-like, the south-facing plaza is designed to accommodate a variety of outdoor activities as well as provide panoramic views of the park and surrounding landscape. As a publicly accessible cultural facility, the city hall is a new symbol for Libreville—a place to enjoy and contemplate culture, the city itself, and nature and a place that provides an unparalleled setting for passive relaxation, active participation, and chance encounters for all people.

02 Ground floor axonometric, showing public plaza and public interface at street level
03 Perspective of entrance plaza
04 Aerial view of model, showcasing roofscape
05 Final model with roof removed, revealing interior spaces
06 Reverse Nolli map of the Boulevard Triomphal

02

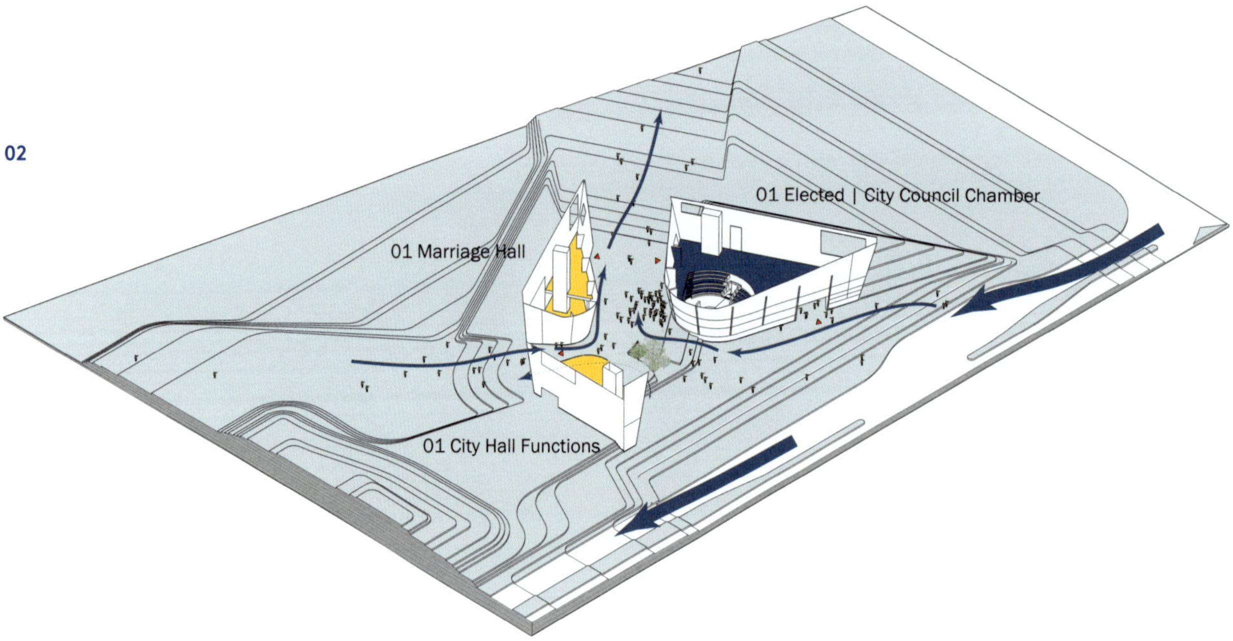

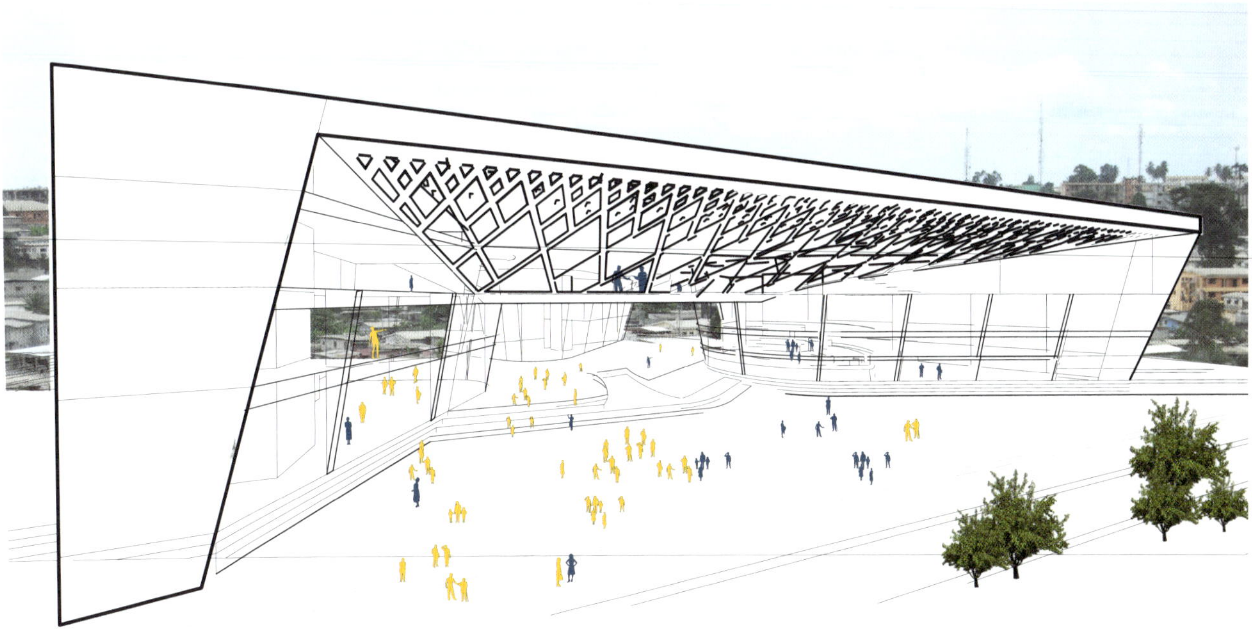

03

04

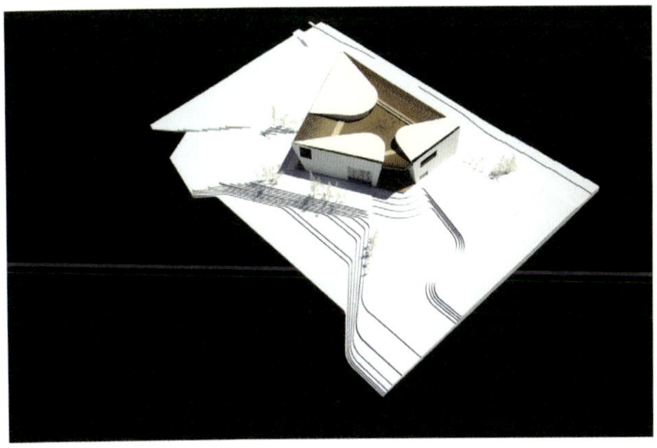

05

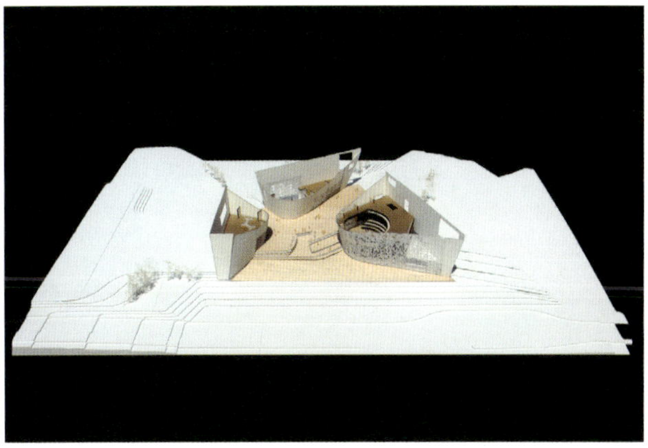

06

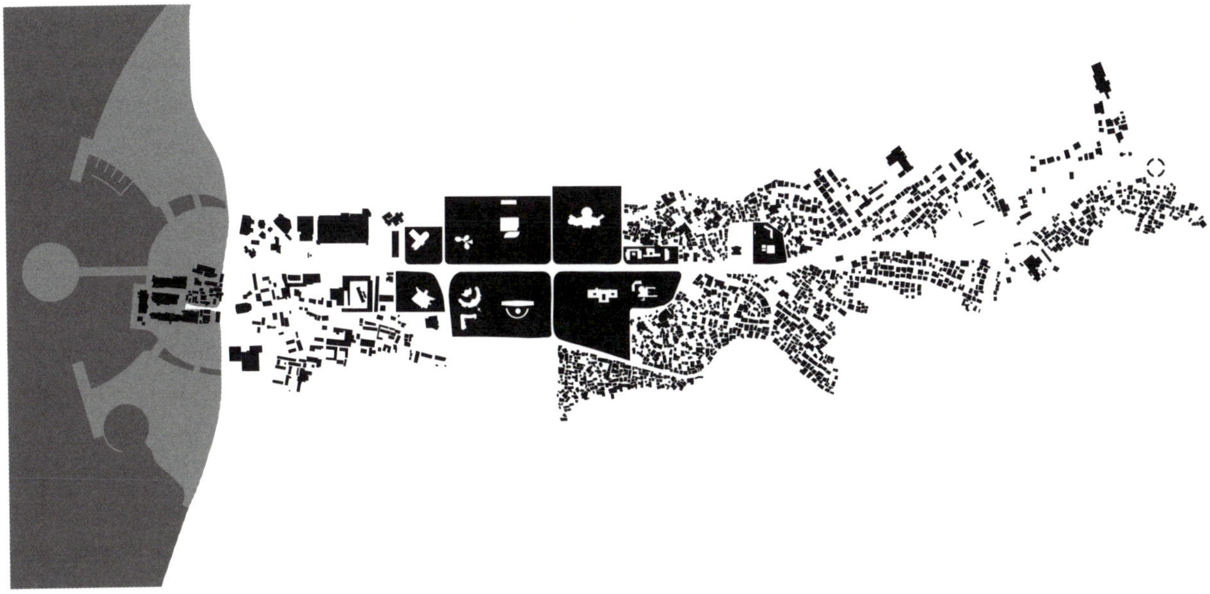

03 RE-IMAGINING *SOCIAL SPACES*

Despite the city's lack of infrastructure and formal gathering spaces, the residents of Libreville have found ways to create some of the most vibrant spaces in the city. They gather at markets on the side of the road, build informal settlements due to housing shortages, congregate to celebrate a diversity of religious practices, and connect through mobile devices when internet access is otherwise unavailable.

These projects attempt to develop and celebrate the ways in which people have created vibrant communities within the city. The schemes provide spaces in which people can exchange goods and ideas. Located near the Boulevard Triomphal, the buildings not only provide public spaces that connect to a major thoroughfare that currently lacks any, but, standing alongside government buildings, they also are symbolic images of the positive developments of the city.

HOCHUNG KIM

MARKET = STREET= HOUSING

Libreville's informal, wonderfully chaotic markets are the lifeblood of the city's community and culture. While the street vendors comprise an improvised network of goods and services, the market sites themselves offer a place for people to work, shop, interact, or just hang out. Often located near housing developments and, especially, the informal settlement areas, the markets currently are also a cause of traffic congestion. This project attempts to produce a new housing typology that capitalizes on the symbiotic relationship between the existing market and the residential housing.

Forming a new housing typology is pressing because Gabon has a housing shortage of about 200,000 houses, with 160,000 in Libreville alone. While the government proposed to build around a thousand houses in 2012, five thousand in 2013, and up to seven thousand in 2014, in 2012, it was able to build only about twenty houses. About 75 percent of Gabon's 1.5 million people live in cities, and, in Libreville, around 40 percent live in slums, with limited or no access to water, sanitation, and other basic services. The government has proposed to build satellite cities in Angondje, Cap Esterias, and Andem, with the nearest one being fifteen kilometers away from the city center with the adoption of Smartcode—a Transect-based code as defined by new urbanism; however, there is little direct relationship to the

01 Section perspective, showcasing the streetscape rising into the building

02 Aerial view of building within site context

01

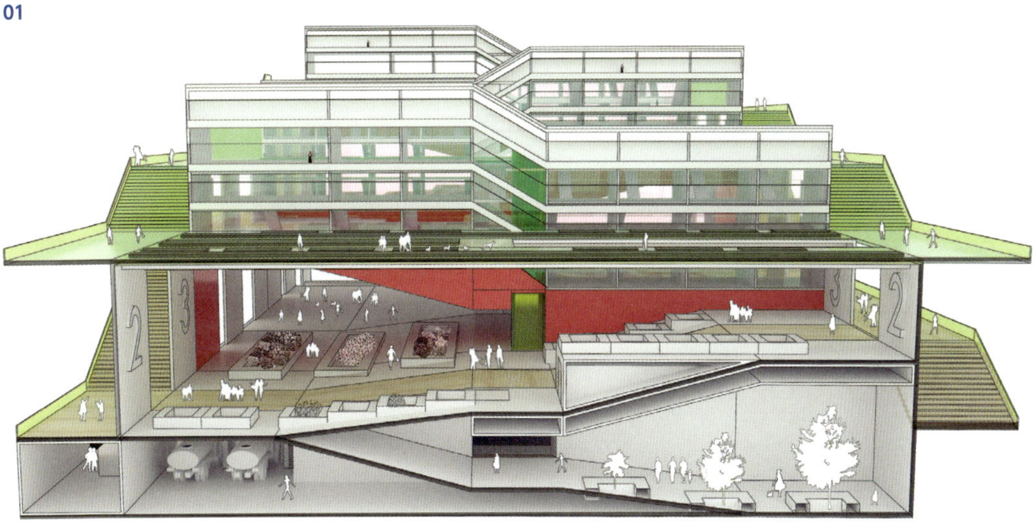

02

HOCHUNG KIM

existing environment. It acts like a copy-and-paste system that can be stamped on a city anywhere.

Furthermore, the city lacks basic infrastructure to connect to the new suburban communities. As an alternative, this proposal brings together the informal settlement population and the Boulevard Triomphal to form a model for the future of housing in Libreville. The proposed site will replace the Mbolo Casino Market, a warehouse shopping center. Studying potential elevational relationships between the circulation and market, there are two ways the market and housing can be organized. Instead of creating a vertical elevator core, the streets loop around the housing units and are laid in parallel relationship with the market, thus transforming the street into a market. By creating a stepped form, the proposed building also provides opportunities for people from informal settlement to enter underneath the market and housing units. By integrating the housing and market, the place becomes active and provides for convenient advertising for each vendor, boosting overall sales and helping the residents to afford their apartments.

---

03 Final model, showing the building in its context
04 Rendering of plaza level under the elevated housing and market
05 Cross-section perspective, showing how the housing and market spaces are integrated
06 Exploded axonometric, showing the plan of each level within its vertical circulation context

03

04

05

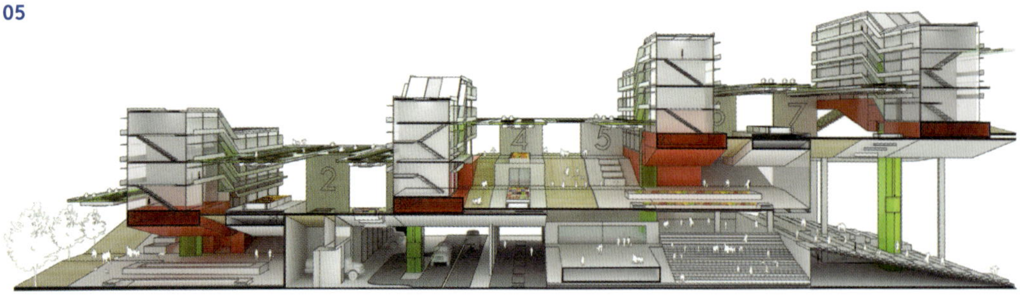

06

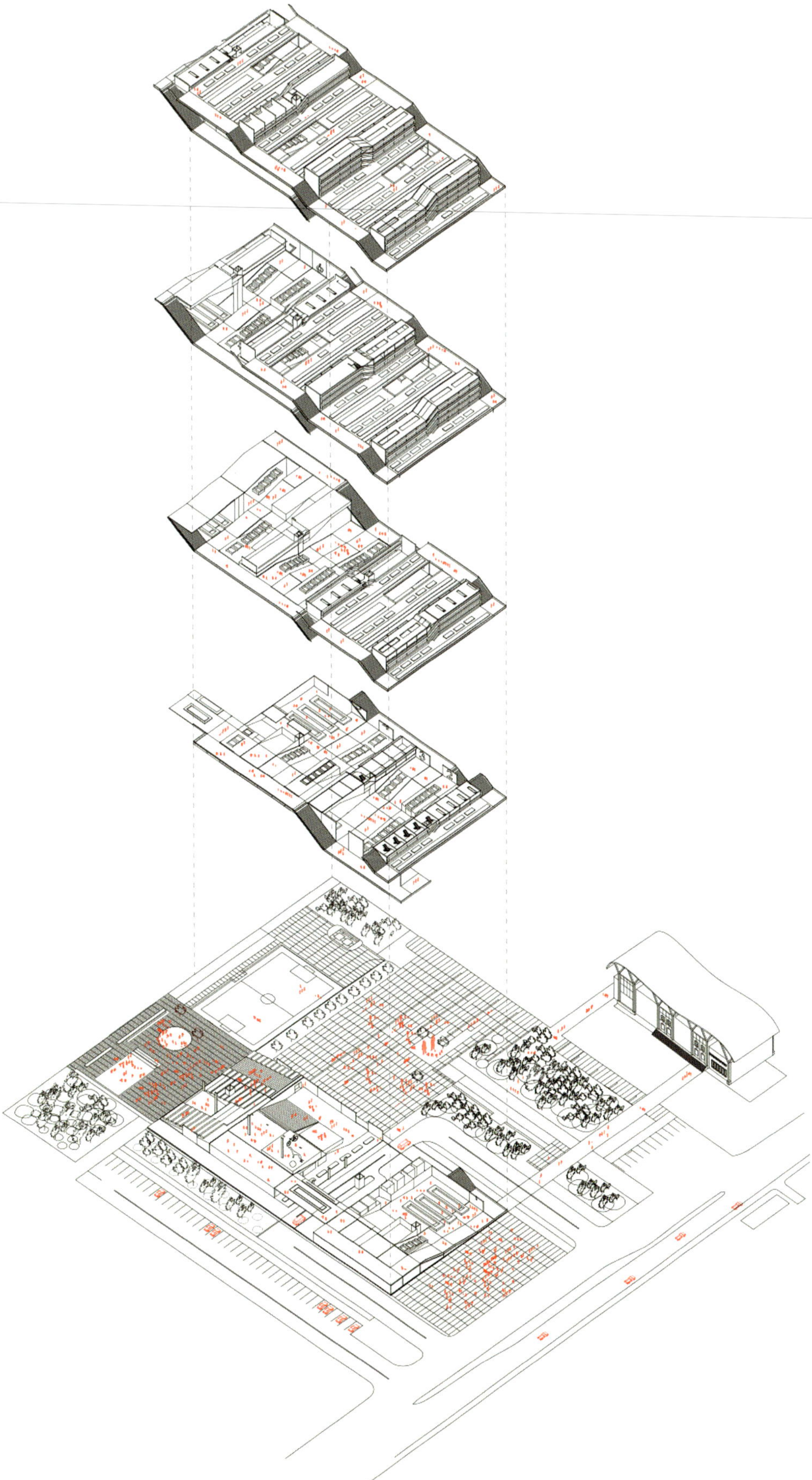

JACQUELINE KOW

INTERFAITH GABON

The Boulevard Triomphal is a major governmental axis that lacks any public and social infrastructure for the city of Libreville. To address this issue, this project proposes an interfaith chapel right off the boulevard. Religion has always played an integral role in the community and culture of the country, and with increasing religious diversity in the country, the city seems primed for an iconic building that celebrates and preserves the religious cultures of the country. From the indigenous religion of Bwiti, originating from the rain forest; to the growth of Christianity, due to the country's history of being a French colony; to the recent growth of Islam after the discovery of oil and the country joining OPEC, the acceptance of religious diversity within Gabon is a cultural aspect that should be celebrated. In studying several religious typologies and recognizing the opportunity for taking advantage of exterior space, the building is centered around two types of ritual space: the courtyard and the chapel. While these spaces allow for all liturgical practices to occur, the interfaith chapel does not valorize a specific religion or practice.

Because of the lack of specificity, the forms of both the chapel and courtyard are shaped by the spatial demands of the supporting programmatic spaces. The interfaith chapel goes beyond being just a religious space: it is also a piece of social infrastructure, which is currently lacking on the boulevard. The seven-story building includes a youth club, an auditorium, exhibition space, and a library, all of which allow for different means of engagement with the city's religions. At the top of the building, a public platform allows for one to look back onto the rest of the city and back down on to the central chapel.

01 Early study model, showing formal strategy
02 Site plan, showing the project's relationship between the Boulevard Triomphal, the city hall, and the surrounding informal settlements
03 Section through courtyard and chapel

01

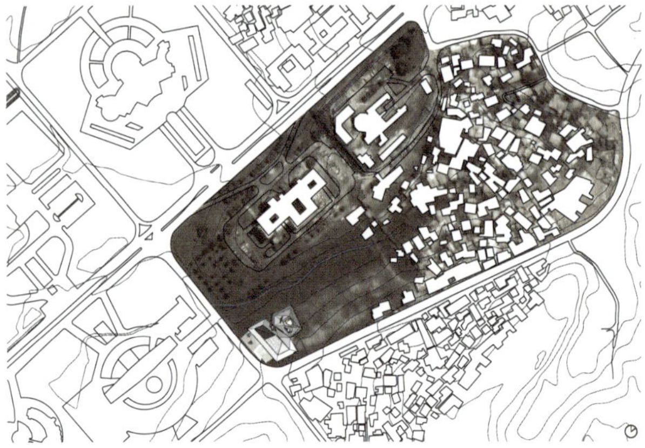

02

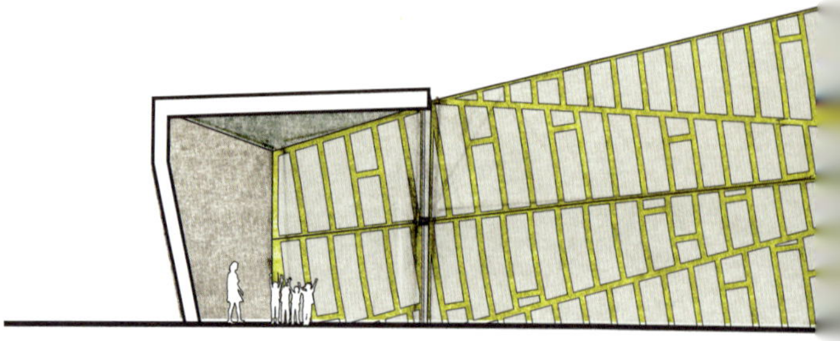

03

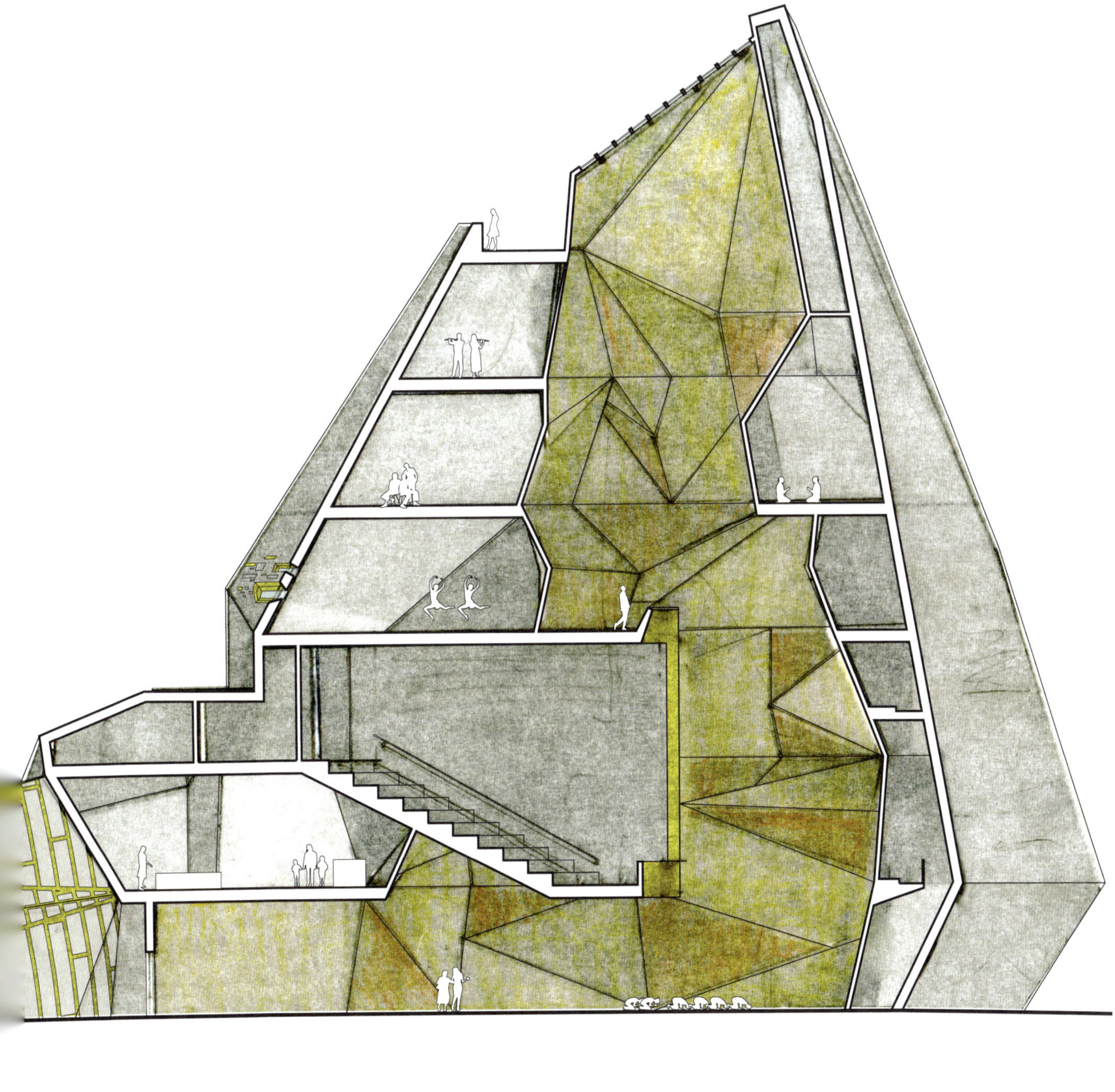

04

05

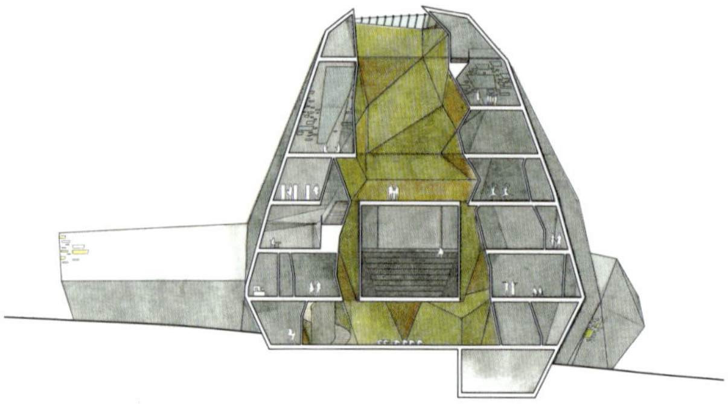

06

04 **Final model**

05 **Cross-section through the chapel and floating auditorium**

06 **View looking up from within the chapel**

YOOJIN HAN

THE INCUBATOR

Fifty percent of the Gabonese are under the age of nineteen, and 97 percent of the youth are literate. The recent explosion of the mobile phone has opened up opportunities for small-business development. To capitalize on this, the project creates a start-up incubator to inspire and attract young Gabonese entrepreneurs. Located within proximity to the Ministry of Finance and the Radio Television Gabonaise buildings, the project proposes to be a joint venture between the two.

The building sits atop a stream that runs between the government ministries and informal settlements. The ANGT has a plan to develop the stream as a focal point of a pedestrian-friendly development alongside the vehicular Boulevard Triomphal. The start-up incubator is a place where neighborhood residents and government ministers can meet, eat, and play, as well as provide a shaded pedestrian park, which can be enjoyed by the University Omar Bongo students and the people who work at the new commercial port development, Port Mole. The five-story building contains colocation workspaces, presentation and meeting rooms, and media resources for the entire population of Libreville.

01 Sectional axonometric, showing how the atrium connects to smaller meeting spaces

01

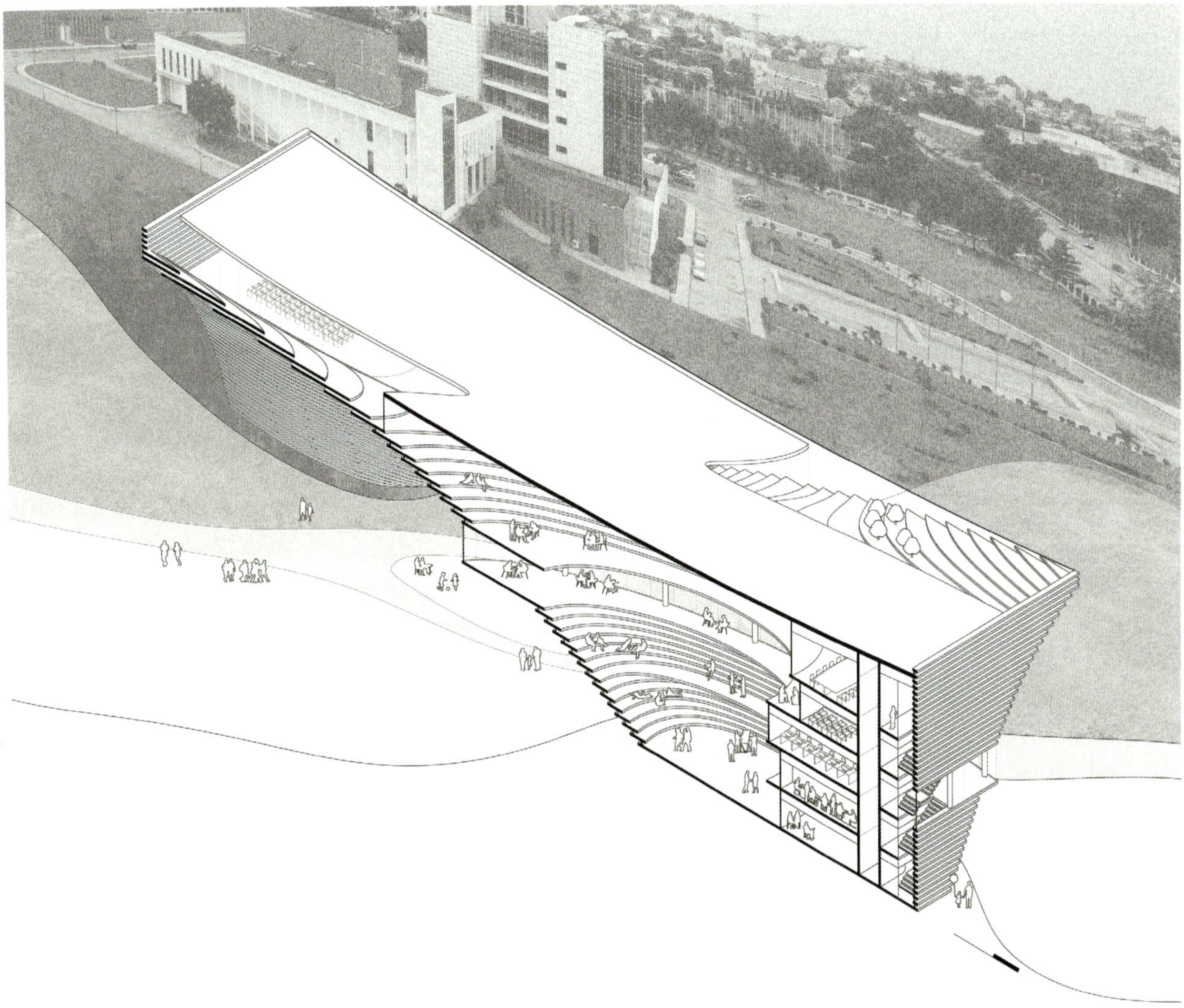

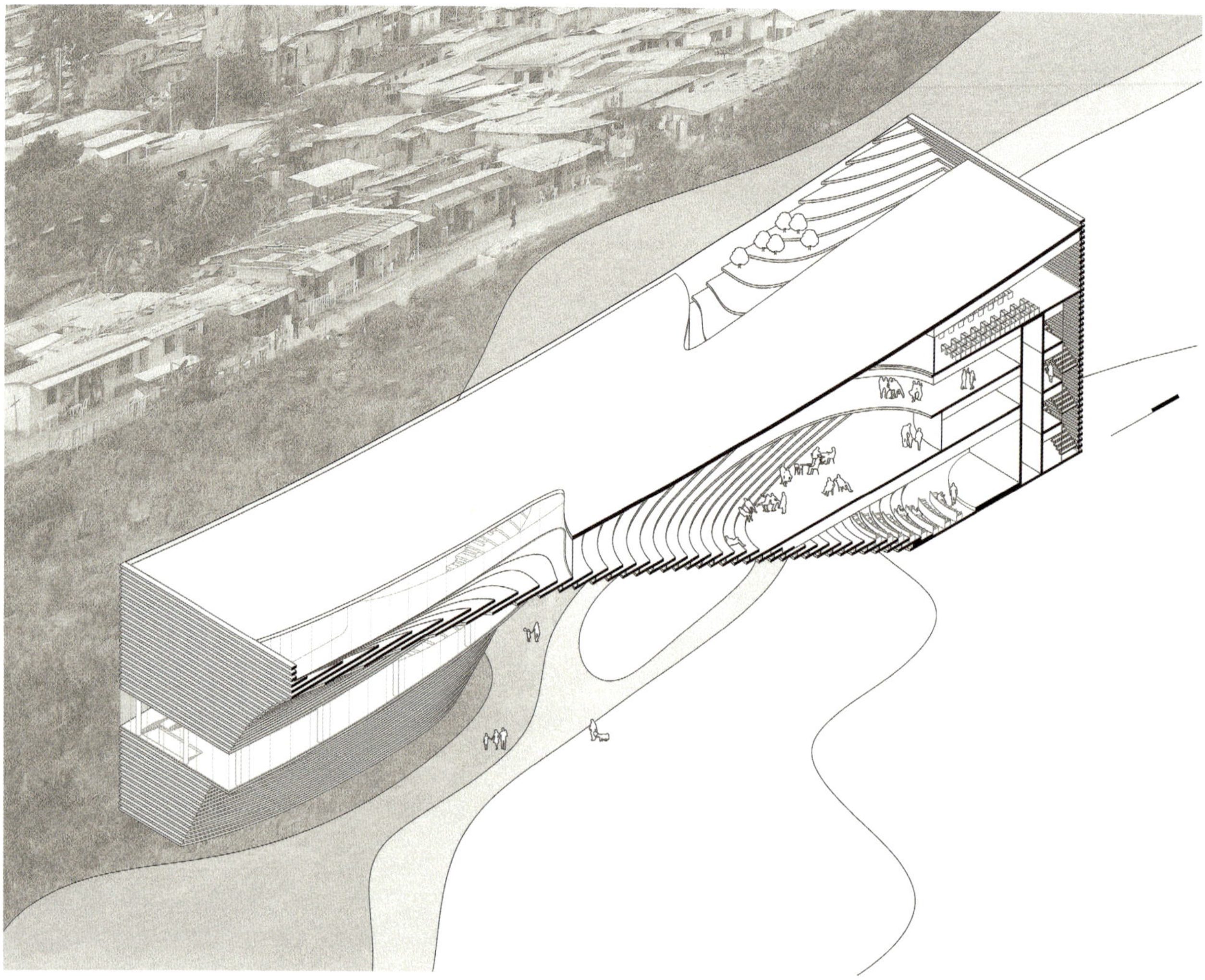

02

03

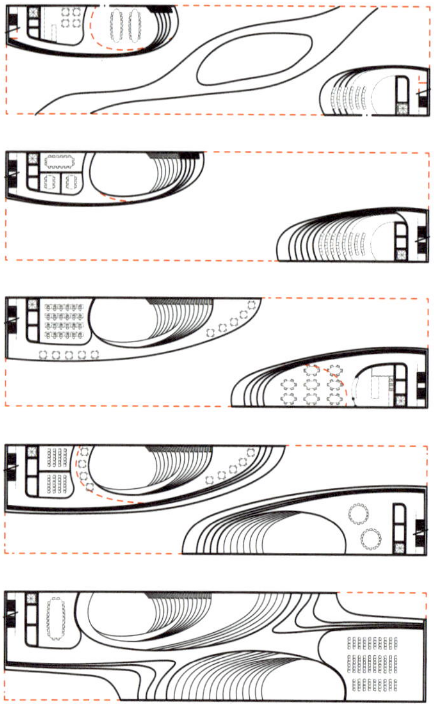

02 Sectional axonometric, illustrating how the building's formal strategy creates seating and collaborative space

03 Final plans, showing the different programmatic spaces within the two legs of the building

04 Final model, showcasing how the building goes over the stream

05 Final model, showing the relationship between interior and exterior

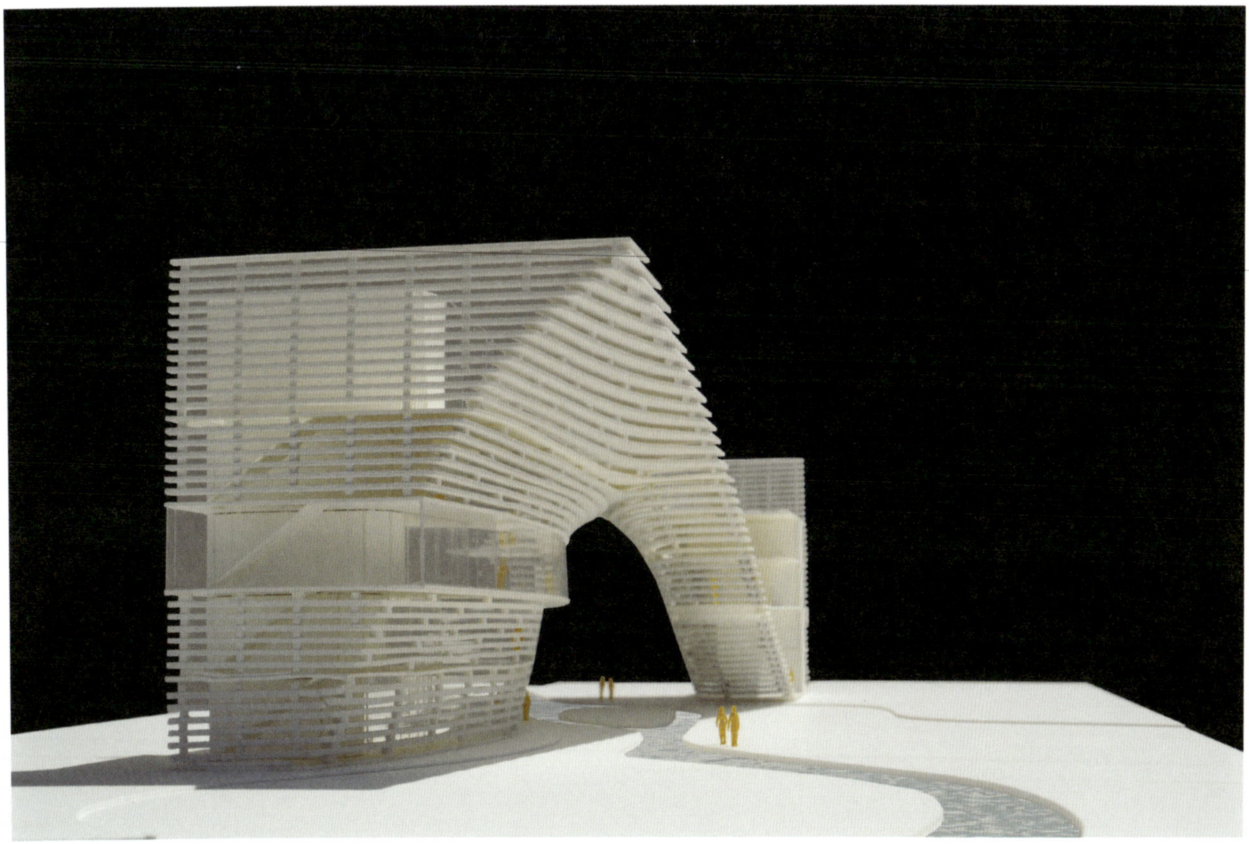

04

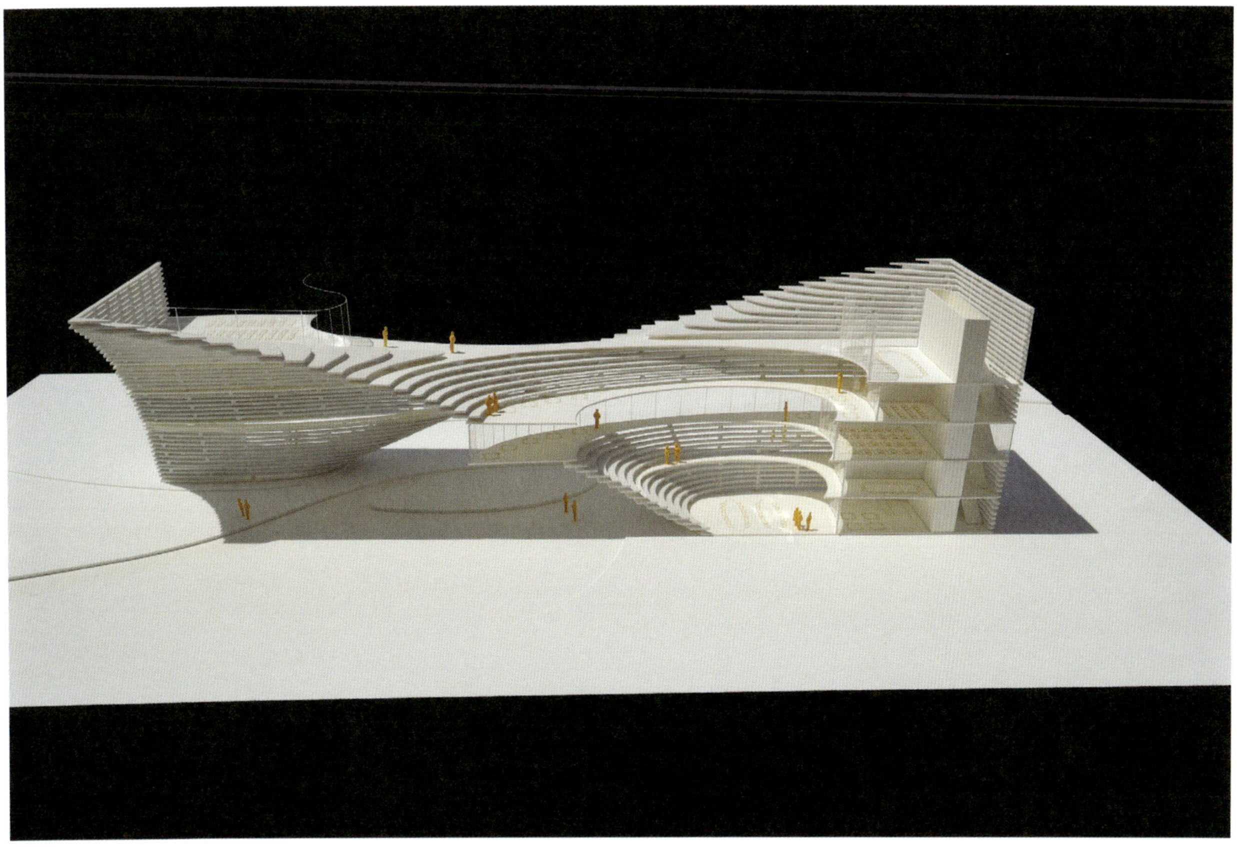

05

LISA GRAY AND ALAN ORGANSCHI

TIMBER INNOVATION

INTERVIEW

LISA GRAY *AND* ALAN *ORGANSCHI*

Lisa Gray and Alan Organschi discuss their practice with Nina Rappaport.

Nina Rappaport Looking at your early design-build work, you focused on construction, in light of Alan's training as a carpenter, and the idea that everything can be tested in a feedback-loop process, prototyping as you proceed. How did this approach inform the design and the materiality of, for example, wood in your projects?

Alan Organschi An underlying anxiety in the architecture profession is that architects are increasingly marginalized by the commercial construction industry, removed from the aspects of conception and design relating to structure, material, and detail and relegated, instead, to the specification and arrangement of commercial products. Lisa and I were inclined to try to work around or tease apart the increasingly tight technical configurations of building products and assemblies to understand the principles and processes underlying their shape and detail and to experiment with their architectural implications. As a result of this inclination—formed in part, I guess, by my own background in construction—we made a workshop part of our practice from the outset. This enabled us to physically test our design ideas, experiencing, at a real scale, both the feasibility of the material details and their architectural and spatial effect. The benefits were huge. We learned to better predict where conflicts would arise, due to the limitations of a material or the complexity of an assembly process, but we also got to assess the relationship between technical effort and architectural effect. In a sense, we got to rehearse our approach to architecture. There was also a downside, of course: this early experimentation took its toll in the time pressures and cost impacts it introduced into the process. It was hard to reconcile it with the conventional expectations of an architectural design-and-construction project. When you're forced to conceive of a design solution and then actually execute its construction, design conceptualization can become something of a casualty in the rush to advance the process. I'd say we're still learning how to integrate concept and execution a little more seamlessly.

Lisa Gray I think there's important feedback between the parameters of a project and its most appropriate and compelling set of solutions. When a design problem comes to our studio, it's perhaps a bit reflexive for us to imagine how it might be solved in wood because we have special experience with it and feel it's a great material for a host of environmental reasons. But it's not really an ideological position for us. We love the character and potential of any material and the interplay of different materials—both as a subject of our practice as well as an experience in our buildings. Each project has its own particular set of conditions, of course, so wood may not always be the right choice. But our early experience with wood and structural timber has proven to have placed us at somewhat of an advantage now that the material is experiencing something of a technical renaissance.

NR How did your shop, JIG Design Build, become a separate entity from your architecture firm, Gray Organschi Architecture, and how do the two practices relate?

AO Although the work of Gray Organschi Architecture and JIG is still deeply intertwined, we were forced, because of the increasingly stringent and costly insurance requirements for an architectural practice doing construction, to draw a clear professional distinction between our roles as designers and builders. In a move that coincided with formalizing our contract with the city of New York through the Department of Design and Construction's Design Excellence program, we decided to partition the business. It turned out to have made good financial sense because, now, JIG is doing its own fabrication projects and construction management. Dan Kazer, technical director of JIG, is currently supervising a private-house project, and Parker Lee, our senior design associate, is performing under JIG as the construction manager for the Steep Rock Bridge. In the future, we may decide that JIG can perform work for other architectural design firms. As a matter of daily practice, though, everybody in the office is involved in some aspect of fabrication or construction, so the professional segregation of the businesses isn't reflected in our approach to the work or the spirit of the workplace.

LG In fact, I'd say that we're increasingly interested in building projects that we don't touch at all. We realize that, as architects, we may actually have more agency orchestrating a large group of players with specific skills than when we are doing it all ourselves. The kinds of public buildings we're taking on are obviously going to be bid and executed by others. But we feel our experience with our own construction projects can inform our role there.

NR How is your own work shifting in the direction of larger projects?

LG We've proposed, for instance, using curved glue-laminated timber elements as the structure for the South Shore Little League Grandstand, in Staten Island. It's a

01

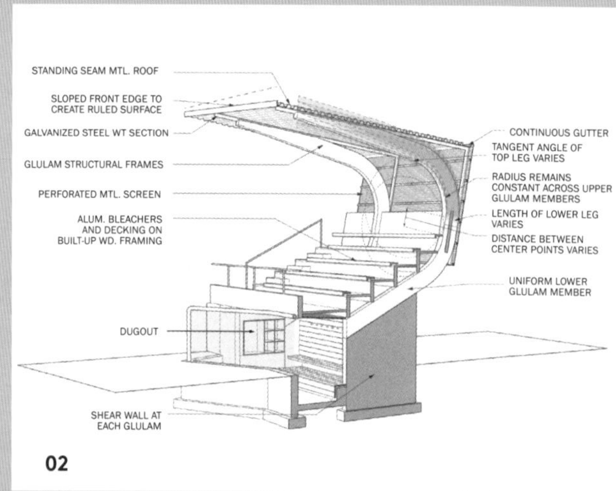

02

material that's still considered unconventional for the DDC and for construction in New York City, in general. We felt the material was a perfect solution to the cantilevered canopy called for in the client's brief, and we were able to insist on using it because of our connection to the engineered wood industry and our ability to demonstrate construction detailing and sequencing. Although the glue-laminated timber suspension bridge in the Steep Rock Preserve, in Washington, Connecticut, is small in scale, it's logistically quite complex and entails a significant incursion into a beloved public landscape and ecologically sensitive site. Our design calls for a sequence of carefully planned operations that reduces our construction footprint. By prefabricating parts in a factory and delivering them under a just-in-time regimen, we not only reduce the costs of site labor but also our impacts on the river and adjacent wetlands. So, this approach provides us the kind of direct feedback offered by doing the heavy work of construction, as well as a lot of lessons in thinking of design as the coordination of discrete components and the orchestration of a variety of players, each with their own strengths and weaknesses. The bridge construction created the kinds of demands we face when designing from a remove, with limited control of the means and methods that characterize more conventional delivery methods of larger architectural projects. Those methodologies that we were able to rehearse in the workshop, we now are better at predicting through drawing. But the approaches adopted and the techniques refined in each case constantly loop back to inform one another.

NR As a couple that has succeeded in working together for nearly twenty years, how do you divide the work, in that Alan teaches and Lisa doesn't?

AO I think this question is a moment to actually demonstrate our managerial hierarchy. Lisa, you go first.

LG Of course, we have different predilections and areas of expertise, but we both have a very roll-up-the-sleeves and hands-on approach to all the tasks required of a design office. Out of that mind-set has evolved an office structure that reflects our different approaches. As it evolved, we both felt strongly that pulling back from trying to build everything we design would allow us to test our abilities and exercise our interest in work at a larger, public scale. But work at the more intimate scale of houses and within the close, personal relationships we develop with our residential clients will always be part of our practice.

NR Is it difficult to maintain design control as you jump to larger projects?

AO Each time we jump scale, we stumble and make mistakes. When we can't control implementation, we have to be more innovative in the way we develop the design and its documentation to keep the work buildable but still formally, spatially, and materially rich.

NR A good example of this is your environmental Common Ground High School, in New Haven. The building itself is a kind of blackboard, a learning tool for the students and the teachers. Was the project also a learning curve for you? For example, how did you use it to integrate your interests in ecology and materiality, and what form is it taking?

---

01 Storage Barn

02 Construction diagram of the Joseph A. Verdino Jr. Grandstand

03 Footbridge at Green Hill Brook

03

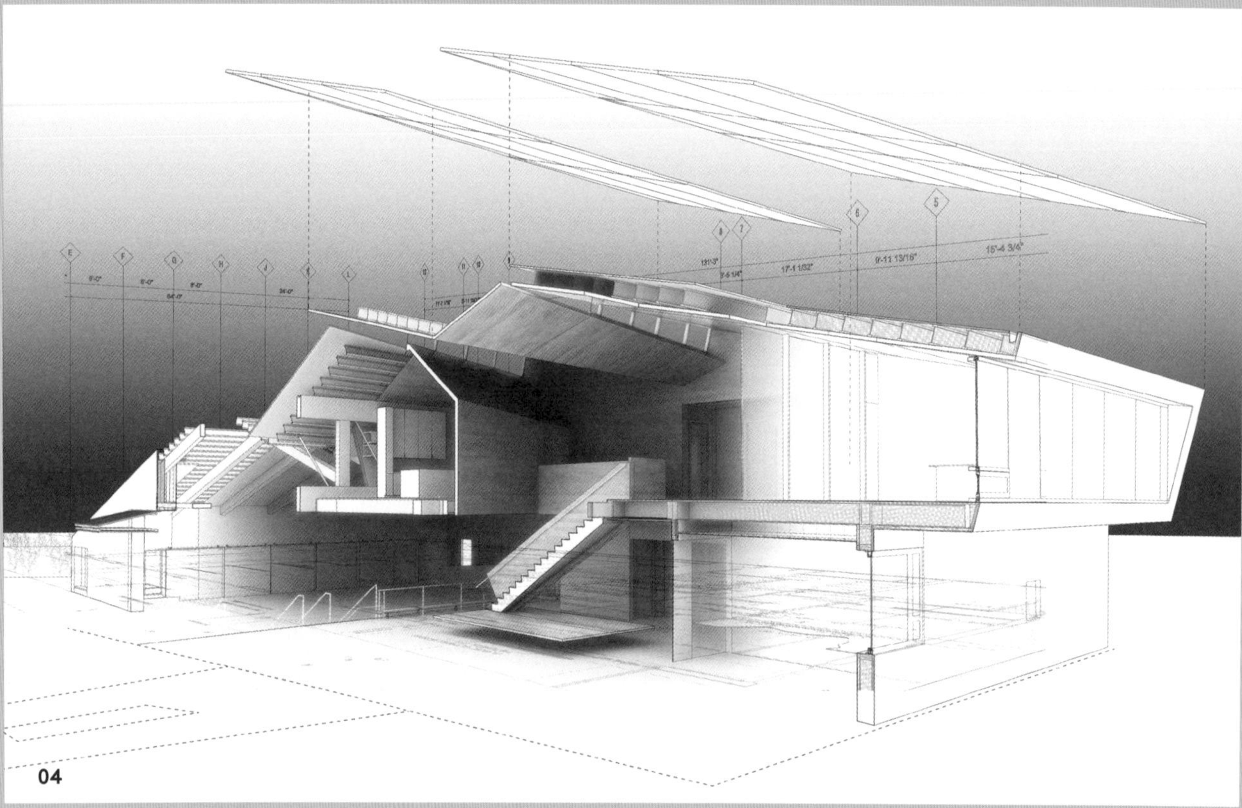

04

AO The new building at Common Ground High School offered us the rare opportunity to work closely with dedicated teachers and deeply engaged students to craft a special architectural design. Their challenge to us was to make a building that is healthy for both the school community and our global environment; durable in its construction, using sustainable systems and renewable materials in a legible and innovative way; flexible enough to adapt to the school's rich and constantly evolving curriculum; and respectful of the buildings and spaces that give this emerging institution its character. The goals for this new addition to their working "classroom," a landscape that includes farm buildings, gardens, forests, and wetlands, was a building that would teach about the complex and potentially convivial relationship between the built and the natural environment. We tried to focus that discussion through the way the building would be constructed, adding our own concerns about the global provenance and environmental efficacy of different structural materials and assembly techniques to the conventional "sustainability" checklists. Working closely with the engineer Chris Carbone at Bensonwood and our industrial partners at Nordic Engineered Wood, we developed a design that incorporates structural mass timber—cross-laminated timber panels as well as more conventional glue-laminated members—in what we believe to be a unique and innovative solution. And, of course, then we had to push this new method through a gauntlet of building, regulatory, and school-funding reviews as well as a construction bidding process that was entirely unfamiliar with what we were proposing. The learning curve was steep, to say the least.

LG It's a privilege to work with mission-based clients; this particularly well-informed and thoughtful group selected us because they felt we would help them to realize a building that would express their objectives. A high-performance building like this one costs more, and it's extraordinary that a publicly funded Connecticut school could become a model for a new environmental building culture.

AO That's an important point: In our more public projects—whether the Little League Grand Stand, the new high school, or the Jesuit home and community center—we've been fortunate to have clients who are trying to convey a message to a larger community, a message about who they are and what they want to be. It makes the design process more than a pragmatic exercise in programmatic organization and cost savings. These groups came to us with clear constraints and demands, but they asked us to make something beautiful that tells the

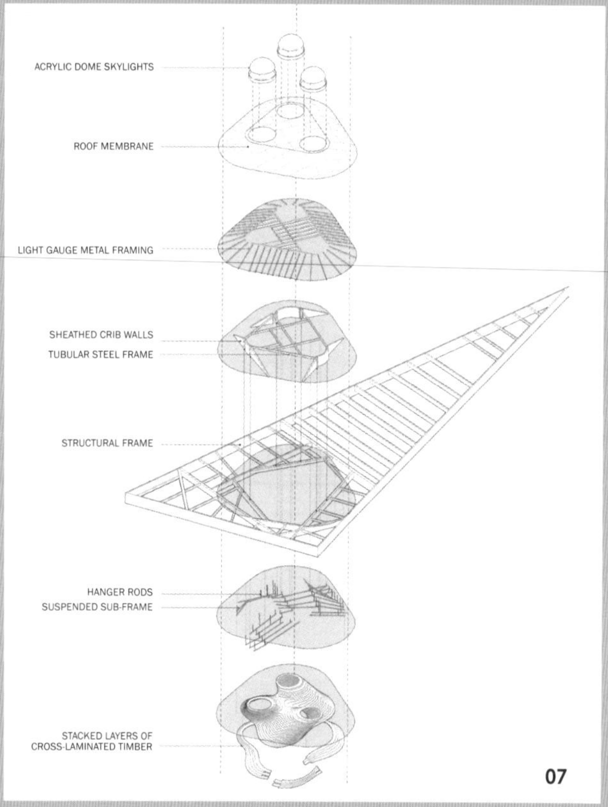

story of their community and institution. Their mission, and the particular sites they chose to build in, formed the conceptual basis of our work with them.

NR Alan, how has your research into the properties of high-performance timber been incorporated into the school building?

AO The project brief challenged us to make a building that articulated environmental principles to the students who would use it. From early on in our practice, we were forced to contend with the provenance and properties of material. Where does it come from? How do you get it here? What will it do when you change its shape or apply it in a particular way? Slowly and with some soul searching, we shifted those questions from the more immediate and individual issues of craftsmanship to the larger issues of environmental impacts and resource allocation. The school was a chance to use new material systems with the lowest possible embodied energy and CO_2 emissions while still achieving the highest feasible standards for air quality, thermal performance, and day lighting. The story of a panel of cross-laminated black spruce is pretty straightforward, easily traced, and with very visible and, therefore, comprehensible environmental impacts. The process of assembly is obvious; the experience of it in the spaces of the finished building is unmediated. The students can look out a window and see a tree. They can make the connection. It's pretty elemental.

LG In our first ten years working on houses, we learned from construction managing and design-building that we needed to design the whole building delivery process, not just the building form and organization. And I'm very interested in all of these processes. What do you set in motion when you make a set of drawings, and what are you really asking people to do? How conscious are you about the requirements that you are proposing? I think the architectural profession has to take ownership of the huge amount of consumption we're demanding.

AO Lisa used the term *orchestration* earlier, and that idea has characterized the improvisational side to our work. We

04 Exploded axonometric section of Common Ground High School
05 Interior of cottage
06 Stacked layers of cross-laminated timber of carousel shed roof for the Mill River Park Pavilion
07 Diagram of roof assembly for the Mill River Park Pavilion

are not manufacturers of building products. But we like to understand the processes so we can manipulate them, when possible. Not everything can be a one-off—although, as designers, we do like to try to reinvent the wheel from time to time.

NR How has your education at Yale and your teaching of the Yale Building Project influenced you? What drew you back to New Haven, and how has the place shaped your firm's identity?

AO At first, for us, New Haven was going to be merely a way station between larger cities, but then we realized the benefits it could provide us. A small city affords direct contact with decision-makers. It opens up interesting conversations that can go somewhere fast. Our reason for coming wasn't even connected to Yale at first, except, I guess, because it was familiar and, therefore, easy.

LG New Haven and Yale are distinct entities, of course, but they mix in interesting ways. It's a place where you can have wonderful space that's not that expensive, which was very important to us when we started out. We came back from Berlin, in 1994, wanting to hang our own shingle. I think that's part of the culture at Yale, or maybe we went to graduate school here because we were already wired that way. And because of the school's academic life and several significant firms that are here directly because of it, there's a pretty strong architectural culture that still puts us in striking distance of New York clients. The school is also an incredibly rich resource, obviously. We realized that it was a great set of opportunities for us.

AO As a small city with a powerful educational institution, New Haven has both history and promise as a kind of urban architectural laboratory; we think that promise is starting to manifest itself in small but exciting ways. To be honest, I didn't come back to New Haven to teach at Yale. We first discovered the great opportunities it afforded a young practice, and teaching here followed later. I had incredible classmates at the school—one of them is now my partner—and some really important teachers. Yale was quite different in tone when we were there; it was a make-your-own-way kind of place. Dean Stern has changed that culture to a degree—tuned it, professionalized it, taught it some manners. But the essential DNA, which obviously has informed our current practice, is still intact.

NR What was the focus of your advanced studio this semester?

AO Our studio explored the architectural potential of new timber technologies in contemporary architecture. We asked our students to design one of four urban building types, developing its structural morphology, applying it within a dense city district, and, ultimately, beginning to assess its environmental and social impact on a small, former manufacturing city. The background for the work was a recent challenge by U.S. Secretary of Agriculture Tom Vilsack and the U.S. Department of Agriculture to fund and develop proposals for high-rise and long-span timber architecture in order to reinvigorate a declining rural manufacturing sector while responding to America's growing urban population and the environmental imperative of reducing CO_2 emissions in the building sector, one of the largest contributors of greenhouse gases.

LG The program was the creation of a live-make district on a site along the Mill River, in New Haven. We called it a Timber Innovation District, which is centered in the once robust but now struggling manufacturing and residential areas that bracket the moribund English Station power plant, on Ball Island, that once provided energy to the city. We conducted the semester as a research studio, one that would introduce students to new construction technologies in timber and challenge them to produce urban architectural design that might address both a global ecological crisis and a more local socioeconomic one. One line of inquiry was an examination of the technical and architectural potential of contemporary precedents in Europe and Australia, where some of the most compelling work in timber is currently underway. Another was the study of programmatic hybridization, using a much wider historical range of architectural precedents, which encouraged our students to question the kinds of horizontal zoning habits that many small cities in the U.S. still cling to. In support of this research, the studio traveled to Helsinki, Switzerland, and Austria to examine historical and contemporary large-scale urban architecture constructed from timber, as well as the political, economic, and cultural apparatus that generated it. From a conceptual standpoint, this represents the underlying motive of the semester: the formation of a design culture that responds to a new technology, driven by an abundant and renewable material resource, supported by an economic policy initiative, and aimed at the potential ecological synergies between dense cities and healthy, potentially productive forest landscapes.

---

08 Cottage, showing the interplay of glazing and wood to dematerialize the building's seams

TIMBER *COLLOQUIUM*

WITH U.S. *AGRICULTURE* SECRETARY VILSACK

On April 14, 2015, the students and faculty of the Louis I. Kahn Visiting Assistant Professorship studio welcomed U.S. Agriculture Secretary Tom Vilsack and officials from the United States Department of Agriculture and the Connecticut Department of Energy and Environmental Protection for a presentation and discussion of Mill River's Timber Innovation District.

Alan Organschi Secretary Vilsack and guests, we invited you here today to see some of the work of the Louis I. Kahn Assistant Visiting Professorship studio but, more importantly, to discuss how it reflects upon, and has implications for, a rapidly changing academic and professional design culture. We conceived of the studio as a means to shape a response to what we consider a critical policy initiative by Secretary Vilsack and the USDA, one that seeks to improve the health and resiliency of North American forests, transform and strengthen our rural economies, and minimize the impacts of—and we would argue, possibly even capitalize upon—the rapid urbanization of the U.S. and global populations.

The simultaneity and interconnectedness of these three objectives suggest the radical shift we see in both architectural pedagogy and practice, a shift that dissolves disciplinary boundaries by calling for the convergence of the fields of climatology, silviculture, forest and material science, commercial manufacturing, structural engineering, architectural design, urban planning, political economics, and governance.

Put plainly, the topic here is plant fiber—for the purposes of this discussion, wood—and the way we apply it in the formation of the built environment.

Tom Vilsack Let me emphasize this point to the students: it will not be enough to come up with an incredible design. You also need to come up with a messaging campaign. What convinced you that this was possible?

Perry Wexelberg (Student) Seeing how these timber systems were made and how they manifested themselves in architecture was what really sold me on the idea. It's very similar to a steel framing system. These new systems were deployed in ways that made buildings that were familiar but were also better.

Ben Smith (Student) I was convinced when we visited some of the manufacturing facilities and mills where they are actually producing things. It seemed like a very dignified job that was honorable and exciting. As someone who comes from a part of the country where people don't have work, it's exciting to think about a potential future when people can learn this new trade.

PW Some of the systems combined timber and concrete. This could potentially be an intelligent political move. Timber will not completely displace the concrete industry; rather, it will work with the concrete industry to make composite systems that perform at an even higher level.

TV Five or six years ago, when we started to raise the issue of local and national food systems, there was an immediate negative reaction by production agriculture and groups representing traditional agriculture. However, we responded with the message that we were proposing a complement to traditional agriculture, that would not only allow it to stay in business but also allow it to broaden. In the case of the timber industry, eastern Kentucky, which is devastated economically, may have a way of saying, in effect, to the concrete industry, "We are not going to put you out of business, but you are not going to be over here in eastern Kentucky—we are. So, why wouldn't you want us to encourage new kinds of construction and new job opportunities? Over time, there should be enough business for all of us."

AO I think Perry's point is very important in terms of gaining momentum. Timber engineers and people in this field are looking at ways to integrate these materials in the most efficient assemblies. When they see the excitement of a timber building that goes up in New York City or San Francisco, they are going to want to get in on the action.

TV The next time I have an opportunity, I'm going to suggest less spending on political campaigns and, instead, putting a couple million dollars into something like this. They could actually build something that would create the momentum for this to really take off.

TIMBER CITY *INNOVATION* DISTRICT

Introduction

The Gray Organschi studio explored the potential of new timber technologies in contemporary high-performance urban architecture in an experimental timber district in and around Ball Island on the Mill River, in New Haven. Through the design of four urban building types and their associated structural morphologies, students tested the capacity of a natural building material to produce beautiful and innovative architecture in the contemporary city.

It has often been observed that wood is one of the oldest materials in our building culture, but it is also notable that—for well over a century, as the processing and construction technologies of steel and concrete (the two other primary classes of structural material) were revolutionized and then continuously refined—the use of wood and timber has been stuck in a kind of construction limbo, relegated to the limited scale of the craftsman's workshop or, worse, to the relatively light structural demands, but significant environmental destructiveness, of low-rise, suburban sprawl.

It seems ironic that wood and structural timber, by all measures the least energy-consuming and carbon-emitting materials we build with—both in terms of the demands and impacts of their extraction and processing but also in their unique capacity to hold carbon in a structure for as long as it stands—has been used by architects and builders to produce the most land-intensive building morphologies.

Meanwhile, the most environmentally intensive structural materials, steel and concrete, are deployed in the production of mid- and high-rise buildings, dense urban aggregations that are relatively restrained in their use of land, efficient in their deployment of infrastructure, and, compared to suburbia, miserly in their operational demands. Think of it: Out of bad habit, misinformation, and cultural bias, we continue to use this low-impact material to produce sprawl, and we use steel and concrete, material systems with significant environmental footprints, to structure urban density.

This challenge was the substance of the Louis I. Kahn Visiting Assistant Professorship studio. How do we take all the timber that we use to build suburbia and, instead, shift it into new, high-performance configurations and applications to build dense, vibrant cities? How do we transform one of the largest sectors of our economy by providing a strong tug on the rural supply chain and, in doing so, turn our cities from carbon sources into carbon sinks? The introduction of substantial quantities of biomass into the structure of our buildings is a promising means to offset the CO_2 emissions produced in the construction and operation of human settlements.

Background

On March 18, 2014, U. S. Secretary of Agriculture Tom Vilsack announced a new initiative to educate architects, engineers, and builders about the benefits of advanced wood building materials in an effort to bring new structural timber technologies and industrial wood products to the forefront of a national manufacturing renaissance. Noting that one of the world's oldest building materials is now also one of its most advanced, Vilsack described the U.S. Department of Agriculture's new partnership with the U.S. Forest Products Lab and the Bi-National Softwood Lumber Council as an important part of President Obama's so-called Climate Action Plan. This alliance of governmental agencies and commercial manufacturing organizations seeks to develop and promote a host of new building materials and sustainable construction practices, aided by $2 million in federal funding for innovative designs in high-rise mass-timber building and housing development. A series of programs will include design competitions that call for, and building demonstration projects that employ, advanced timber techniques with the goal of reducing greenhouse-gas emissions through increasingly robust practices of sustainable forestry and the expansion of markets for innovative wood products.

In response to this policy initiative, the Kahn studio examined, through students' collective analysis and design work and an intensive travel and research program, the way in which such a political directive might promote a new architectural, engineering, and planning culture, one that addresses both environmental crises and pressing socioeconomic need through the innovative use of an abundant but underused resource.

Program

Although the studio focused on the detailed design of individual buildings, students undertook architectural and technical work within the context of historical and contemporary urban culture and the physical and infrastructural artifacts of the city. Working individually, each student developed one of four hybrid building types,

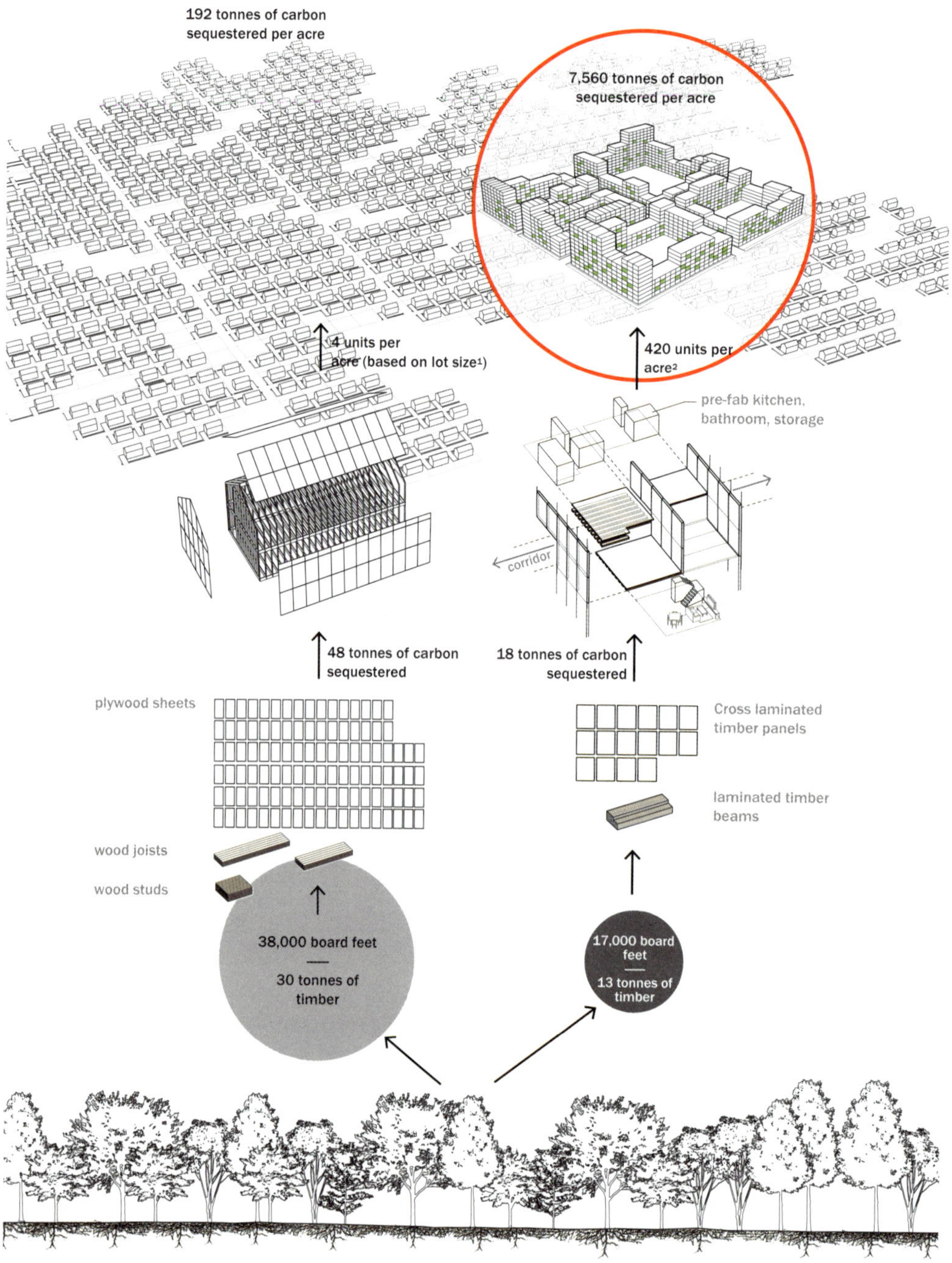

01

exploring new structural morphologies using varied engineered timber systems. Each building type was deployed as an architectural solution to an urban site and resolved within a shared plan for a mixed industrial-residential zone, creating hybrids of the following programs:

Live-work housing (mid-rise, repetitive span)
Manufacturing-market space (flexible space, repetitive long span)
Vehicular and service infrastructure (dynamic, heavy loading)
Recreational facilities (long span)
Commercial office and retail (repetitive, flexible structure)

Although the studio worked collaboratively to knit individual projects into a cohesive site plan, each student was expected to develop her or his building to a high level of resolution in terms of the following criteria:

Sensitivity to the ecological characteristics and vulnerabilities of a coastal, riparian site;
Responsive and appropriate urban place-making within the guidelines of a city-planning district framework;

Structural feasibility using contemporary timber construction technologies;
Operational impacts, as they relate to the performance of the building envelope;
Architectural quality.

As a preface to this architectural exploration, two short exercises—an analysis of contemporary precedents of timber building and an analysis of a hybrid-program precedents—introduced the students to the techniques and principles of mass-timber manufacturing, recent demonstration projects in high-performance wood construction, and hybrid building types—all of which they developed during the course of the studio.

Site

New Haven's history of nineteenth-century masonry and heavy-timber construction, as well as ongoing research at the Yale School of Architecture, the Yale School of Forestry and Environmental Studies, and the Global Institute for Sustainable Forestry, make the city an ideal venue for the architectural exploration of low-impact urban building. In addition, the Yale Corporation's investment in global forests and the city's re-emerging manufacturing infrastructure combine to provide institutional support and an economic rationale for experimentation with timber design, manufacture, and construction. New Haven is a place where dense urban development might function to mitigate, rather than exacerbate, greenhouse-gas emissions from the building sector.

The Mill River district, centered at the English Station power plant and bounded by Grand Avenue and Chapel Street, had been identified by the city of New Haven and its Economic Development Corporation as a new industrial village, already home to 3,000 light-industrial jobs with ready access to mass transit, industrial rail systems, a commercial waterfront, and Yale University's scientific research infrastructure. In an extensive report prepared by the urban planning consultancy UTILE and business development adviser Ninigret Partnership, the area was identified as a future site of unconventional mixed-use buildings and new architectural types—live-work and live-make buildings—which would provide a blend of residential, commercial retail, and the "fashion risk" industrial sectors, which specialize in mass customization. The city has embraced this proposed mix of industrial work and residential space as a potential antidote to the kinds of gentrification common to urban waterfronts. The district's ecological zone, a brackish, riparian wetland prone to tidal surges and vulnerable to impacts related to building and infrastructural development, provides an optimum condition for the exploration and implementation of resilient, dense, coastal urban

01 Diagram from *Timber City: Architectural Speculations in a Black Market* by Alan Organschi, illustrating the difference in carbon-sequestering density between conventional single-family home construction and multifamily mass-timber construction

02 Aerial view of the Mill River district

development. Sited in a tidal floodplain, burdened with polluted soils, and technologically obsolete, the now moribund English Station power plant remains the district's contested centerpiece. Located at the mouth of the Mill River and exposed to the winds off Long Island Sound, the low-lying land offers exciting opportunities for alternative forms of energy production.

In selecting a site in New Haven as the subject of the semester's work, the studio encouraged students to test and confirm their design premises through repeated visits at different stages of their project's development. A primary research trip sought to place the USDA challenge and the work of the studio in a global context. Additional daylong research trips to manufacturing and fabrication plants and current building projects near New Haven served to supplement students' understanding of the potential of these new technologies in an American building culture.

Research Trip

A study trip examined two specific "cultures" of timber building design that, today, are connected through a shared manufacturing base and economic and political union. Both Finland and Austria have experienced a resurgence in wood design and architecture, fueled by ample forest resources and silvicultural infrastructure as well as robust traditions in building with wood. Today, Finnish and Austrian architects, engineers, and researchers work at the forefront of new mass-timber technologies, charting an alternative course in the design of dense urban building and infrastructure that is reinforced through methods of embodied energy and emissions analysis, measures that seek to mitigate the building sector's global environmental impacts.

Finland's innovative wood design culture is rooted in the soil of twentieth-century Finnish independence, a conscious, mid-century effort by the national government to build a political and industrial apparatus that is geared to develop new, value-added manufacturing products wrought from the country's vast natural material resources. Today, the region around Helsinki and Jyväskylä is a locus of sustainable building and urban development. A competition for a new Guggenheim Museum in the capital's south harbor district is one of

03–05 Images of the Mill River District

06 Studio travel photos of Swiss, Austrian, and Finnish projects

06

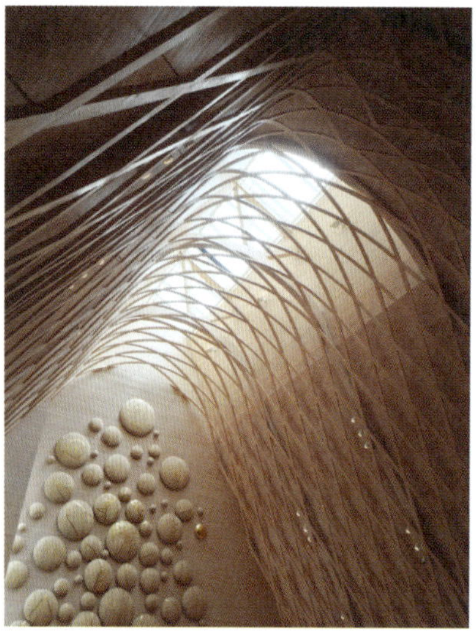

07

the most highly publicized examples of the new Finnish imperative to build in wood. However, over the past decade, more significant, albeit lesser known, work in mid-rise timber building and sustainable city planning has put Finland at the epicenter of a movement that combines techniques in high-performance wood design with low-impact urban development.

The contemporary boom in new timber technology and sustainable architectural design in Austria, Switzerland, and Germany is founded on those countries' tradition of timber construction and culture of wood craftsmanship. Vorarlberg, a province at Austria's western edge that borders Germany and Switzerland, is home to innovative wood architecture and state-of-the-art producers that now export mass-timber construction products and techniques world-wide. Most notable in a contemporary urban context of timber is the work of CREE, a research wing of Herbert Rhomberg's development consortium, that has produced several prototype projects, accompanied by rigorous impact analysis, including the eight-story timber Life Cycle Tower and the newly completed Illwerke Zentrum Montafon, a five-story office headquarters of the central hydroelectric energy plant for the state of Vorarlberg. Ongoing research at ETH Zurich and the University of Stuttgart's Institutes for Lightweight Structures and Computational Design, as well as sophisticated manufacturing facilities in Switzerland, provided the opportunity to examine the pathway from structural timber design to building production and performance.

The Technical, the Social, and the Ecological as Themes in Urban Innovation

The studio investigated hybrid urban building types and examined how the varied structural demands associated with different building uses and occupancies (high-rise housing and office space, repetitive commercial retail space, long-span manufacturing space, and so on) might combine with new timber technologies to produce innovative architectural solutions within dense cityscapes. Within the nine assigned sites in the Mill River development zone, each student proposed a mix of building uses they thought would be relevant to contemporary urban economies and lifestyles and appropriate to the character of the neighborhoods directly adjacent to their sites. Students were challenged to address the ecological characteristics and vulnerabilities of a coastal riparian wetland site and, through their architecture, seek potential solutions to the restoration and reinvigoration of a damaged industrial city. In an effort to measure both the impact and efficacy of their designs, the studio challenged the students to quantify the atmospheric carbon sequestered in the structural timber assemblies that comprised their buildings.

07 Left and middle: OOPEAA, Kuokkala, Finland
Right: Petajavesi, Finland

STUDIO WORK

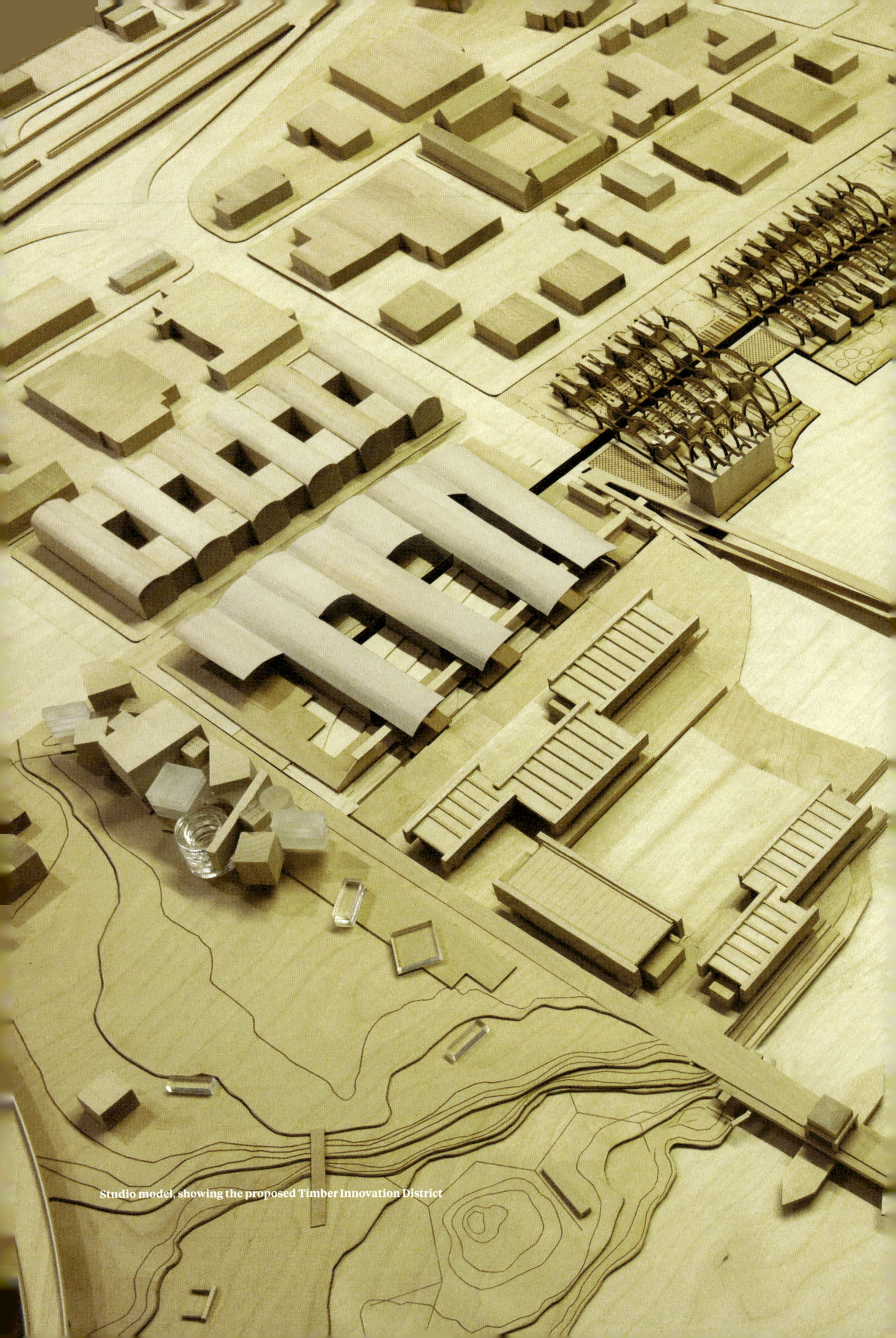

Studio model, showing the proposed Timber Innovation District

01 LIVING AND *WORKING*

Working on contiguous sites edged on one side by a low- to mid-rise residential district and, on the other, by the eastern bank of the Mill River, four students investigated contemporary modes of urban life and work, exploring new building types while testing the architectural means of combining, in timber, the long structural spans of commercial workspace with the shorter, repetitive spans of housing. The four projects developed dense architectural aggregations of dwelling and working program: cohousing with office space, live-make configurations of housing with workshops, and a live-sell building that combines a public marketplace with attached apartment units and private gardens. The four students collaborated to continuously weave public space through their buildings and along the water's edge in an effort to enlist public support and political motivation for the remediation and preservation of the Mill River ecosystem.

HAELEE JUNG

LIVE-MAKE-SELL MIXED USE

Carbon Sequestration: 3,630,000 kg of CO_2

This proposal for live-make housing recognizes current movements in housing design that combine living and working spaces, bringing them close together in the form of life that was common before industrialization. While this elision solves many of the problems caused by the contemporary separation between living and working spaces, including reducing the time and cost of commuting and helping to balance family and career, the strategy is limited to only those jobs that require relatively less space and equipment and that create little noise and dust so that they can coexist with residential life. However, as part of the Timber Innovation District, we suggest that, as a major industry, light manufacturing can coexist with residential life. This project seeks to create a convivial form of interaction between living and making while ameliorating the undesirable living conditions that could result from an overlap between residential and production spaces.

The project proposes, along the river, two parallel buildings—one for residences and the other for light industry—that are structurally separate but programmatically connected through the pushing and pulling of differently sized units. Project elements reach out to each other, creating public space that weaves through the two structurally independent buildings. On the ground level, a wide public promenade connects Grand Avenue, the major commercial street on the north side of the district, to the residential neighborhood on the east. On both sides of the street, shops become a platform for product exhibition and direct interaction with customers. On the levels above, individual units create semipublic platforms across which residents and workers can commute between the two buildings and enjoy the outdoor floating gardens.

Adjusting the architecture of each element to the distinct program it houses becomes possible through the separation

01 Diagrammatic façade, showing the coexistence of residential and industrial life

02 Site model, showing building in relation to all of the studio's projects

01

02

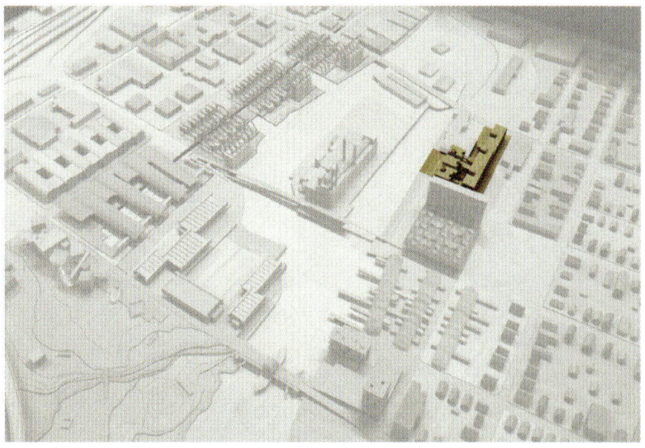

of structure. Cross-laminated timber (CLT) slabs comprise the residential building, while mass-timber post-and-beam construction forms the industrial building, accommodating the different loading conditions and higher ceilings required by large equipment. The load of residential units is carried through prefabricated, vertical CLT walls, the openings of which create continuous spaces across the walls. Exposed CLT texture provides warmth to the interior. Heavy glulam posts and beams on the industrial side gain rigidity and strength from a concrete decking system, suggesting a way for the existing concrete industry to coexist with a revivified twenty-first-century timber industry. Residential units are adapted from Le Corbusier's Unité d' Habitation and occupy the whole width of the residential building, allowing for cross-ventilation and double-height living spaces. These double-height spaces increase the spatial quality of the otherwise simple, repetitive housing units, letting in ample light and providing great views toward the river. The parallel timber-frame structure is a flexible, open structure that provides residents the opportunity to build and customize their own workshops. This live-work housing, located at the intersection of the Mill River district's industrial side to the west and its historic residential side to the east, creates a visual dialogue between, and an expression of, two different program types within two hybrid buildings. The apartment wing affords sweeping views of the river and the industrial site beyond, while the industrial wing, in effect, advertises the workshops, fabrication, and materials for the houses to its east.

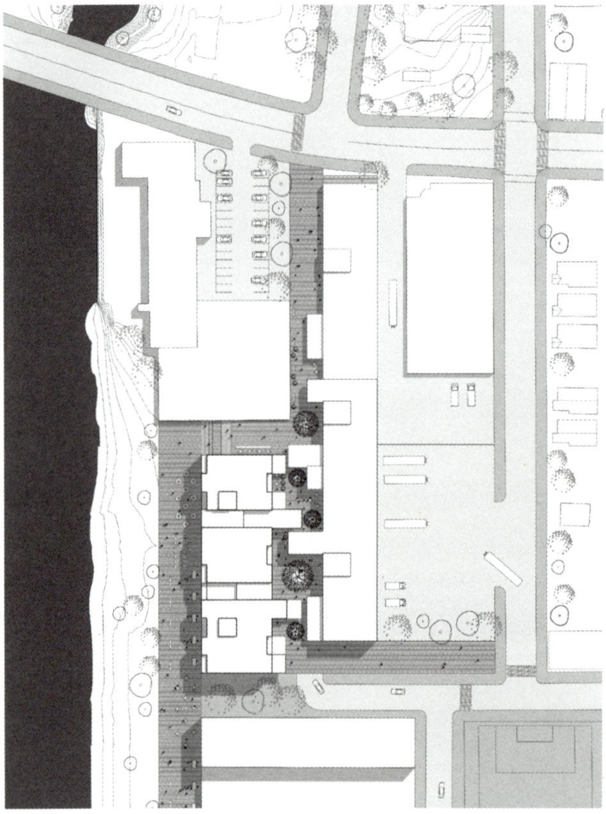

03

03 Site plan, illustrating how the two parallel buildings interact and form the public space between them
04 Building section, revealing double-height spaces and the floating, semi-public platforms
05 Rendering showing the volumetric interplay between the two buildings and the contrast between the two structural systems

04

05

PERRY WEXELBERG

PUBLIC MARKET COMPLEX

Carbon Sequestration: 3,630,000 kg of CO_2

This proposal uses contemporary timber manufacturing technologies to express a new vision for urban wood buildings. In contrast with the way wood is typically used in stick-frame construction, this building expresses wood as a monolithic structure. The structural assembly system of large, cantilevering box beams made of laminated timber trusses and cross-laminated-timber (CLT) panels allows for a thickened plane of deep wooden coffers supported on a field of hollow timber pylons. This monolithic expression of timber creates an exciting indoor-outdoor market hall, with high ceilings and a grocery store floating above.

Currently, the Mill River area is home to several food manufacturing facilities that produce bread, coffee, and chocolate. The public market complex forms a large, new public space that connects the Fair Haven neighborhood to the waterfront and creates a dynamic retail space for new and existing food businesses. The open plan of the hall allows for market stalls, providing retail space for existing food businesses and for home-based food production start-ups. Each modular market stall can be occupied by up to four vendors. This configuration enables a business to start small, using only one corner of a stall and growing to use the entire stall. The market hall becomes an incubator for food businesses as well as a grand public space that is enriched by the possibilities of contemporary timber construction.

The second level houses a grocery store, which lies within the roof structure of the market hall. The grocery store, oriented toward the Fair Haven neighborhood, overlooks an existing soccer field. A large landscaped stair cascades down from the grocery store and transforms into bleachers as it nears the field. The programs of the grocery store that require more open space are placed along the building's edges, where large cantilevers allow for more open floor plans, while the aisles are organized within the deep structural grid box beams. Punched windows in the beams create a visual connection between the grocery-store shoppers and the market hall.

Above the grocery store, there is a garden roof and a ten-story apartment tower. A series of clerestory windows are set into the roof's planting beds, allowing light to penetrate down to the market hall. Each apartment is a two-story unit, with the kitchen, dining room, and living room on the first floor and private bedrooms on the second floor. Each first-floor level has a large balcony with space for socializing and planter boxes, while each upper level

01

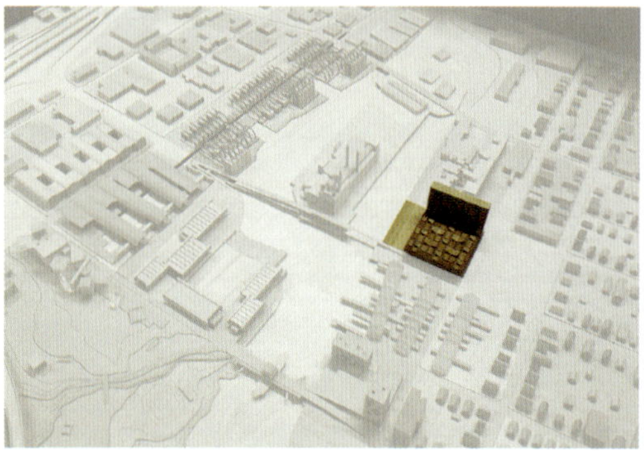

02

03

includes a smaller, more private balcony. These south-facing balconies are shaded by a wood louver system that formally resembles the clerestory of the green roof. The angular formal similarity allows the louvers of the tower façade to frame views and let morning and afternoon light in while blocking the most intense midday summer sun. The planters on the balconies also create a relationship between the roof and the apartment façade.

The market hall, the grocery store, the garden roof, and the apartments become a series of layers, each of which is connected to the urban context in a particular way. The market hall faces the Mill River and becomes a part of the public promenade along the riverfront. The landscape stairway connects the Fair Haven neighborhood to a desired amenity, the grocery store. The planted roof of the grocery-market hall is connected both visually and programmatically to the planted balconies of the apartments. The building is sensitive to its context while expressing advanced mass-timber construction and stimulating a new urban economy and lifestyle.

01 Site model, showing building in relation to all the studio's projects
02 Detail of model, showing view of roof garden and skylights
03 Detail of model, showing monolithic expression of the interior
04 Building sectional axon, revealing the different layers of the building

04

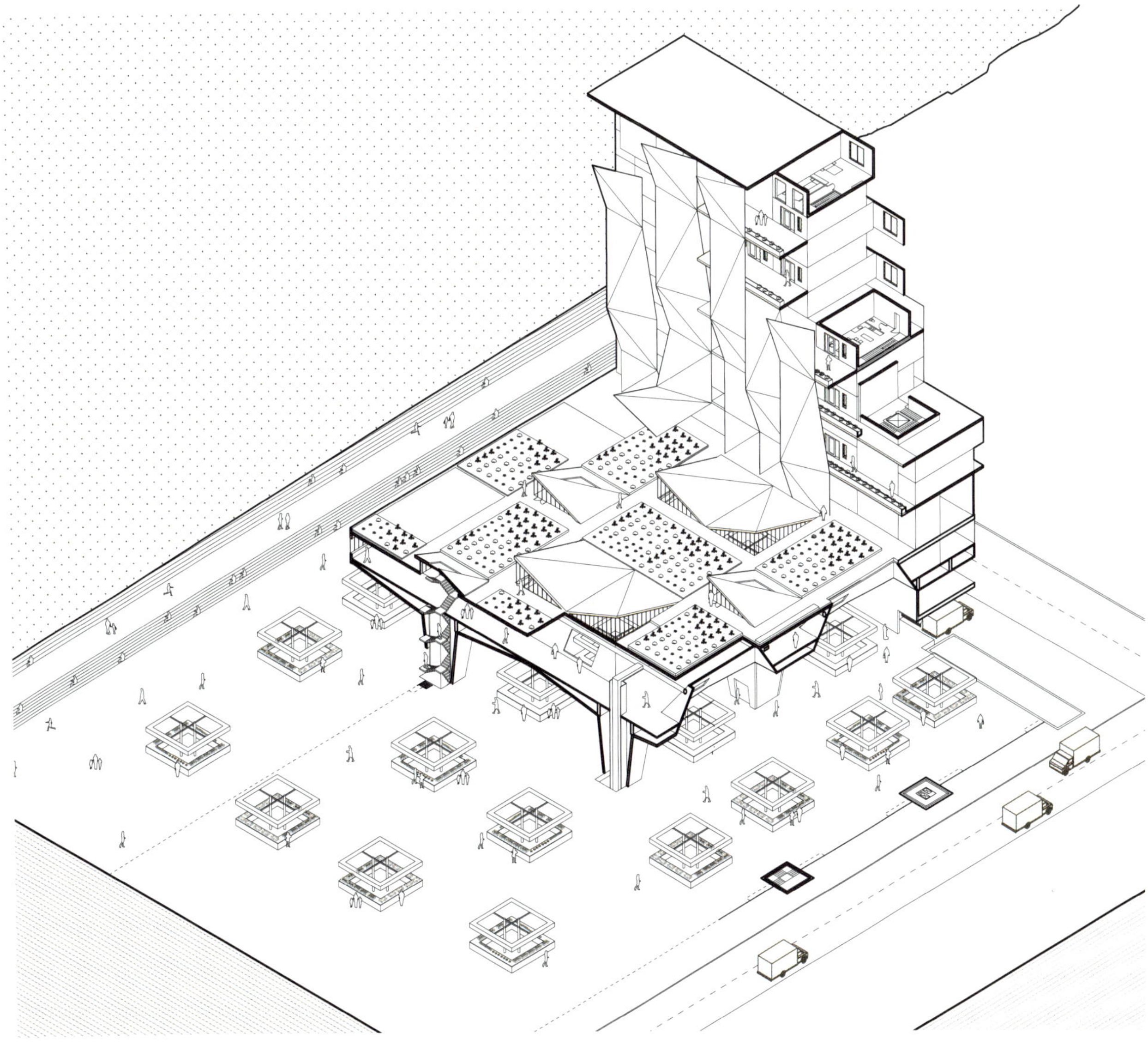

05 Building section, revealing clerestory windows giving light to the market hall

06 Model, showing formal connection between market hall and apartment tower

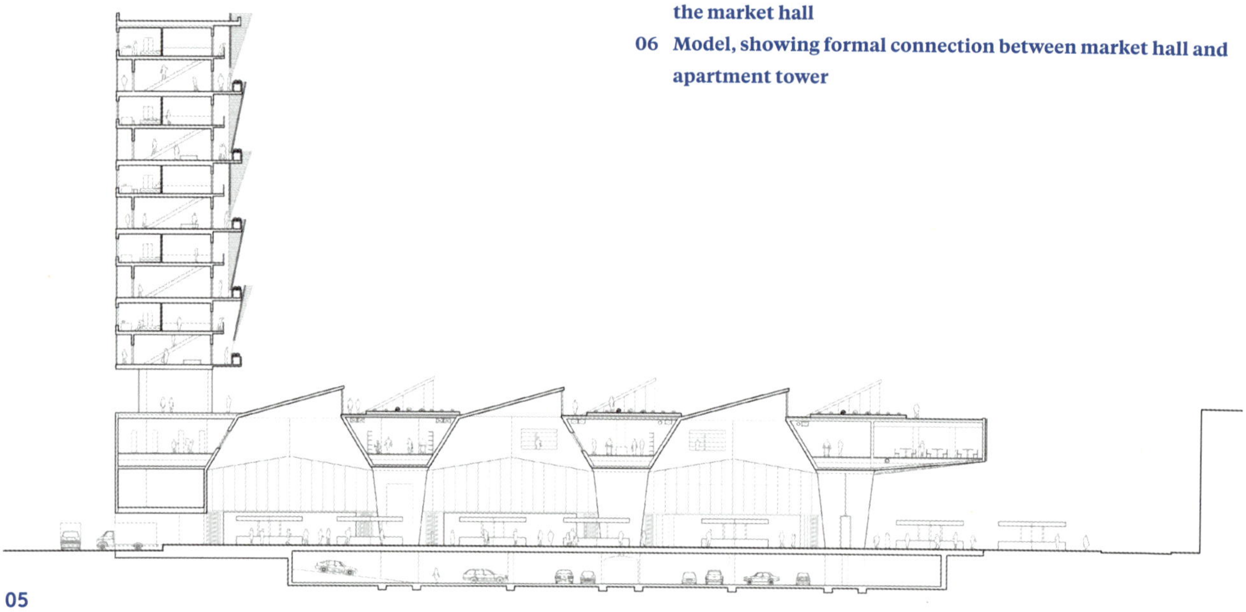

05

06

BEN SMITH

RESIDENTIAL-MANUFACTURING BLOCK

Carbon Sequestration: 5,360,000 kg of CO_2

Over the past fifty years, the American home has gradually become a place of consumption and self-expression. The commoditization of the home has changed the way that we build cities and how we interact with one another. American urban sprawl and interpersonal connections are held tenuously by the tendrils of highways and internet cables. This porject's building looks to older historical models—the Roman domus, the nineteenth-century New England fishing cottage, and the informal settlements of Mumbai—for examples of means and modes of living. The proposed cooperative combats the city's uncontrolled spread by reincorporating a place of production into the domestic space.

The cooperative mediates between two scales, domestic and manufacturing. Light manufacturing takes place in large, translucent shed structures that are composed of a series of glulam portal frames that parallel the river; dwelling occurs in the smaller, prefabricated, cross-laminated-timber box beams that run perpendicular to the river. Supplies for the shops are delivered at the south end of each shed and move north along the river. Residents arrive from the mews that runs down the center of the complex and, upon entering their home, gain a view to the street or the waterfront. The adaptable system logic

01 Plan, showing live-work divide in New Haven

02 Typical plan of system

03 Site model, showing building in relation to all the studio's projects

01

02

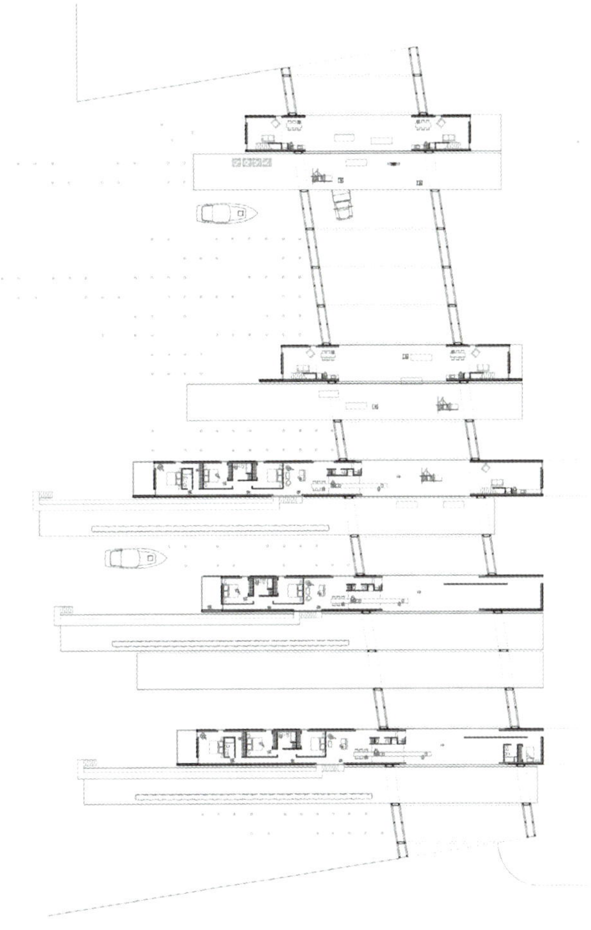

03

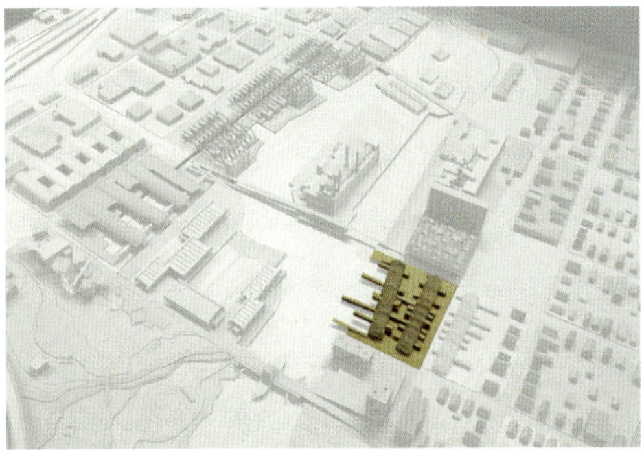

BEN SMITH

of the cooperative allows for multiple housing options, including loft spaces, single-family homes, and group housing. Individual units comprise three parts: the shop, the dwelling, and the hybrid space. Existing between the shop and the dwelling, the hybrid space acts as an extension of both.

The Mill River district is currently home to a variety of light industries, including sewing, printing, and carpentry. The cooperative augments these existing industries and allows makers and craftsmen to work and live collaboratively. The reintroduction of productive space into the domestic space generates revenue and extends the function of the dwelling. This elision of programs also erodes the work-live separation produced by current zoning practices and reactivates the urban environment. Rather than becoming inactive during periods of disuse, the cooperative transforms multiple times throughout the course of the day, alternating between its domestic and productive functions.

Located along the edge of a flood zone, the building responds to the likelihood of rising sea levels. The site gradually slopes down toward the Mill River, and the cooperative sits lightly on a restored wetland. Floodable program spaces, such as parking and delivery, are located at the level of the river, while the domestic space and the production floors are located at street level, fifteen feet above the flood zone. The building proposes a new way to build and live in cities, one in which we are more thoughtful about, and responsive to, the environment and one in which we can increase community interaction and reactivate moribund portions of our cities.

---

04 Section sketch

05 CLT domestic bars intersecting with translucent production sheds at the water's edge

06 Interior view of production space

07 From top: axonometrics for a loft, for a single-family unit, and for an extended family unit

08 Structural section model

04

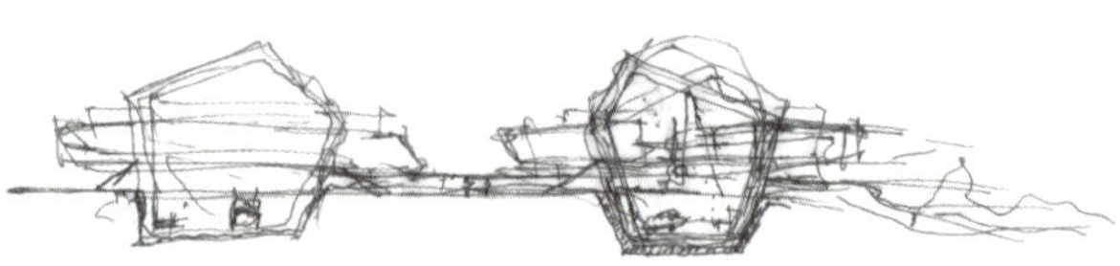

05

06

07

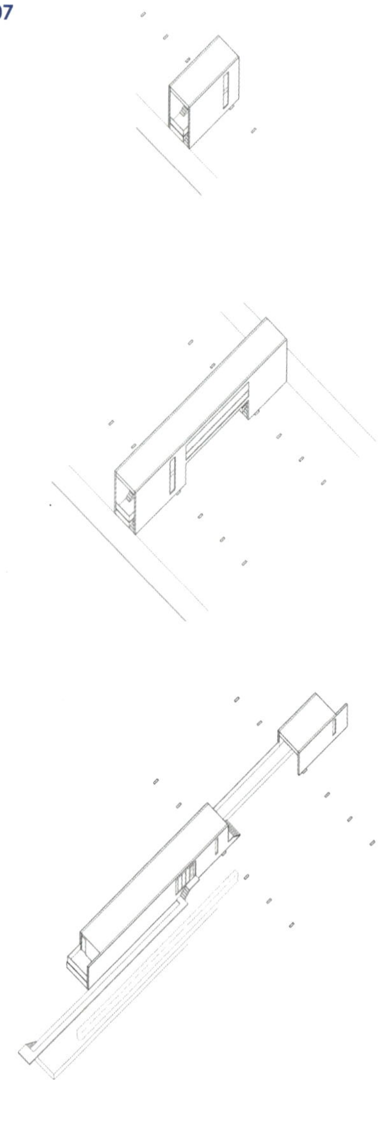

08

AMY SU

LIVE-WORK TOWER

Carbon Sequestration: 6,850,000 kg of CO_2

This site at the intersection of Mill and Chapel streets serves as an important marker for the proposed Timber Innovation District. To draw attention to the district along Chapel Street from downtown New Haven and from I-95 to the southwest, the site contains a twelve-story tower and a six-story slab building. The two buildings are linked by a publicly accessed plinth that provides pedestrians with an elevated view of the river and separation from traffic on Chapel Street. Additionally, a pedestrian pathway connects the plinth directly to the Chapel Street Bridge. As the southernmost lot of the residential half of the Timber Innovation District, both buildings comprise a mixture of live-work spaces, with additional commercial spaces at the street level and parking spaces underground.

In the two buildings, the idea of combining live and work programs is re-imagined and varied to create a diverse community of people. There are three types of living arrangements: co-living units consist of minimal private units—dorm-style rooms—and maximum shared spaces, including cooking, dining, social, and work areas. Co-working units have larger private spaces that include private bathrooms and kitchens with shared work areas. Live-work units include entirely private apartment units with personal work spaces. Three sizes of private living units thus allow for three types of functions.

A mixture of the three types of living units is organized within each glulam tray-assembly system. Three levels of living units are stacked between two glulam superfloors. Outside the individual unit boxes, the leftover spaces become shared spaces for occupation and circulation. The tower contains skip-stop elevators that bring people to the first level of each tray unit; stairs are used to reach the second and third stories. Therefore, each tray assembly becomes a newly defined neighborhood unit. All shared surfaces are created either from the stacked and offset unit boxes or by the superfloors themselves. In the tower,

01

02

03

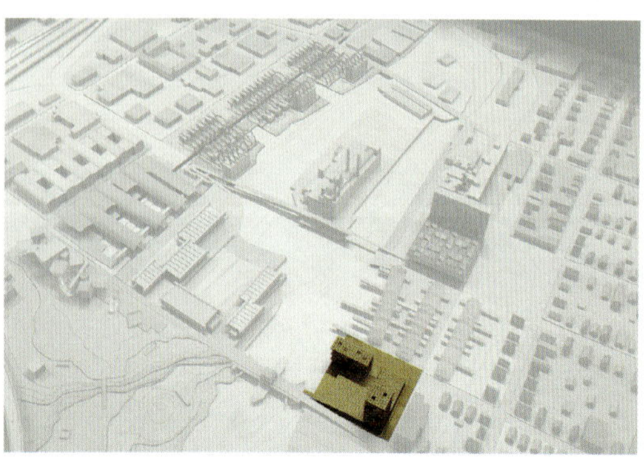

there are four sets of stacked tray units, creating twelve total stories, which are all linked by two cores containing elevators and utilities. The cores also provide structural stability to the building. The slab building consists of the same supertray system in a different configuration: a two-by-two assembly that creates six total floors. The living units are prefabricated CLT boxes, manufactured in the Timber Innovation District. Then, the boxes are transported and set into place on the site.

A high-performance building envelope encloses all the shared spaces throughout the buildings. In certain sections, the envelope is offset ten feet from the perimeter of the building to create outdoor spaces, both shared and private. The buildings, made up of prefabricated parts and a repeated structural system, allows for efficiency in the construction process, while the diverse combinations and arrangements of living units provide space for a redefined model for living and working.

01 Site section, showcasing the grouped living units and the superfloors

02 Final model, showing the cores of the towers with one module of three floors on a glulam superfloor pulled off

03 Site model, showing the building in relation to all the studio's projects

04 Diagram of module types

04

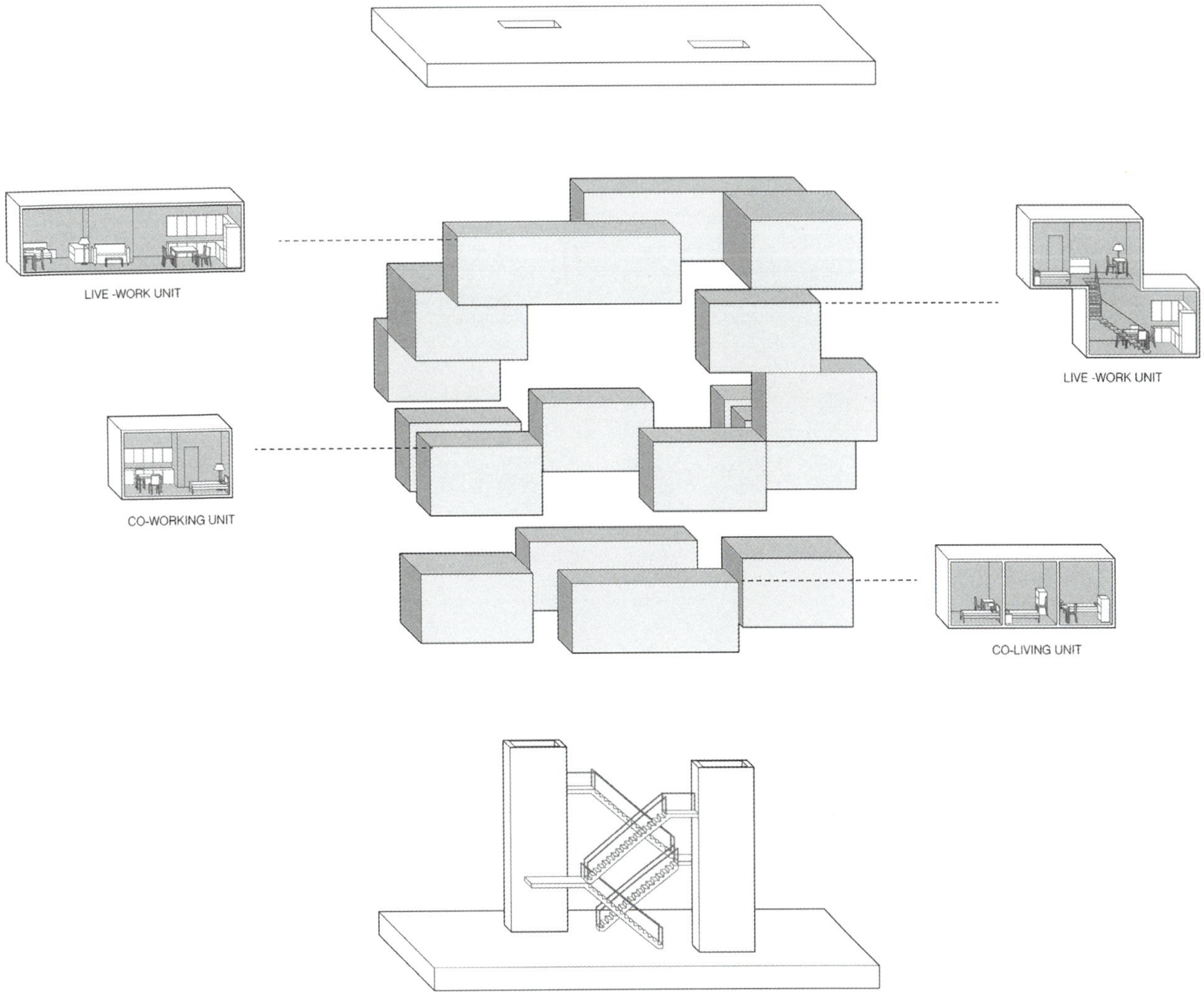

02 INDUSTRY *MADE PUBLIC*

On the western bank of the Mill River and occupying low-lying industrial brownfields exposed to coastal storm surges and prone to flooding, three students sought to infuse new industrial buildings with readily accessible public space. Each developed long-span structural prototypes in mass timber, aggregating them into replicable systems for the enclosure of expansive spaces for heavy-materials handling and assembly. Each sought to weave the remediation of the coastal wetland with the productive economies of urban industry. Two of the projects examine current commercial technologies in mass-timber production, focusing on different techniques of adhesive-laminated wood to produce large structural members of significant dimension and load-bearing capacity. The third project seeks to expose and celebrate the processing of industrial waste for public energy production, creating new public infrastructure that would bridge the residential neighborhood to the east and the industrial riverbank to the west while publicizing the relationship between urban life and the physical resources it demands. At the urban scale, each architectural proposal seeks to transform historically segregated spaces of industry and infrastructure into places of public education and even spectacle.

BOYUAN ZHANG

MANUFACTURING FACILITY

Carbon Sequestration: 5,400,000 kg of CO_2

This project for a manufacturing facility along the Mill River results from three parallel studies: an exploration of the material properties of cross-laminated timber (CLT), the development of a structural system suited to the tectonic character and structural properties of CLT, and the adaptation of that long-span structural system to a specific urban site.

Cross-laminated timber is an engineering product made of alternating layers of wood that take the shape of planar panels. A natural development from single-axis glue lamination, cross-lamination produces a two-way system that behaves like a shell structure with strength in two axes. Drawing inspiration from the folding-paper system of Poul Henningsen's origami lamp at Alvar Aalto's studio in Helsinki as well as from recent mass-timber techniques developed in other parts of Europe, this project combines the system of a folded-plate structure with standardized repetitive panels of cross-laminated timber to achieve long spans while minimizing component depth. The modular, prefabricated panel system also enables fast, in situ construction and has the flexibility to be expanded into larger manufacturing units or converted into other uses that require long-span interior space.

Taking one typical bay as a structural unit, the folded-plate system responds to functional, urban, and environmental requirements. It achieves a long span (more than 60 feet), providing clear spaces for manufacturing. A simple tilt in its geometry admits daylight through large clerestory lights. Since much of the site is located within the flood zone, the building's main manufacturing level must be elevated above

01 Model, showing typical structural bay
02 Site model, showing the building in relation to all the studio's projects

01

02

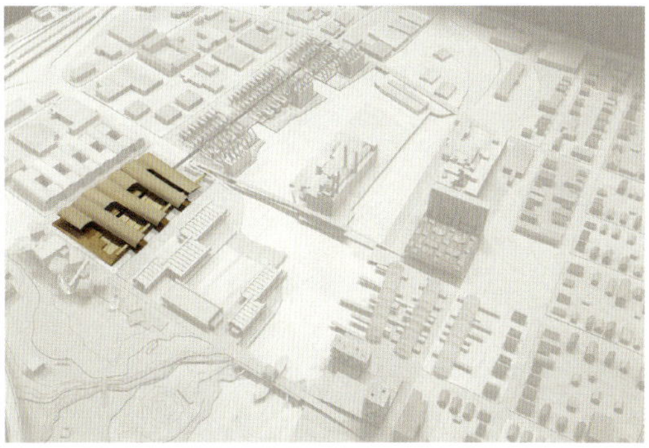

the 500-year floodplain. So, the relatively lightweight system allows the entire building to rest on a foundation of wood pilings, with carbonized surface treatment to resist decay. The folding system of the structure also helps to direct stormwater off the roof into constructed wetlands that lie between each manufacturing hall.

The detailing of each individual panel also takes into consideration construction efficiency and material economy. The symmetrical layout of each bay reduces geometrical irregularity. Each roof panel is constructed as a stressed skin system, employing CLT panels as its top and bottom skins and, to give rigidity to the panel edges, glulam stiffeners.

The manufacturing plant is sited at the prominent corner of Chapel Street and East Street, facing the proposed Timber Innovation Center across Chapel to the south and adjacent to the Waterfront Recreational Center to the east. Serving as a transition from the vehicular traffic along both streets, the manufacturing plant's forecourt introduces a pedestrian wetland walkway that runs northward to the river's east bank. The architecture offers both a public space and an inviting urban image at this major intersection and seeks to mitigate the large industrial scale of the manufacturing halls.

In addition to addressing the structural and economic challenges of commercial long-span structures, mass timber offers a materiality that is warm and familiar, casting a new light on the image of urban industrial buildings. While the folded-plate structural system adds an unconventional but pleasing rhythm to the streetscape, the building's public program of exhibition and demonstration areas alters the old dialogue between industry and community. The building offers both the proverbial fish and the fishing pole, providing New Haven's construction sector with new industrial products and creating job opportunities.

03 Fabrication sequence
04 Exploded diagram, revealing the spatial organization within the structure
05 Plan, showing main level within the urban context
06 Interior rendering of a manufacturing hall

03

04

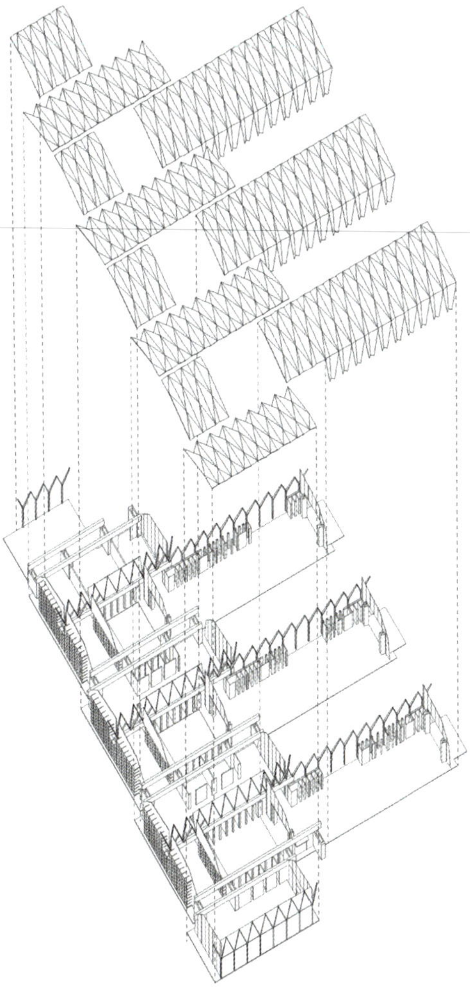

05

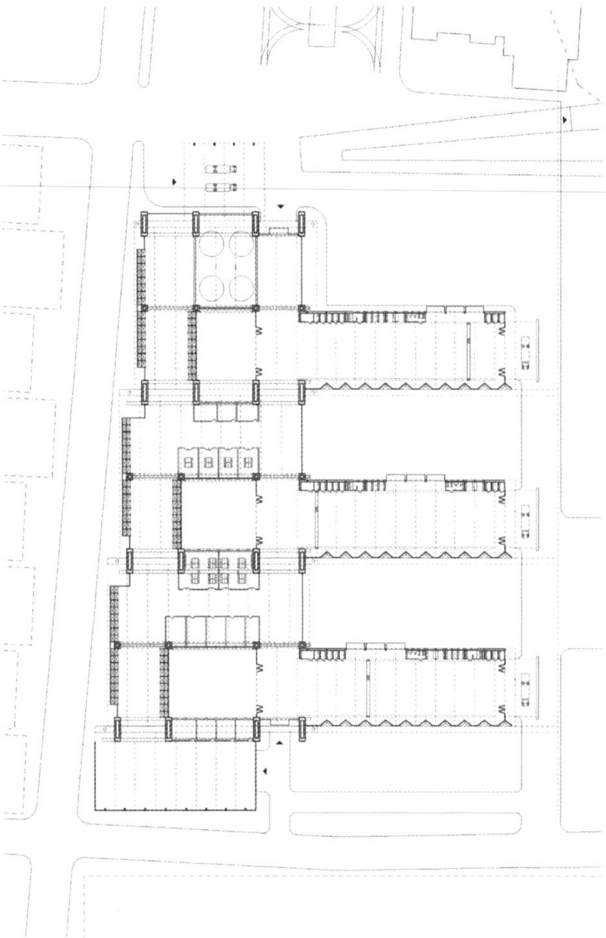

06

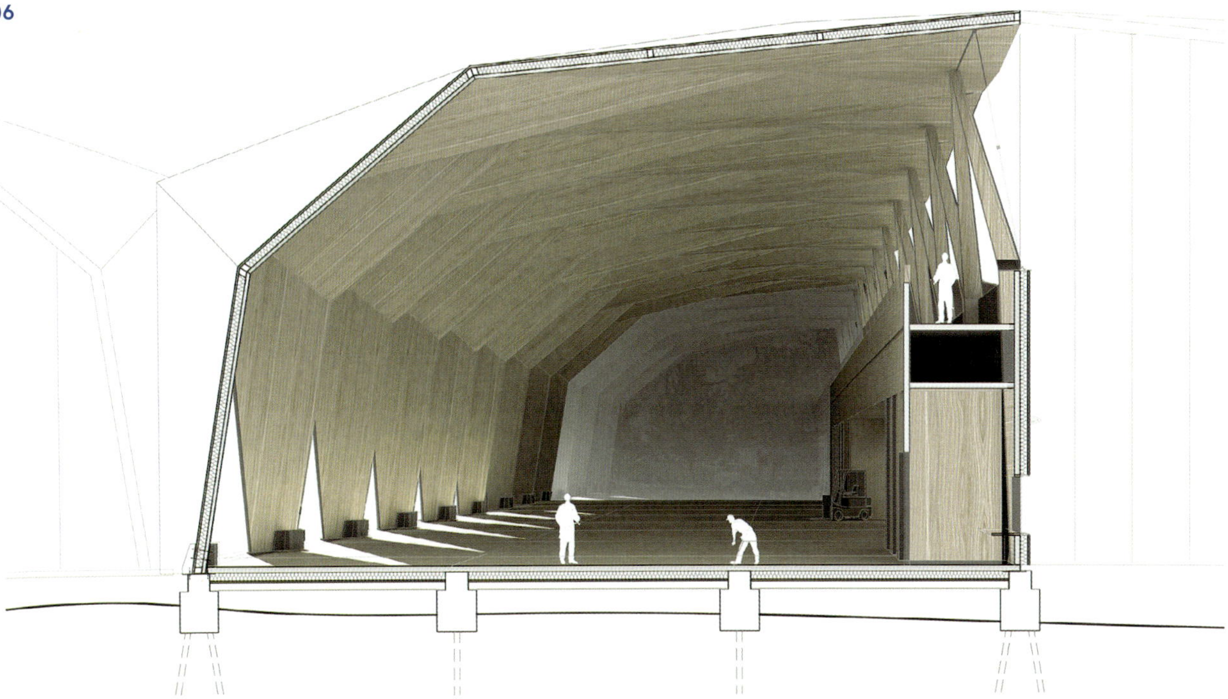

MENGRAN LI

MANUFACTURING FACILITY

Carbon Sequestration: 4,570,000 kg of CO_2

This project celebrates the architectural potential of the forest-products industry while seeking to remediate the damaged ecology of the wetland and flood zone of the Mill River, in New Haven. New timber technologies, especially long-span, glue-laminated timber, form the conceptual premise and fuel the exploration of this high-performance timber-product manufacturing facility, an architectural response to the USDA initiative to bring new structural mass-timber technologies and industrial wood products to the forefront of a national manufacturing revival.

The site for this project, identified as a test location for new, unconventional mixed-use building types, is located in between downtown New Haven and Fair Haven and bordered by East Street to the west and the Mill River to the east. Located within a light-industrial zone with a long history in timber construction, the site has ready access to mass transit and industrial transportation. In order to test the architectural potential for merging industrial building with public educational and commercial space, the project uses a parcel to the north of the designated site. This tactic allowed the structural prototype to proliferate, demonstrating its adaptability to different kinds of streets and presenting a commercial face and public entrance along the once vibrant but now dilapidated Grand Avenue, which forms the northern edge of this new district.

01 Site model, showing building in relation to all the studio's projects
02 Cross-section, showing the change in density across the site
03 Longitudinal section, showing how the canopy allows for daylighting
04 Detail of final section model, focusing on glue-laminated timber

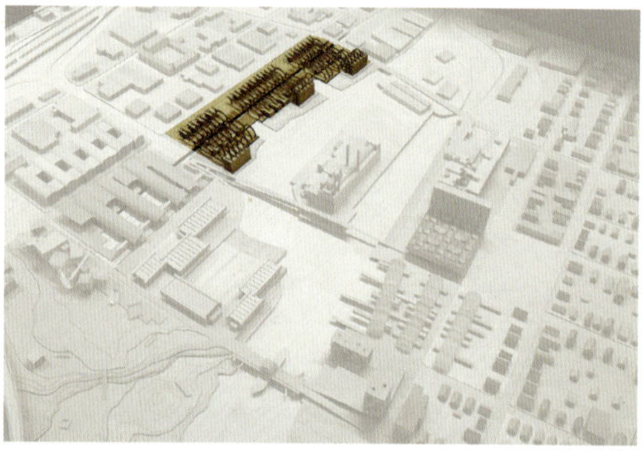

01

02

03

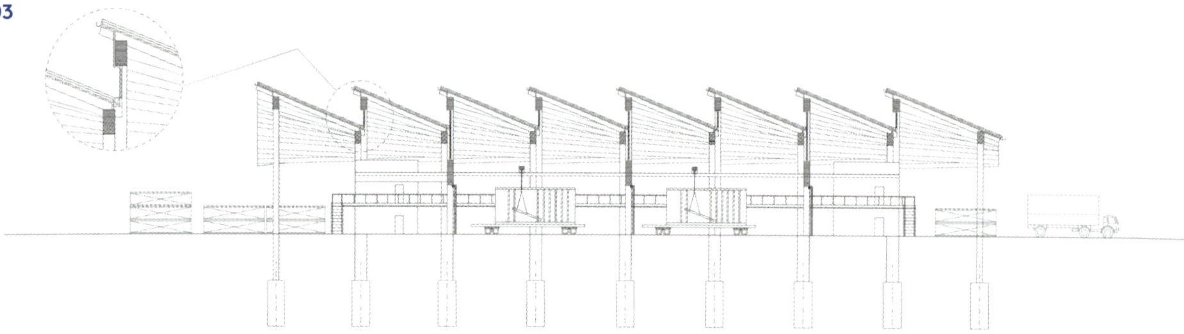

04

MENGRAN LI

The design inspiration was derived from the glulam precedents by Alvar Aalto and by some high-density, urban wood structures, encountered during the studio trip to Europe. As a result, the giant, glue-laminated "bents" demonstrate the potential of long-span contemporary timber construction, using lamination—and de-lamination—as a means of changing structural shapes in response to varying structural demands.

By creating a large-scale, expressive timber structure formed in undulating and arching long-span, glue-laminated timber, the project accommodates a variety of programs for the receiving, processing, manufacturing, storage, and transport of timber material. The configuration of the factory allows for the production of prefabricated building modules and large-scale timber building components, and the existing, on-site freight rail tracks connect to a network that extends to Vermont, an important supply artery from areas with rich timber resources.

Facing the river, the density of the building increases sharply and features research-and-design laboratories and multistory office spaces, serving manufacturing engineers and administrators, as well as an array of waterfront education and exhibition spaces. This area within the plan has excellent views of the river and the historic English Station power plant. Its adjacency to the wetland brings the ecology of the place into sharp focus while offering a site for both leisure and recreation to the researchers, employees, and visitors.

Along the busy industrial corridor of East Street, the project offers a street-front supply market under its cantilevered roof canopy, a pedestrian mall that, on the weekends, sells artisanal goods and home building supplies.

Supported by the arching glulam bents, the giant roof canopy captures both rainwater and daylight through the careful calibration of topography and apertures, admitting ambient northern light for factory halls and limiting the stronger southern sunlight to the exterior courts, formed by the freight-rail platforms that pass through the complex. In the building's public and administrative areas, skylights and bridges penetrate the roof canopy to introduce daylight and provide circulation throughout the building. Along the river, a wetland park for site visitors and the plant's employees offers a network of pedestrian paths that also serve as a series of stormwater catchment and absorption zones, interweaving the river's renewed habitat with this new industrial architecture.

05 Early study model

05

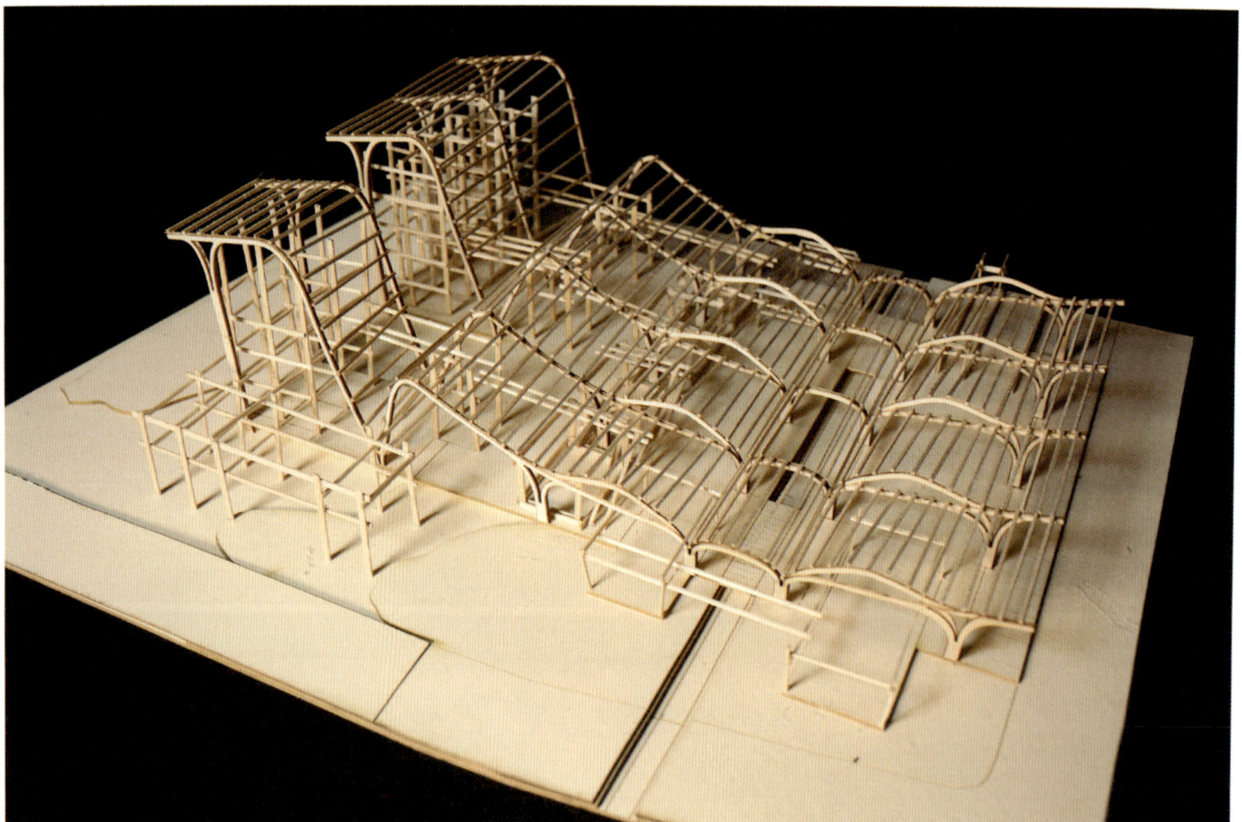

MAYA ALEXANDER

PUBLIC RIVER CROSSING

Carbon Sequestration: 2,770,000 kg of CO_2

The proposed bridge is a crucial link within the Timber Innovation District, connecting the recreational and manufacturing programs located on the west side of the river to the market and housing, located on the east side. However, instead of serving simply as a connection between two areas, the bridge creates a third space that has its own unique functions and programs while answering the logistical demands of nearby industry and the recreational needs of the residential sector. Its prominent location within the district and its visibility from the Interstate 95 corridor create a prime opportunity to raise awareness of the structural potential of mass timber.

As with the vernacular covered bridges of New England, the crossing uses the structural logic of the timber truss. Employing this time-honored structural type and the massive glue-laminated beams that serve as its deck, the bridge is able to span the river with nearly 100-foot sections. A secondary timber mesh provides resistance against lateral forces and creates an enclosure within the bridge's lower section, which is used to transport waste to Ball Island from the adjacent timber manufacturing facilities. Located in the middle of the Mill River Basin, the island houses English Station, a former coal- and then oil-fired power plant that now stands as an abandoned relic in a brownfield site. By reconnecting the waste stream from the timber manufacturing facilities to the power plant, repurposed as a biomass incinerator, the project gives a new role in the city to this prominent relic of New Haven's industrial past.

Unlike its historical counterparts, the bridge takes advantage of both the roof and road decks. At the recreational park, visitors gain access to the bridge through

01 Site model, showing the building in relation to all the studio's projects
02 Site plan, showing the building form spanning the river
03 Full model

01

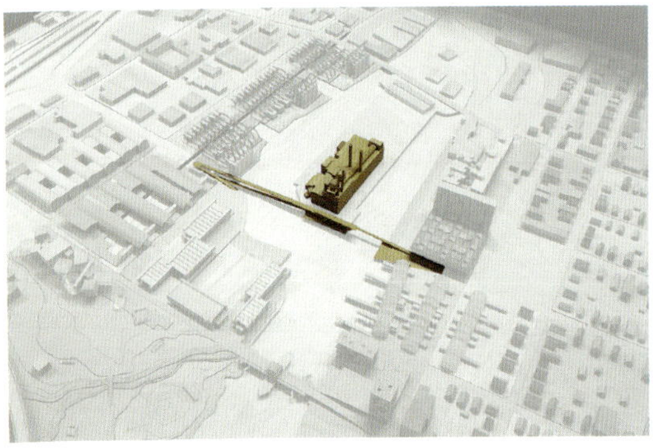

02

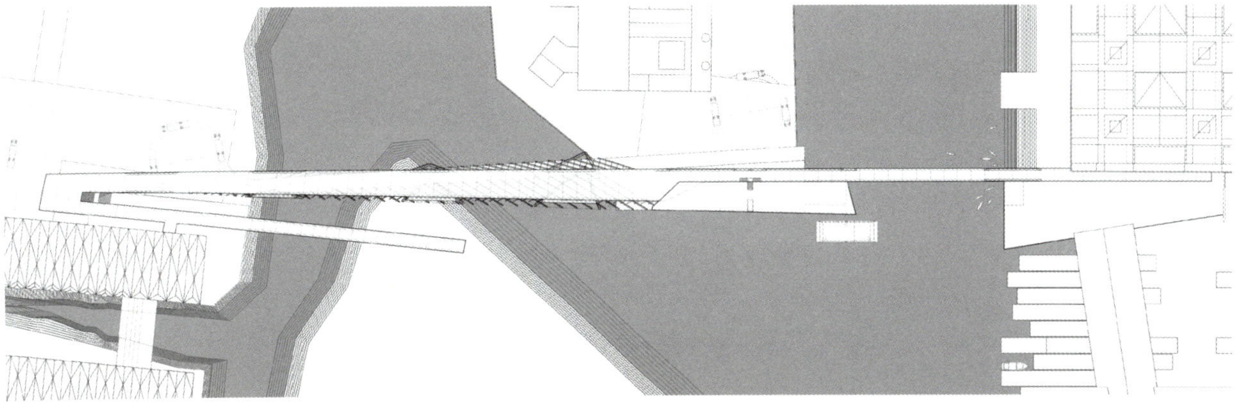

03

an entrance ramp that gently climbs to a viewing platform overlooking the loading docks of the manufacturing facilities. From this vantage point, visitors can see the delivery and handling of raw timber products as well as the wood waste bound for Ball Island. From the viewing platform, the bridge spans over the first leg of the river, allowing visitors a close-up view of the power plant while keeping them clear of the heavy vehicular traffic. In testing the limits of a new material-structural system, the bridge also creates opportunities to engage the public in the on-site manufacturing activities.

As the bridge passes over Ball Island, the structural system changes, and the industrial link terminates. Here, glulam piers support pedestrian access. The raised structure connects visitors to an open-air market and provides for the docking of small watercraft. These series of transitions and connections in both the horizontal and vertical dimensions of the site provide a crucial experience of this newly combined river and industrial waterfront, an important part of the revitalization of the Mill River district.

04 Final model, showing bridge in context
05 Circulation sketch, illustrating how a third space can be inserted between two ends of the bridge

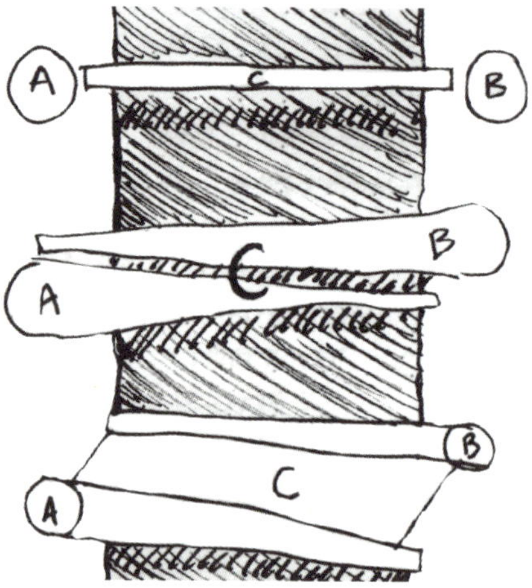

04

05

03 DEMONSTRATION *AND EXHIBITION*

On the two sites most in need of environmental remediation and most vulnerable to coastal flooding, two students explored the creation of monuments to public work and recreation. Bracketing the heavily trafficked corridor of Chapel Street—and in the spirit of the major public buildings and facilities that punctuate its two-mile length—two new buildings structured in mass timber form a gateway to the Timber Innovation District. Each offers New Haven's citizens and visitors resources and respite. On one hand, the project offers visitors educational information about emerging technologies and sustainable economies based in timber; on the other, the project offers an escape from the rigors of work through sport and urban recreation. Integrating resilient landscape strategies that seek to remediate and restore once-damaged ecologies, both projects propose new building types that explicitly link the materials and structure of dense urban construction with the forest and wetland ecologies that are its source. Material durability, strength, and fitness are monumentalized through programs and spaces for the research, development, and demonstration of emerging timber technologies and new wood products and for the pleasure and health benefits of physical activity and play.

KAROLINA CZECZEK

WOOD INNOVATION RESEARCH AND DESIGN CENTER

Carbon Sequestration: 6,320,000 kg of CO_2

The Wood Innovation and Research Center is designed to house exhibition spaces, event venues, flexible workspaces, and workshops that explore the possibilities of wood as a building material. Additionally, its extensive wood structure itself promotes the use of timber in large-scale developments and in public-use buildings. The building form, a collage of volumes enclosed by a structural grid, corresponds to the mix of different programs and acts as an anchor and signature structure for the whole development.

Each program component is housed in a specific volume that represents different types of wood structures. Programs such as event and exhibition spaces are enclosed by solid, cross-laminated-timber volumes, while programs that require daylight are housed in volumes created with trusses. The scattered volumes are all connected and supported by a "superfloor" structure, which is made of long-span, glue-laminated-wood trusses. The interstitial space between the volumes becomes an area of informal interaction for building visitors and acts as a gallery of diverse wood structures and finishes. The structural thickness of the superfloor is also used for distribution of services around the building. The interstitial spaces and the terraces on top of selected volumes are enclosed by glass envelopes, supported by structural façade mullions made from of tall-wood columns. Volumes scattered inside the building create two different conditions by intersecting

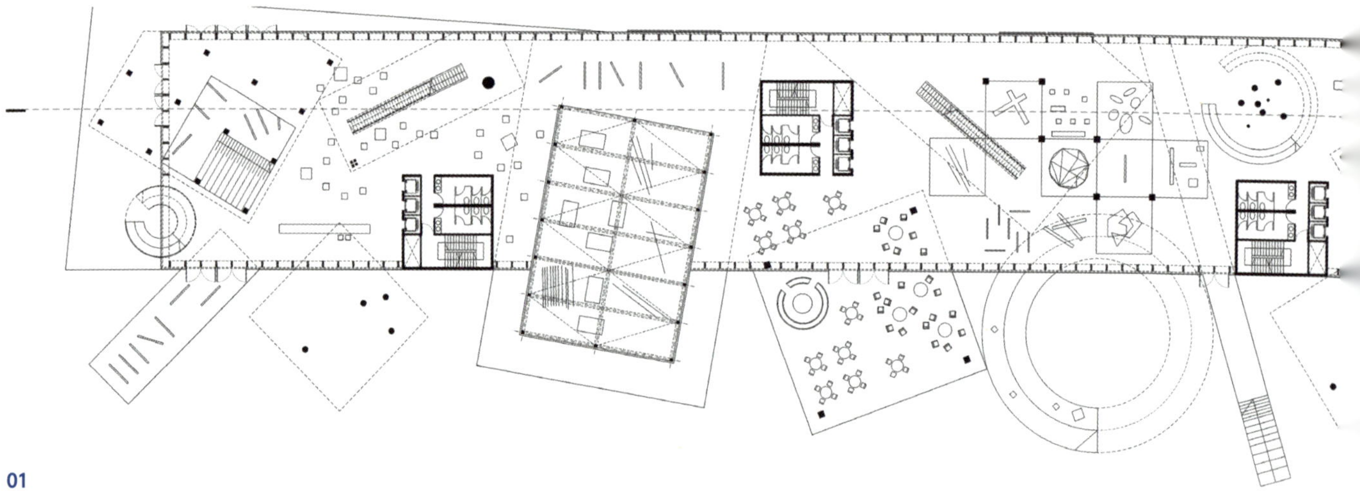

01

02

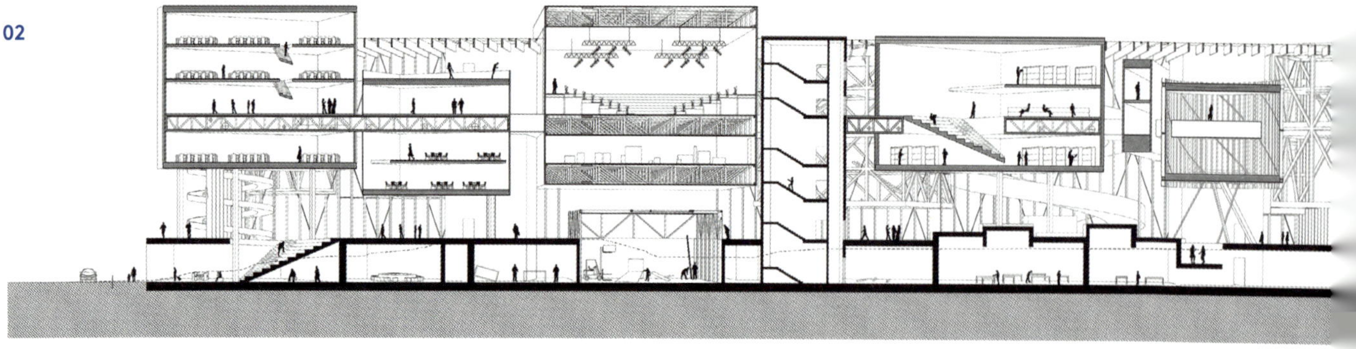

the building façades. On the front, along Chapel Street, volumes are cut by the façade to create a continuous street front and expose their interiors to the outside. At the back, the same volumes protrude from the façade's enclosure.

The building is placed on a plinth that extends from the street and allows for an uninterrupted flow of visitors. The outdoor part of the plinth can be used as a sculpture garden, an amphitheater, or a playground that contributes to the building's public program. In the rear of the building, the plinth becomes more fragmented and begins to disintegrate into the landscape, which is designed as a wetland park. This part of the project takes advantage of the site's location within the district's ecological zone—a brackish riparian wetland prone to tidal surges. A series of follies, boardwalks, and floating platforms are distributed throughout the site, which is planted with locally sourced plants and trees.

The location of the building in a post-industrial area provides an optimum condition for the exploration and implementation of resilient, dense, coastal urban development. Here, the building and the wetland park become a discussion platform, encouraging architects, engineers, biologists, and ecologists to engage the possibilities of wood for the future of the construction industry and as a means of mitigating carbon emissions.

01 Ground-floor plan, showing the collage of volumes interacting with the structural grid

02 Building section, revealing plinth level

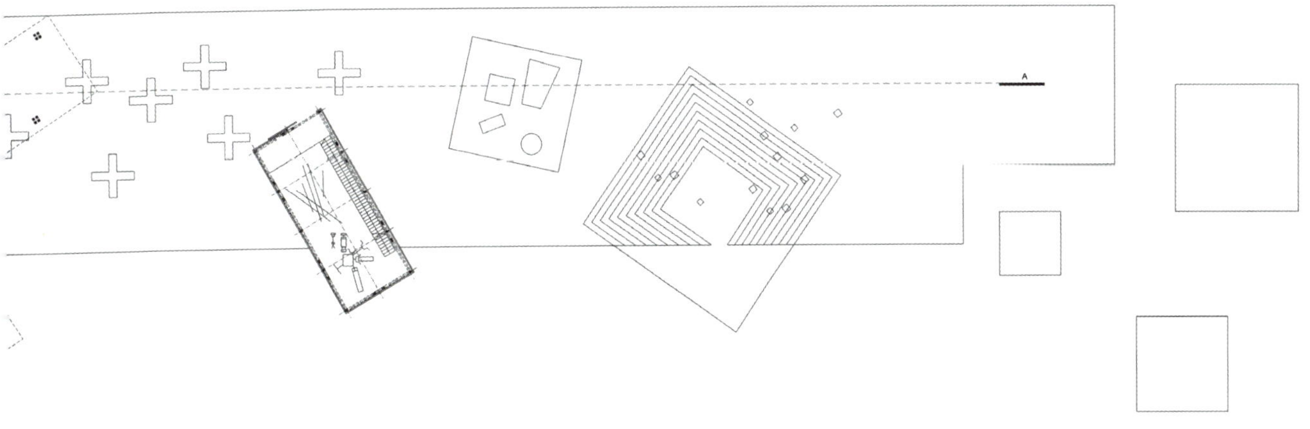

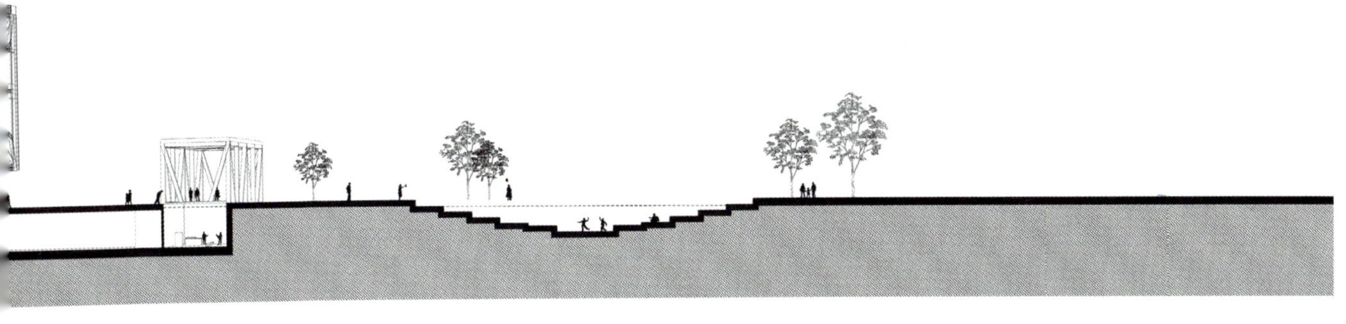

03

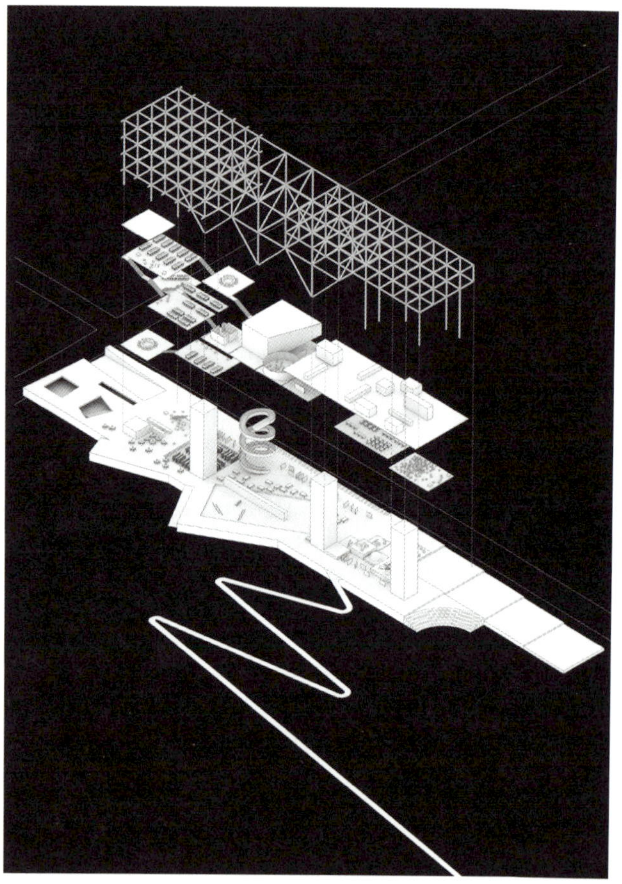

04

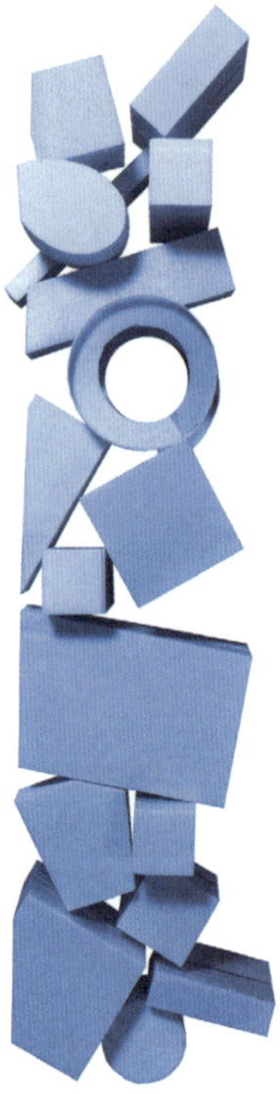

05

06

03 Site plan, showing relationship between highway and waterfront
04 Exploded axon
05 Massing model, showing the collage of volumes
06 Site model, showing building in relation to all the studio's projects

PETER MCINISH

PUBLIC ATHLETIC FACILITY

Carbon Sequestration: 4,160,000 kg of CO_2

This proposal for a recreation complex in the Mill River district brings together a wide array of athletic activities, distributing them within a series of pavilions that mediate the transition from a neglected New Haven thoroughfare to a newly remediated wetland edge. Conceptually, the project becomes a bookend to one end of the Chapel Street corridor by striking a similar cadence with the scale of the other bookend, the Yale Bowl and its recreational program, creating spaces through the manipulation of the ground plane.

Situated between the educational, retail, and industrial areas to the west and the mixed-use and residential areas to the east, the project site is transformed into a wetland park; for public circulation, the park has raised pathways along the riverfront and between the pavilions. Each pavilion is raised on an elevated plane that, through its manipulation of the site's topography, produces seating and observation areas for inside and outside events. Across the change in grade from the road to the river, these earthen striations step down, across the site, to floodable levels of wetland habitat, capable of bearing both tidal fluctuations and storm events.

Hovering above this newly shaped topography, the repeated structure of the recreation halls allows for long spans in both directions. By adapting construction methods at the forefront of timber bridge design, the spans across the gymnasium spaces are carried by a series of massive timber box girders, comprising glulam members and cross-laminated-timber structural sheathing. At ground level, this produces unimpeded and largely uninterrupted views of the Mill River district, its renewed wetland ecology, and the overlap of activities within each sports hall. The sections of the proposed structural members are large

01 Site model, showing building in relation to all the studio's projects

02 Interior perspective

01

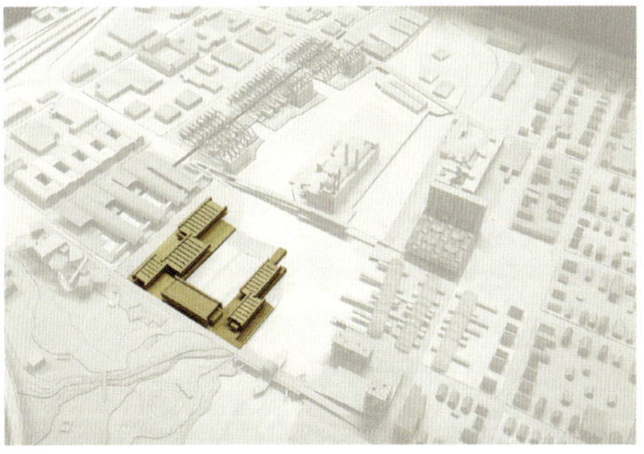

02

enough that each can be selectively used to house and distribute mechanical systems for the complex and can even become occupiable space for visitors, spectators, trainers, and officials. Exterior screens of burned wood—in the Japanese tradition of *shousugi ban*—give the massive structural spans a shadowy depth and a strange, delicate aspect.

The overall structural bay's dimensions accommodate activities that vary in scope, from yoga classes and swimming to indoor-outdoor archery competitions. In addition, the depth of the major structural members makes it possible for a variety of discreet overhead daylighting strategies, which impart differences in the atmospheric quality of each sports hall: for example, concentrated skylights for the natatorium, but a factory ceiling over the archery range. Thus, experientially, the project is a patchwork of large but simple wooden rooms, each seemingly levitating above its own bespoke section of the ground plane and, in some instances, the river itself. On the eastern side, for instance, a pair of pavilions float above the water's edge to form a boathouse and rowing facility, encouraging the active use of the river itself as an urban resource. By pairing ecological sensitivity with a simple structural ambition, this project seeks a rich interaction with its delicate site and its placement within the larger Mill River district plan.

---

03 **Structural model**

04 **Section through pool**

05 **Boardwalk**

06 **Site section, illustrating topography that produces seating and observation areas**

07 **Site plan, showing how the building allows for unimpeded views of the Mill River district**

03

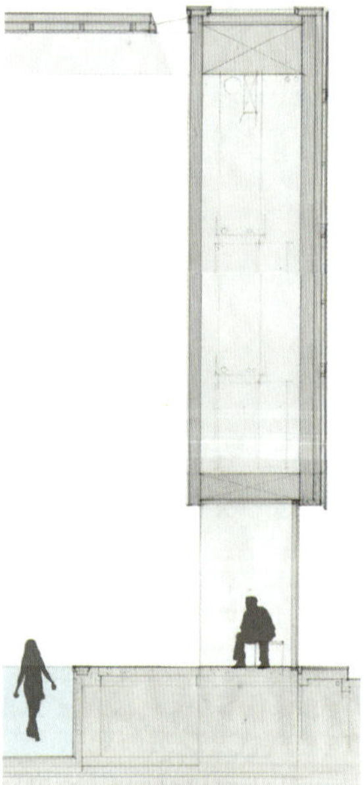

04

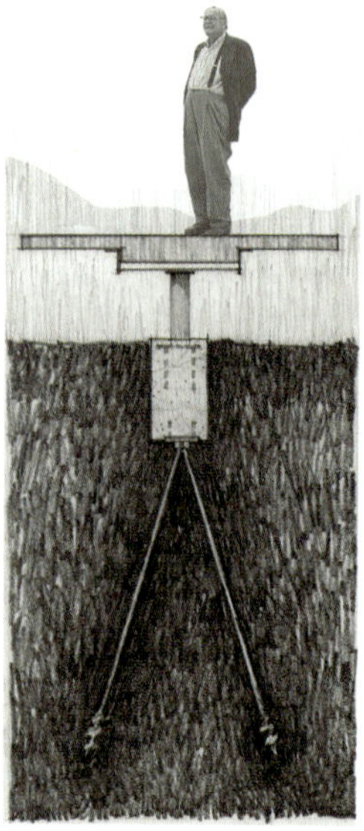

05

06

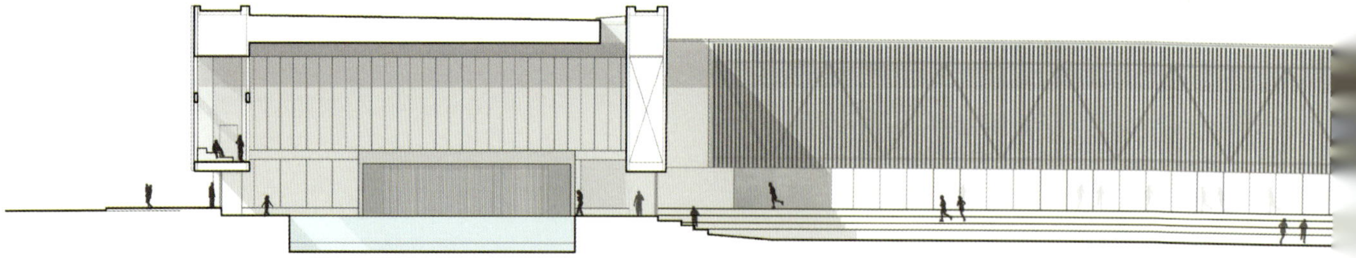

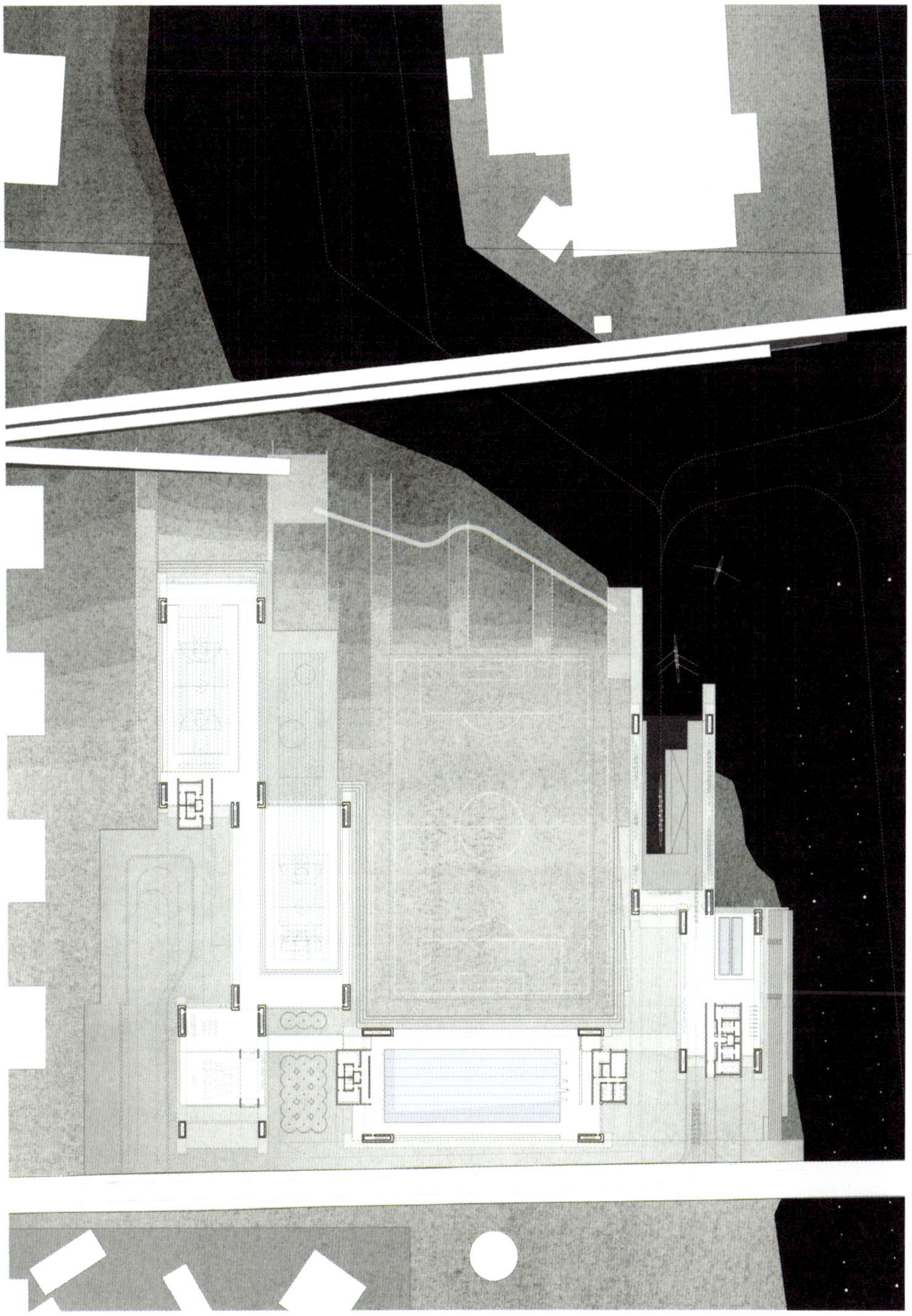

07

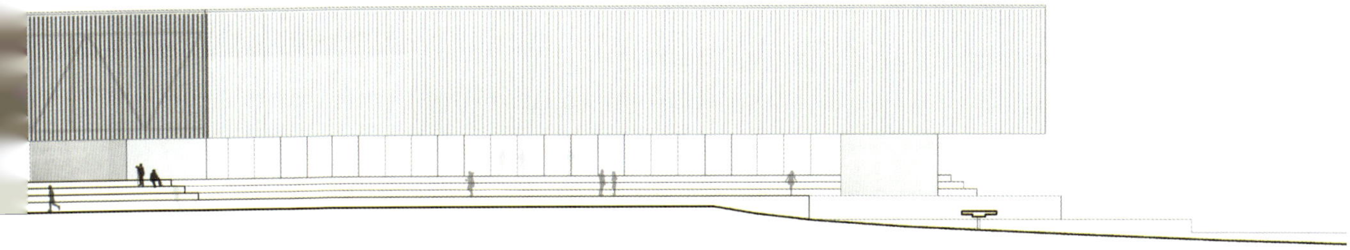

IMAGE CREDITS

Gray Organschi Architecture: 114, 115, 116, 117, 119, 124
Gray Organschi Advance Studio: 126, 127, 128, 129
Google Maps: 125
Iwan Baan: 56
P-A-T-T-E-R-N-S: 10, 11, 12, 13, 14, 15, 18, 19, 20, 21
Robert Adams: 57
WORKac: 58, 62, 64, 66, 68, 69